D1121967

Thomas Merton's Art of Denial

THOMAS MERTON'S
ART OF DENIAL

The Evolution of a Radical Humanist

David D. Cooper

THE UNIVERSITY OF GEORGIA PRESS
ATHENS & LONDON

R0122164642
HUMCA

HOUSTON PUBLIC LIBRARY

© 1989 by the University of Georgia Press
Athens, Georgia 30602
All rights reserved
Designed by Louise M. Jones
Set in Palatino with Cartier display
The paper in this book meets the guidelines for permanence and
durability of the Committee on Production Guidelines for
Book Longevity of the Council on Library Resources.

Printed in the United States of America
93 92 91 90 89   5 4 3 2 1

Library of Congress Cataloging in Publication Data
Cooper, David D.
Thomas Merton's art of denial:
the evolution of a radical humanist / David D. Cooper.
p. cm.
Bibliography: p.
Includes index.
ISBN 0-8203-1094-8 (alk. paper)
1. Merton, Thomas, 1915–1968—Criticism and interpretation.
2. Radicalism in literature.   3. Humanism in literature. I. Title.
PS3525.E7174Z63 1989
818'.5409—dc19
88-17230 CIP

British Library Cataloging in Publication Data available

For Christina

CONTENTS

ACKNOWLEDGMENTS

This study began several years ago when I was asked to review a collection of newly released books by and about Thomas Merton. Since then, a near-tsunami of biographies, critical analyses, reminiscences, primary source materials, reprints, and ephemeral bric-a-brac have spilled over the floodgates of Merton studies. Even more books and collections have been recently launched upstream. Such a lively dialogue surely stands as a testament to Thomas Merton's durable and enduring message for our increasingly confused and troubled era. I hope this book contributes something to the dialogue. I hope too that my critical perspective, while no doubt bound to stir some controversy, will nonetheless help clarify Thomas Merton's message as I trace its genesis and chart its evolution through his inner conflicts, self-doubts, and ambivalences—a crucible of creative inner divisions, as it seems to me, that is the wellspring of Merton's humanist legacy for our times.

Since that inaugural review essay, I have accumulated a sizable ledger of research debts, both to institutions and to individuals.

For permission to include material in this book revised from previously published essays, I thank the publishers of the journals and anthologies in which the material originally appeared. Portions of the prologue are revisions of an essay published in *Cithara* (1981); portions of chapter 7 are based on an essay in *Toward an Integrated Humanity: Thomas Merton's Journey* (Kalamazoo: Cistercian Publications, 1988); and sections of chapter 8 are revisions of essays published in *New Oxford Review* (June, 1986) and *The Thomas Merton Annual*, vol. 1 (New York: AMS Press, Inc., 1988). I also thank my colleagues at the University of California, Santa Barbara and the Robert M. Hutchins Center for the Study of Democratic Institutions for their participation in dialogues and colloquia where I first presented some of my work in-progress.

Thanks, too, to the Trustees of the Thomas Merton Legacy Trust for permission to quote from unpublished Merton material, and to Bellarmine College and the staff of the Thomas Merton Studies Center, the official repository of Merton's papers, where I conducted the bulk of my archival research. The University of California Academic Senate, Santa Barbara Division, awarded me several grants for research travel. The University of California, Santa Barbara library staff provided expert technical support, especially the Interlibrary Loan Office. James Birchfield (the University of Kentucky Libraries), Steven Corey (Special Collections, the University of San Francisco), and the Special Collections staff at Columbia University deserve mention for their research assistance. To the monks of Gethsemani I offer my humble thanks for their hospitality, tolerance, and permission to examine the Abbey's Merton collection. In addition to Arthur Callard, the following individuals were kind enough to share with me their private collections and their special insights into Merton based on personal friendships: W. H. Ferry, James Laughlin, and Mrs. Carolyn Hammer.

Several meetings with a community of Merton scholars throughout the past few years have given me support, impetus, and inspiration. That community includes Anthony Padovano, Lawrence S. Cunningham, Victor Kramer, Dewey Kramer, George Kilcourse, M. Basil Pennington, Paul Wilkes, Christine Bochen, Glenn Hinson, Patrick O'Connell, Ron Seitz, Bonnie Thurston, Sr. Mary Luke Tobin, and Walter Capps.

The criticism and advice I received from several readers have made this a better book, although my grateful acknowledgment of them here does not imply their endorsement of my views: John Giles Milhaven, Hyatt H. Waggoner, Harry E. Reese, Frank McConnell, Michael O'Connell, Donald Pierce, and Nick Tingle. Thanks as well to my students in the Thomas Merton Seminar, Spring 1986, who listened with patience and spoke with insight, enthusiasm, and critical good sense.

Dr. Robert E. Daggy, Monsignor William H. Shannon, and Brother Patrick Hart—the triumvirate of Merton Studies—have given so unstintingly their knowledge, insight, wisdom, and resourcefulness that I can never repay my debt. I am especially grateful for something that means more to me than their scholarly expertise: their continued warm friendship.

My thanks, finally, to the University of Georgia Press: to Mary McFeely for her expert copy editing, to Debra Winter for her patience, and to Elizabeth Makowski for her enthusiasm.

And to my wife, who has brought a halcyon calm to the stormy seasons of one man's life, I lovingly dedicate this book.

LIST OF EDITIONS CITED

AG *My Argument with the Gestapo: A Macaronic Journal*. New York: New Directions, 1975.

AJ *The Asian Journal of Thomas Merton*. Edited by Naomi Burton, Brother Patrick Hart and James Laughlin. New York: New Directions, 1973.

BW *Bread in the Wilderness*. Collegeville, Minnesota: The Liturgical Press, 1971.

CGB *Conjectures of a Guilty Bystander*. Garden City, New York: Doubleday & Co., 1966.

CP *The Collected Poems of Thomas Merton*. New York: New Directions, 1977.

CWA *Contemplation in a World of Action*. Garden City, New York: Image Books, 1973.

DofS *Day of a Stranger*. Edited by Robert E. Daggy. Salt Lake City: Peregrine Smith, 1981.

DQ *Disputed Questions*. New York: Farrar, Straus & Cudahy, 1960.

FA *Figures for an Apocalypse*. New York: New Directions, 1947.

F&V *Faith and Violence: Christian Teaching and Christian Practice*. Notre Dame, Indiana: University of Notre Dame Press, 1968.

Ground *The Hidden Ground of Love: The Letters of Thomas Merton on Religious Experience and Social Concerns*. Edited by William H. Shannon. New York: Farrar, Straus & Giroux, 1985.

LE   *The Literary Essays of Thomas Merton.* Edited by Brother Patrick Hart. New York: New Directions, 1981.

L&L   *Love and Living.* Edited by Naomi Burton Stone and Brother Patrick Hart. New York: Farrar, Straus & Giroux, 1979.

NVA   *The Nonviolent Alternative.* Edited by Gordon C. Zahn. New York: Farrar, Straus & Giroux, 1980.

Raids   *Raids on the Unspeakable.* New York: New Directions, 1966.

SecJ   *The Secular Journal of Thomas Merton.* New York: Farrar, Straus & Giroux, 1977.

SofD   *Seeds of Destruction.* New York: Farrar, Straus & Giroux, 1980.

SJ   *The Sign of Jonas.* New York: Harcourt, Brace & Co., 1953.

SP   *Selected Poems.* London: Hollis & Carter, 1950.

SSM   *The Seven Storey Mountain.* New York: Harcourt, Brace & Co., 1948.

TMR   *A Thomas Merton Reader.* Edited by Thomas P. McDonnell. New York: Harcourt, Brace & World, 1962.

Woods   *Woods, Shore, Desert.* Santa Fe: Museum of New Mexico Press, 1983.

WS   *The Waters of Siloe.* New York: Harcourt, Brace & Co., 1949.

ZB   *Zen and the Birds of Appetite.* New York: New Directions, 1968.

Thomas Merton's Art of Denial

PROLOGUE

Shortly before Christmas in 1946, Thomas Merton's literary agent forwarded his manuscript of *The Seven Storey Mountain* to the publisher Harcourt, Brace. Merton had not published a great deal by this time. His friend James Laughlin at New Directions had issued Merton's first three volumes of poetry. Merton's only other substantial publication prior to the arrival of his manuscript at Harcourt, Brace was *Exile Ends in Glory,* a melodramatic hagiography that he wrote at the request of his religious superiors, who also assumed the responsibility of nursing it into print.

One can imagine the excitement of the young monk whose spiritual autobiography was now in the hands of a prominent publishing firm. One can as easily imagine the anticipation of a young *writer* who had spent the last five years in the obscurity and isolation of a cloistered religious community tucked deeply into the Kentucky woods, a community whose commitment to silence ran so deep that its members were forced to communicate with each other through the use of a cryptic sign language. In spite of his relative inexperience as a published writer, however, Merton knew that it would take the editors some time to assess the merits of *The Seven Storey Mountain.* He reports rather sarcastically in *The Sign of Jonas,* his journal covering this period, that "I knew quite well that publishers always make you wait at least two months before saying anything about your manuscripts" (20).

So it came as a great shock to Merton when at dinner one evening, only one week after his agent had sent off the manuscript, the Father Prior handed Merton a telegram from Harcourt, Brace. Merton's excitement quickly paled into an understandable nervousness and anxiety. It produced a ritual familiar to any writer. First he insisted quietly to himself that he would wait until after dinner to open the telegram. Although he strained to listen intently to the words of a lay brother reading passages out of the *Liturgical Year*, an uneasy anticipation continued to knot up inside him. "My heart," Merton later admitted, "sank into my dinner." And while that telegram loomed as an insurmountable distraction and smoldered there on the rough plank of the refectory table, all sorts of frightening scenarios unfolded before him. "The first thought that came to my mind," he recalled, "was that the manuscript . . . had been lost."

With a precarious patience Merton finished his dinner and returned to his pallet in the cloister where he opened the telegram. It was from Robert Giroux, then an editor at Harcourt, Brace. It contained only five words, five extraordinarily simple words that would have an undreamed-of impact on the next twenty-two years of Merton's life. "Manuscript accepted. Happy New Year."

Two years passed before the actual publication of *The Seven Storey Mountain*. Not only did Merton have to carry on business with his New York publishers, who by all accounts treated him with great respect, but he also had to deal with the editors of his religious order, the Cistercian censors. They were much harder on him. In April 1947 the censors rejected the book. Interestingly enough, they were not as concerned with the propriety of a cloistered religious entering the public literary arena as they would be when they rejected *The Sign of Jonas* a few years later. The censors argued, rather, that the book, purely from a *literary* perspective, was, as Merton reports, "unripe for publication." "I am held to be incapable of writing an autobiography 'with his present literary equipment' and I am advised to take a correspondence course in English grammar" (40). At the request of his Gethsemani superiors Merton set about to revise the manuscript, to "tone it down" and readjust its content to conform more uniformly to the needs of a projected audience that Merton would describe, with no little ridicule of the censors' underlying conservatism, as running a narrow gamut from "nuns in Irish convents" to "young girls in boarding schools, whom the censors are afraid to scandalize" (50–51).

Merton's editorial efforts proved successful. The censors eventually granted an imprimatur and on a hot, muggy day in July 1948 the Abbot of Gethsemani handed Merton the first copy of *The Seven Storey Mountain* and told him to look it over. This would be the beginning of that New Year Robert Giroux promised Merton in 1946, for Merton soon discovered that he was virtually an overnight literary success, with all the attention, praise, gossip, and correspondence accorded to a best-selling author. Even as early as July, three months before the release of the book, three book clubs negotiated with Harcourt, Brace and guaranteed the sale of fourteen thousand copies. A second printing was already in the works. Paperback rights were assigned. And by 1952, the book had gone through sixteen printings and several foreign editions had already appeared. When thumbing through that first stiff copy of *The Seven Storey Mountain*, Merton could sense that the book would have a profound impact on his life. Intoxicated by the feel of the hefty volume in his hands, he mused in *The Sign of Jonas*, "Look out! Maybe this business is going to turn your life upside down for true!" (110).

The publication of *The Seven Storey Mountain* did indeed turn Merton's life upside down, but in not nearly as ebullient a way as the above quote suggests. Instead of inspiring Merton with self-confidence, instead of flooding the writer with the warmth of a responsive and sensitive readership, the publication of his autobiography sunk Merton quickly into a deep conflict. It was a New Year for Thomas Merton, but not a happy one at all. The significance, then, of that humid day in July 1948 is not that it introduced an important new writer onto the postwar American literary stage. It marked, rather, the beginnings of a crisis in Merton's life, a crisis that extended well beyond the immediate conflict Merton faced as a cloistered monk whose name suddenly topped the best-sellers list and pestered him for the next several years, culminating eventually in two nervous collapses and a stretch in a Louisville hospital.

In an effort to define the nature of this crisis, we can turn to the events surrounding the arrival of Giroux's telegram. At about the same time Merton's manuscript arrived at Harcourt, Brace, Merton himself was preoccupied with addressing the radically different business of his spiritual life. In his journal, for example, he despondently admonishes his "Lady, Queen of Heaven" to "pray me into solitude and silence and unity" and begs her to help him "be content with whatever darkness surrounds me." On the morning of the day Giroux's telegram arrived, Merton jotted down a list of things he felt he could profit by; among them was his wish "to let people know, in what I write, that the contemplative life is quite easy and accessible and does not require extraordinary or strange efforts, just the normal generosity required to strive for sanctity" (55, 20). But Merton had spent five hard years in the monastery by this time, an already arduous climb that had only advanced him to his simple vows. Surely he must have realized by now that his daunting goal of sanctity in the contemplative life was not nearly as easy and accessible as he hoped his readers would believe. In a journal entry dated Christmas Eve, 1946, Merton acknowledges that it takes "a faith and simplicity without which it is hard to live the contemplative life." His rejoinder speaks for itself: "I do not know if I shall ever be able to do it." Moreover, just a week after the delivery of Giroux's telegram, the Father Abbot announced in Chapter that Merton had made his petition to be admitted to solemn vows, an important new stage in Merton's monastic journey and its ultimate destination of total self-detachment— something which, at the time, certainly ran counter to the self-absorption of a newly-published autobiographer. So at a time when Merton's commitment to the affairs of the religious life began to make heavier demands on his spirituality, the newfound affairs of his budding literary career confronted him with demands of an entirely different order. The conflict between these two sets of demands, each pulling at Merton from contradictory directions, constitutes, in part, the core of the crisis of Thomas Merton's middle years.

The crisis can perhaps best be seen through the somewhat risky procedure of bifurcating Merton's personality during these years. On the one hand, there is the Thomas Merton who entered the Abbey of Gethsemani fully equipped with the instincts of a writer and published poet. When he first visited the Abbey in 1941, he was boiling over with language and the inspiration to record what he discovered there. As he says in *The Secular Journal*, April 7, 1941, "I should tear out all the other pages of this book, and all the other pages of anything else I have ever written, *and begin here.*" Note too what Merton says about the "logic of language" in another entry of the same journal: "The logic of the poet—that is, the logic of language or the experience itself—develops the way a living organism grows: it spreads out toward what it loves, and is heliotropic, like a plant. A tree grows out into a free form, an organic form. It is never ideal, only free; never typical, always individual" (24). That three volumes of published poetry preceded the appearance of *The Seven Storey Mountain* suggests that Merton's poetic roots were indeed flourishing, nourished by his freedom to write about those things he loved. Some critics have argued, in fact, that Merton let his poetic canon grow uncontrollably, like a vine sorely in need of pruning. The fact remains, however, that this exuberant and prolific young poet was a much different person from the monk who emerged in 1947, the monk who implored his superiors to demand that he *stop* writing, the monk who began to pray for silence beyond words, and the monk who would insist, in a 1947 essay on poetry and the religious life, that the contemplative who fancied himself a poet must assume only one course for the benefit of his own sanctification: the uncompromising sacrifice of his art. Looking back a few years later on this period of conflict between his monastic calling and his literary agenda, Merton writes: "An author in a Trappist monastery is like a duck in a chicken coop. And he would give anything in the world to be a chicken instead of a duck" (*SJ*, 89).

After all, from the very beginning of his tenure at the Abbey of Gethsemani Merton entered into a tradition of Christian mysticism that could only exacerbate the self-division he encountered upon the publication of his popular autobiography. The apophatic tradition, as it is commonly called, established the foundations of ascetic discipline that Merton embraced enthusiastically as a young convert bent on fleeing the nihilistic aimlessness he had come to associate with secular life.[1] The tradition derives its name from the Greek *apophasis*, meaning denial or negation. The apophatic mystics' insistence that language could not be used to describe the ultimate monastic goal of union with God clearly presented Merton with a formidable conundrum. How could he continue to follow his literary inclinations when faced with the central premise of the apophatic program and its claim that the contemplative must approach his God-encounter by first transcending ideas, images, metaphors, and sense impressions? Since self-expression loomed as a major roadblock toward self-transcendence, the monk, in short, must extinguish the temptation to name what the apophatic mystics insisted was Unnameable.

Clearly, Merton's love of language, his poetic instincts already flourishing in several volumes of poetry, the entire thrust of his literary education at Columbia University and his subsequent teaching of writing and literature at St. Bonaventure, not to mention the spare moments he longed for as a young novice when he could get to work on the sizable manuscript of his life story—all of these clashed, with increasingly little hope of reconciliation, with Merton's radical conversion to apophatic theology. It set him on the horns of a dilemma which he would struggle with throughout the early and middle years of his monastic life. Unable to give up writing completely and yet

convinced that continued writing would only frustrate further progress in the contemplative life, Merton faced an identity conflict in
these years, essentially a crisis of ambivalence. Even after the publication of *The Seven Storey Mountain* and Merton's plea in its epilogue to
be free of the writer's shadow that darkened the monastic way, it
seems curiously counterproductive that he would immediately sign a
long-term contract with Harcourt, Brace for the delivery of four more
books. The ambivalences deepen as we consider that the royalties
Merton collected during these years, including the huge sums from
the sale of *The Seven Storey Mountain*, were accumulating in the Abbey
coffers and being used to purchase the tractors and jackhammers that
Merton spoke of with such contempt because they destroyed the am-
bience of solitude and silence he longed for as a monk. The monk, as
it turns out, bemoaned precisely those kinds of thriving projects at a
rapidly expanding monastery which were bankrolled, in large part,
by the writer who, in spite of himself, could not turn down a contract
offer.

The crisis of language—the central dilemma of the poet/priest—
was nowhere more apparent than in the journal prose of the period
and in Merton's halfhearted decision to abandon the writing of
poems. Saturated with the clash between the monk's spiritual demands and the creative needs of the writer, *The Sign of Jonas* (1953)
reveals Merton wrestling, in nearly all of its daily entries, with a
growing conflict between a monk's hunger for humiliation and an
author's hunger for admiration, what Merton called "the dialectic between silence and utterance" (*SJ*, 266). Caught in the whorl of this
dialectic, the poems were simply filtered out. After purging himself of
the poet's temptation to articulate the monk's unnameable quest for
God, Merton's tenacious inborn need to fulfill his authorial self-image
was still partially satisfied by an ambitious agenda of prose projects.
But even these were viewed with skeptical ambivalence. While the
poet was silenced altogether, the monk frequently referred to the du-
ties of the prose writer as a "penance" and a "cross." In the words of
Leon Bloy, which Merton quoted as an epigram to what he promised
would be the last volume of poetry to appear after *Mountain*, "When
those who love God try to talk about Him, their words are blind lions
looking for springs in the desert" (*CP*, 196).

It was indeed a desert period as far as Merton's poetry was concerned. The poet who burst through the Abbey gates in 1941, bran-

dishing words like six-guns and celebrating poetry as heliotropic and free, soon entered into a spiritual landscape so arid and barren that it could not nourish "the logic of the poet." Instead of the poem representing, as it had in 1941, a natural heliotropic bending toward the light of knowledge and the beauty of creation, poetry, for Merton, became obscured by the apophatic mystic's mute quest for God.

A cursory glance at the prodigious *Collected Poems of Thomas Merton* quickly reveals, however, that the bulk of his poems were written after 1957. Not only did Merton return to poetry writing after an eight-year hiatus, but at the same time his principal interests as a prose writer shifted significantly. He turned away from meditative tracts on the contemplative life. Instead, he began producing works of trenchant social criticism much more responsive to the modern intellectual climate than the earlier antiworld jeremiads—such as in *Mountain*—which were shaped by a reactionary, premodern eschatology that treated post-Augustinian intellectual history with intolerance and suspicion. A similar thematic and ideological turn is evident in the post-1956 poetry where the axis of Merton's social discontent shifts from righteous indignation over the moral iniquity of secular life (*Figures for an Apocalypse*) to existential protest against the dehumanizing, self-destructive proclivities of modern mass culture (*Cables to the Ace*)—from *contemptus mundi* and its vapid stereotype of world rejection, in short, to a radical new Christian humanism which could accommodate and endorse the post-Christian critiques of such figures as Marx, Freud, Bonhoeffer, and Camus. Such bibliographical observations alone suggest that Merton eventually reconciled a crisis of self-division that tore at him during those years when his natural bent as a writer was crippled by self-denial. Thomas Merton gradually emerged, that is to say, from a crisis of identity denials and passed through a catharsis that integrated him at a higher personal unity where, in a manner of speaking, the silence of the monk could live compatibly with the racket of the writer. Instead of seeing the artist as an impediment to the spiritual ascent of the contemplative, Merton began to confront the possibility that art could play an important role in the growth of a more integrated man. In admonishing his readers to accept their own deficiencies, Merton states, in the prologue to *No Man Is an Island* (1955): "We will see that we are human, like everyone else, that we all have weaknesses and deficiencies, and that these limitations of ours play a most important part in all of

our lives." Perhaps it could be said that before 1957 the priest despised, rejected, and subjugated the weaknesses and deficiencies of
the writer, while after 1957 the writer, as it seems to me, began seriously questioning the rigidity and feigned perfection of the priest.
This inner dialogue produced a less perfect priest and a less repressed
and dogmatic poet. And it contributed to the evolution of a more perfect human being—an evolution that this two-part study of Thomas
Merton seeks to explore. My inquiry into Thomas Merton's journey
from a young contemplative's monastic asceticism to a mature social
critic's world-affirming Christian humanism is driven by a question
that has always flanked Merton scholarship with gnawing persis-
tence: What factors account for the transformation of a caustic young
man, who haughtily turned his back on the world and joined a monastery with his Bible dog-eared at the Apocalypse, into a world-
embracing humanist called to rededicate himself, as he put it in a
letter to Dorothy Day, "to face the big issues, the life and death issues
. . . on which the very continued existence of the human race depends"? (*Ground*, 139–40).

Looking back on the books, articles, and poems he wrote after 1956,
Merton says, in the preface to *A Thomas Merton Reader* (1962), that they
"are, perhaps naturally, the ones that seem most significant to me."
Those readers upon whom Merton exerted considerable influence
may agree, perhaps as naturally, with his own assessment here, especially those of my generation who turned to Merton during the 1960s
not particularly for a message of world renunciation and denial, but
rather in an effort to cope with what Merton himself so accurately
described as "turbulent, mysterious, demanding, exciting, frustrating, confused existence in which most definitions, explanations, and
justifications become incredible even before they are uttered" (*CWA*,
160). We turned to a man who had somehow managed to emerge
victoriously from his own personal crisis and begun to speak with
great conviction about such things as personal authenticity, the search
for a radical self, and the necessity of engaging man's inhumanity to
man instead of tolerating it with passivity, ignorance, or guilt. We
turned to a writer who insisted that we liberate ourselves from the
superficial, transient freedoms of modern life and overcome the
temptation to give in to ontological diets and deals peddled either by
conventional prescriptions or those circulating in the marketplace of
pop fashion—the delusions, the mystifications, the stubborn, fab-

ricated dreams lying at the heart of the American cult of success. We
stacked our reading shelves, not with the writings of a young Catholic
proselyte who scolded the secular era for its apostasies, but with later
books like *Raids on the Unspeakable* (1964), where Merton wrote in the
stabbing prose of a street fighter (not in the lofty encomiums of a
Trappist cenobite) and squared off against human alienation, not godlessness, as the agent infecting the malaise of modern life. We read
Conjectures of a Guilty Bystander (1966), with its sweeping and unrestrained vision of the world in the 1960's, and *Contemplation in a World
of Action* (1965), with what Jean Leclercq described as its "prophetic,
mobile, even flying . . . [message] to fulfill man's hope" (*CWA*, 11). In
short, we turned to a writer who, in the best tradition of his American
forebears, had positioned himself on the fringes of American culture
and who understood and accepted the obligations of his marginality:
namely, to critique the center of American society and the failure of its
political and social institutions to further the aims of democratic egali-
tarianism as well as the failure of its religious institutions to redress
human suffering and fulfill the claims of Judeo-Christian humanism.

Taken in the balance, then, these later writings of Merton's and the
vision they articulate serve only to frustrate any attempt to enter into
and understand the Merton of what I've called the missing years—
those middle years of Merton's monastic experience when his self-
image as a writer narrowed, as Merton himself later said, to "the official voice of Trappist silence" and when the Christian humanist's social witness was obscured by the antiworld diatribes of an angry
Cistercian misanthrope. The life that Merton lived and the things he
chose to write about during these years of personal crisis contradict,
in fact, the very spirit of the man many readers turned to during the
1960s in an effort to find, as Merton himself had, an authentic and
productive relationship to the world of their time and not escape from
it into a smug, insulated quietism. Merton's message during the missing years was not "mobile" or "running" or unrestrained and certainly
not "flying," except in the sense of flight from the evils of secularity. A
book like *The Sign of Jonas*—excluding its headnotes and epilogue and
its rare moments of extrospection—reveals a man whose wings are
clipped by his apophatic spirituality, his vision frequently clouded by
life at Gethsemani closing in on him. In other books, like *The Ascent to
Truth* (1951), we find Merton clinging to definitions, explanations, justifications in order to render his world-denying mysticism *credible*, in

spite of undercurrents of self-doubt. Most astonishingly, the poems
Merton wrote before banishing his muse do not engage man's inhumanity to man. Instead, they echo that humanity. In his 1949 reces-
sional volume of poems, for example, Merton's apocalyptic imagination guides celestial shock troops who descend upon a modern
secular Babylon and crush it like a spider; "Blest are they that hate
you," he snaps, "Blest are they / That dash your brats against the
stones" (*CP*, 212). And, of course, the book that triggered the inner
divisions of the missing years was soundly criticized by Merton himself in his later years. He faulted *The Seven Storey Mountain* not only
for its near-bigotry but because he realized he was projecting an artificial public image, that of an over-romanticized, heroic convert fleeing
to the freedom of a monastery, an image that cut against the grain of
personal authenticity Merton spoke of so compellingly years later.

Although Merton expressed considerable regret over the dogmatic
severity and the cold, inhuman hardness projected in his earlier writing, such apologetics cannot easily dismiss the fact that Merton was
nonetheless held in the powerful grip of renunciations during his
most formative years and, more important, that his posture of denial
played a crucial role in the evolution of his mature humanism. The
radical humanism of Merton's later years, that is to say, has deep
roots in the antiworld mysticism of his early monastic commitments,
just as Merton's later vision of the writer's social responsibility sprang
from his forceful denials of the efficacy of art.

For Thomas Merton, the tension between art and spirituality—the
two poles around which he plotted his quest for a durable self-identity—switched polarities during his trials of growth. Art, for the
young monk, loomed as a barrier in his dark search for "a silence
beyond words." Apophatic mysticism compelled him to cut asunder
any bonds that attached him to contemporary affairs and to renounce
poetry—along with social responsibility, humanitarian concern, and
political dissent—as impure distractions alienating him from "the
clean laundries of the saints." For the radical humanist of the sixties—
one of the most prolific writers of the decade— art was worthless
unless its roots dug deeply into human responsibility. One cannot be
an artist or writer, Merton later insisted, "if one is not first of all human, and humanity is not authentic without human concern" (*LE*,
228). Similarly, once Merton came to accept the realities of a post-
Christian era, embraced those realities, and realized that history was

inescapable, then religion, like art, merited no claim on modern life unless it inspired concrete involvement in the common and crucial human problems of history. The evolution of Thomas Merton's radical humanism, then, is a story of withdrawal giving way to engagement, separation giving way to involvement, refusal giving way to affirmation and acceptance, acquiescence giving way to protest. It is a story as well of transformation through personal crisis in which a youthful ideologue, beset by self-division, reassembled from the remnants of inner conflict a higher self-purpose and forged, from the crucible of denials, a radical humanist's "mobile, running, even flying . . . [message] to fulfill man's hopes" during an age itself racked by crisis.

PART ONE

The Crisis of the Missing Years

An author in a Trappist
monastery is like a duck in a
chicken coop. And he would
give anything in the world to
be a chicken instead of
a duck.

1

The Letter Killeth

Dom Frederick Dunne, the Abbot of Gethsemani who received Merton as a postulant in 1941 and later presided over his profession of simple and solemn vows, died in August 1948. "Death succeeded," as Merton put it, while the gentle Abbot was riding a train through the mountains of Tennessee. Dom Frederick's death had a profound impact on Merton. During a period when misgivings over his identity as a writer grew more intense and divisive, Dom Frederick's warm support and continuous encouragement of Merton's literary efforts provided some emotional shelter from such storms of self-doubt. It was Dom Frederick who handed Merton that first advance copy of *The Seven Storey Mountain*. The Abbot knew that Merton was uneasy about the book and wary, even fearful of the consequences of its publication. Although Merton's claim that the Abbot ordered him to write his life story seems disingenuous, Dom Frederick did nudge Merton firmly and never wavered in his persistent counsel that the monk and writer could be fitting companions at Gethsemani. Besides, Dom Frederick, a man of no inconsiderable intellect who came from a literary background, recognized Merton's natural gifts and did not wish to see such talent squandered, especially in light of Merton's often unreasoned appeals to the contrary. Dom Frederick may also have seen in Merton an opportunity to redress the stereotype of Trappist anti-intellectualism. At his direction, Merton set to work on several promotional tracts, including a pamphlet celebrating Gethsemani's centenary and a full-fledged history of the Cistercian Order.

After Dom Frederick's death, Merton reminisced fondly that the Abbot had shaped his monastic destiny while patiently reminding him that a writing career need not frustrate his contemplative life. "Dom Frederick not only 'made' me as a writer," Merton concluded, "but . . . he disposed my life . . . in such a way that I had a greater opportunity to become a contemplative at Gethsemani." With affection and simplicity tempered by extraordinary good sense and his authority as the head of a busy abbey, Dom Frederick "continued patiently and wisely to show me, in every way he could, that this writing was not supposed to interfere with my life of prayer" (*SJ*, 90). When the Abbot died, Merton lost a valuable mentor, a man whose wisdom had helped to quiet the turmoil of Merton's inner divisions during these troublesome early years in the monastery. With Dom Frederick gone, Merton's self-image as a writer would soon turn against him again as a "thirsty traitor, in my Trappist mornings!" (*CP*, 192).

Initially, however, the circumstances attending Dom Frederick's death led Merton to renew briefly his ties with the "world." Busy and eventful days lay ahead. The Vicar General of the Order arrived for the funeral and presided over the business of electing a new abbot. Since the Vicar General spoke no English, Merton was assigned as interpreter and secretary for the duration of the visit. This meant that Merton had to accompany him on an errand into Louisville. It had been seven years since Merton ventured outside the enclosure to do much more than sit in the woods and read or harvest hay. The trip into the city gave him occasion to wonder, then, "how I would react at meeting once again, face to face, the wicked world" (*SJ*, 91).

The impressions of that encounter, as recorded in *The Sign of Jonas*, are somewhat ambiguous due to a dual literary strategy that Merton employs throughout the journal. He sets up a dialogue between the narrative voice of the diary entries themselves and the editorial voice of the headnotes to each part, which looks back on events from a broader perspective of time passed. Writing in a headnote, Merton says that he met the world head-on and found that it was not nearly as wicked as he had anticipated. Merton claims that the trip helped to restore some much needed perspective to the first seven years of his monastic life. He came to realize, upon reflection, that those things he resented about the world when he had abandoned it with much fanfare in 1941—the resentments that yielded the cynicism and self-righteousness of *The Seven Storey Mountain*—were not really immutable flaws of the world itself, but rather, he admits, "defects of my own that I had projected on it." Seeing his distaste for the brutality of city life as rooted in the traumas of past personal experience rather than as a function of the monolithic evils of secular life helped prove to Merton that his interior life had matured and that he had grown. Instead of resorting to the grandiose anticity polemics that dominated the poems in the recently published *Figures for an Apocalypse*, Merton found that much of what he saw in a real city stirred him with renewed compassion, especially the people. "I went through the city," he continues in the headnote, "realizing for the first time in my life how good are all the people in the world and how much value they have in the sight of God." It was as if he began to see with new eyes beyond the superficial "animalistic toughness" of city life, as if "I . . . lost an eye for merely exterior detail and . . . discovered, instead, a deep sense of respect and love and pity for the souls that such details never fully reveal" (*SJ*, 92).

Judging from the tone of the headnote, it would seem that this brief foray into Louisville provided Merton with a much-needed opportunity to immerse himself freely in the impression of his senses and see people and things with greater compassion, openness, and heightened humanity. It also gave him a chance to rediscover the delight he had once experienced in created things, a delight gradually eroded during the previous seven years by the increasing demands of an ascetic life. Perhaps Merton felt, then, the joy of creative affirmations welling up inside of him—affirmations especially of the inherent goodness of common people, which foreshadow the famous humanistic epiphany Merton wrote about years later when, on a street corner in Louisville, he was overwhelmed with a deep love for all humanity.

But turning to the actual diary entry where Merton records the immediate felt impression of the day, there is little sense of this episode being much more, as he says soon after returning to Gethsemani, than "a matter of obedience [that] meant losing a day's work." Although he felt some vague sympathy for the people, nothing about the trip struck him as especially noteworthy. There is no immediate sense of the singular importance Merton gave to the trip when he later reflected on it in the headnote. He makes a rather concerted effort, in fact, to deny even slight expression to any impulse of acceptance or affirmation, preferring to brush aside, with a gesture of detachment, his first encounter with city life in many years: "I felt completely alienated from everything in the world and all its activity" (115).

These contrasting perspectives are integral to a broader pattern of conflicts, examined in more detail in the next chapter, which constitute the narrative architecture of *The Sign of Jonas*. For now it seems clear that the diary text of *Jonas* is shaped by a strategy of denials, whereas the headnotes seek to compensate as commentaries of affirmation. Such an interplay of opposing voices suggests that Merton's perspectives and sensitivities had changed considerably during the four years which separate the diary entry from his drafting of the headnote. But even though Merton sought in the headnote to compensate for his coldness and detachment, he nonetheless made a conscious decision to choke off extrospection as he described his encounter with the city in August 1948. He preferred introspection. He affected an impression of complete alienation by glossing over the experience as a penance. Such a posture of denial and negation followed a course Merton had charted for himself in the epilogue to *The Seven Storey Mountain*: "to be lost to all created things, to die to them and the knowledge of them" (421). Any creative engagement with the "world," especially its humanity and its sensible beauty, was antithetical to the monastic agenda, the enemy of contemplative life.

— 2 —

This strategy of denials informs the poetry Merton was writing during the late forties, especially the poems in *The Tears of the Blind Lions*, published in 1949. These poems are driven by a poetics of negation quite appropriate for a poet who wished to surrender all attachments to the light of created things, preferring instead "the infinitely productive darkness of contemplation." Shortly after the Louisville visit, for example, Merton wrote a poem about the city entitled, "The Captives, A Psalm." If in his diary entry Merton had discounted his experience as a confirmation of his detachment and separation from the world and its confused activity, in the poem he gives much freer reign to his feelings of utter contempt for what becomes "the wild algebra" of an earthly Babylon. There is not the slightest hint of the "deep sense of respect and love and pity for the souls" of the city folk that Merton expressed in his revisionist headnote. Instead, he heaps scorn on "the gorges of a fiery city" and its citizens who "Build themselves each hour another god / and fry a fatter idol out of mud." With a disdain tempered by a rigid Old Testament legalism, Merton lashes out at the godlessness and apostasy that he uncritically associated with secular living. Alluding no doubt to the soul-numbing effect of mass communication, symbolized by the forest of antennas on roof-tops, and the too-worldly ring of conversations overheard in city streets, Merton concludes with Bible-thumping indignation that people "cut themselves a crooked idiom / To the winged animals, upon their houses. / Prayers are made of money, songs of numbers, / Hymns of the blood of the killed." Since paganism is endemic, only an apocalypse can purify these "Bodies . . . grayer than mud" and exorcize misery from "miles / Miles of houses [that] shelter terror."

> Blessed is the army that will one day crush you, city,
> Like a golden spider.
> Blest are they that hate you. Blest are they
> That dash your brats against the stones.
>
> (*CP*, 212)

It would seem, for the time being at least, that Merton still felt there was some peripheral value in the enterprise of poetry writing. The crisis of language had not as yet reached proportions that would soon silence the poet altogether. But it is obvious, especially in the closing stanza of "The Captives, A Psalm," that Merton's reified monk persona is pulling all the strings. Note especially how Merton attenuates an Augustinian polarity between an earthly city—the Babylon of Louisville—and the Zion of Gethsemani into a rigid, stark tyranny of choices.

> May my bones burn and raven eat my flesh
> If I forget thee, contemplation!
> May language perish from my tongue
> If I do not remember thee, O Sion, city of vision,
> Whose heights have windows finer than the firmament
> When night pours down her canticles
> And peace sings on thy watchtowers like the stars of Job.
>
> (*CP*, 212)

The poet's inclination to reach into the light of created things—the heliotropic impulse Merton spoke of a few years earlier—was now on the verge of giving way to a monk's ascension into the peaceful, fecund darkness of contemplation.

I would suggest, however, that Merton's poetics of negation reveals more than monastic detachment. Like other poems in *Tears*, "The Captives, A Psalm" cannot disguise Merton's bitter contempt and haughty loathing for human affairs—the "iniquity," as George Woodcock points out, that Merton harbored for "the metropolis and its culture."[1] The poem expresses a state of being at its core as cold and obdurate and unfeeling as the metallic imagery—"brass traffic," shivering windows, walls, stones, chains—that gives "The Captives, A Psalm" its hard, cruel edge. Such undisguised and arrogant world contempt betrays, I believe, a misanthrope lashing out at the meanness of secular existence where "Old ladies are treasured in sugar" and "Young ones rot in wine" and "the flesh of the fat organizers smiles with oil."

Merton's disdain for modern secular culture in *Tears* carries over from *Figures for an Apocalypse* (1947). In the title poem of that earlier volume, for example, Merton uses the secular/sacred polarity to launch an indignant attack on "the Christless avenues" of the secular city. In part 6, the "boils of Harlem and the Bronx" which infect "The Ruins of New York" are starkly contrasted to "The Heavenly City" of part 8. Fires and lightning strike the city and incinerate its "towers of silver and of steel"—a holocaust of purification that "consigns murderers and sorcerers and crooked leaders . . . home to hell," "while all the Saints rise from their earth with feet like light" (*CP*, 148). This same heavy-handed eschatological imagery surfaces frequently in *The Tears of the Blind Lions* ("The City after Noon," "Senescente Mundo," "On a Day in August"). And Merton brings down "the dark curtain of apocalypse" on the earthly city again in *The Tower of Babel: A Morality* which, although first published in 1955, was written not long after the appearance of *Tears*.

All of the poems in *Figures for an Apocalypse* were written while Merton was working on *The Seven Storey Mountain,* and he wrote most of *The Tears of the Blind Lions* shortly after the autobiography's publication. Inevitably, then, the poetry of this period reflects the dilemma that Merton described in the epilogue of *The Seven Storey Mountain* and one which he continued to wrestle with throughout the pages of

The Sign of Jonas: namely, his "mortal fear" that "this shadow, this double, this writer who had followed me into the cloister . . . bars my way to liberty" and leaves "nothing of my vocation—my contemplative vocation—but a few ashes" (*SSM*, 410). "[W]ill your little shadow," Merton asked in "The Poet, to His Book" (the last poem in *Figures*), "fatten in my life's last hour / And darken for a space my gate to white eternity?" (*CP*, 192). Since the poet—"the stubborn talker"—was lured into "the loud world's corners," since his "rhythms . . . upset my silences," Merton sought, through a poetics of negation, to silence that talker and sever his attachments to the profane world outside Gethsemani where he remained "bound to the earth, in his Egyptian bondage of contracts, reviews, page proofs, and all the plans for books and articles that I am saddled with" (*SSM*, 410). Such an agenda accounts, then, for the dual motifs of negation that surface frequently in the poetry of the late forties: a denial of the ultimate efficacy of language and a total renunciation of contemporary society and its post-Christian secular culture.

Merton's commitment to an apophatic spirituality and its vocabulary of negations is further manifested in certain paradigms of spiritual perfection he celebrates. Throughout the poetry of the late forties Merton turns to the heroic martyrs in several hagiographical compositions: "tremendous prisoners!" Merton writes in a poem to St. Clement, whose "chains shine with hymns" sung from "the base of the prisoner's cliff . . . Deep in the wall of the wounded mountain" (*CP*, 203). By lionizing archetypal ascetic-martyrs, Merton could extol the virtues of suffering and sacrifice, glorify the mortification of sense impressions ("Bones, go back to your baskets," he demands in "Dry Places," "Get your fingers out of my clean skin"), and further promote his reactionary assault on secular values. In his paean to St. John the Baptist, for example, Merton draws all those elements together into a model monastic program for "Those who by vow lie buried in the cloister or hermitage: / The speechless Trappist, or the grey, granite Carthusian, / The quiet Carmelite, the barefoot Clare" (*CP*, 201). Elsewhere, Merton praises other "Voices" whose words burn him "like a branding iron" until, as he writes in a "Hymn for the Feast of Duns Scotus," "I can no longer live in mortal flesh": voices like St. Clare, "the Christ-bearing" Christopher Columbus, St. Malachy, and "the Immaculate Virgin." Almost half of the compositions in *Tears* are devoted to portraits of these "exiles in the far end of solitude." Their spiritual perfection and sacrifice stand in such overt and predictable contrast to the fraudulent claims of mere "mortal flesh" that it creates, quite frankly, some forced and clumsy poetry characterized by severe vacillations between sentimentality and rage. With generic acerbity, for example, Merton attacks the "sarcastic towns" of contemporary America in "Christopher Columbus" where

> . . . the devils are sailing for your harbors
> Launching their false doves into the air to fly for your sands
> They bend over their tillers with little fox faces,
> Grin like dollars through their fur,
> And their meat-eating sails fly down and fold upon your shore.
>
> (CP, 208)

In "On a Day in August," he counters with the "heaven people," "the clean, white saints." While the "sad sour death" of quotidian existence "is eating the roots of our hair,"

> Yet the doors of sanitary winds lie open in the clouds
> To vistas of those laundries where the clean saints dwell:
> If we could only view them from our slum!
>
> (205)

Merton's rigorous separation of the sacred and secular also yields a sense of alienation and loneliness in those poems where he encounters his solitude. In "Song," for example, Merton withdraws into silence, behind "the rude door, my shelter, / And there I eat my air alone / With pure and solitary songs" (197). Solitude shelters the contemplative from storms of distraction. Even his fellow monks who "sit in conference" must be left behind. "Their conversations / Go down into the deep like submarines" as Merton withdraws further behind the barricade of his solitude until "I no longer see their speech / And they no longer know my theater." The implication here is that contemplation is alienation, especially from the distractions of human companionship. And solitude is separation and confinement: "Thus I live on my own land, on my own island."

Whether denying human companionship, renouncing the claims of sense impressions, or condemning the ethos of secular civilization, Merton's poetics of denial produced, above all else, a series of poems which comment on their own impotence. Many of the poems in *Figures* and *Tears* read more like laments on Merton's distrust of language than as meditations on prayer, solitude, and the contemplative life. Words cannot describe or approximate the "acres of night," the "guarded paradise," that "great wordless wilderness" where the monk encounters God. The Leon Bloy epigraph Merton uses for *Tears* is a fitting reminder, then, of the futility of poetry: "When those who love God try to talk about Him, their words are blind lions looking for springs in the desert." These poems become elegies to the poet since, as Merton writes in "A Psalm," "sound is never half so fair / As when that music turns to air / And the universe dies of excellence." (221). Although a poet might faintly "distinguish poems / Boiling up out of the cold forest," those poems could not enter a "Silence . . . louder than a cyclone" in which the monk ached to immerse himself. At a time when Merton believed that further progress in the spiritual life demanded a sacrifice of creative activity, his own poems corroborate that sacrifice by reminding him that "you need no eloquence, wild bairn, / exalting in your hermitage" (201). How could words articulate a silence beyond human speech? What possible claim could the poet have on the monk's "ministry of silence"? If writing a poem is an act of self-revelation and self-discovery, Merton reasoned, it is anathema to a monastic regimen that stressed self-denial and self-transcendence. The poet, therefore, must be allowed no quarter in the wordless wilderness where all Christian mystics have sought exile, where, as Merton writes in "The Quickening of St. John the Baptist,"

> Night is our diocese and silence is our ministry
> Poverty our charity and helplessness our tongue-tied sermon.
> Beyond the scope of sight or sound we dwell upon the air
> Seeking the world's gain in an unthinkable experience.
> We are exiles in the far end of solitude, living as listeners
> With hearts attending to the skies we cannot understand.
>
> (201)

Just as Merton had bid farewell to the poems in *Figures* by complaining of "the prayers and joys you stole from me," so too does he leave *The Tears of the Blind Lions* with a similar vow of protest. The only difference is that Merton generalizes his disavowal to include all acts of creative will. Convinced of the pandemic failure of art, he denies the Muse any claim on his being.

> And I go forth with no more wine and no more stars
> And no more buds and no more Eden
> And no more animals and no more sea:

While God sings by Himself in acres of night
And walls fall down, that guarded Paradise.

(221)

— 3 —

Merton's conviction that creative activity loomed as an obstacle in the spiritual life helps explain the eight-year hiatus between *The Tears of the Blind Lions* and his next volume of poetry, *The Strange Islands* (1957). So persistent were his abnegations of art during the late forties that perhaps the only other thing, besides Dom Frederick's counsel, that sustained Merton's poetry was the presence of certain viable poetic forms in the Judeo-Christian tradition. Many of the compositions in *Figures* and *Tears* were modeled after biblical and liturgical prototypes such as the aubade, the canticle, and the hymn. As songs of celebration derived from biblical antecedents, poems served a liturgical purpose in the life of worship, especially in the ritual cycle of chants integral to the monastic horarium. The psalm in particular became Merton's principal poetic paradigm. In the psalm, the poet's creative self-will lay passive and quiescent, subservient to higher ends. Like Christian sacred art—the psalm's counterpart in the visual arts—the psalm, as Merton said of Byzantine painting, was created in heaven, not made on earth. This hieratic function of psalmody was implicit in *The Tears of the Blind Lions* where, in his poem to St. Clement for example, Merton linked the act of writing a poem to prophecy and divine inspiration. "Poetry, psalms," he writes, must "Flower with a huge architecture." Poems, like the "Words of God" Himself, must raise "their grandeur on the gashed cape" and "blaze like a disaster / In the windows of a prophetic cathedral" (203).

Even if the psalm, however, endured as a legitimate poetic form, Merton was still doubtful whether his own poetry could achieve such lofty standards. The injunction that poetry, like psalms, "shall stand like vineyards / And swing with fruit in other worlds, in other centuries" (204) surely must have intimidated him, for he admitted that even William Blake had fallen short in the Prophetic Books. The problem, as Merton defined it in *Bread in the Wilderness*, his study of the psalms, is that the psalm, while "pure," remains nonetheless an "abstractive intuition of an 'Infinite Being.'" And nothing, Merton argued—no psalm or poem, "no system of asceticism, no mystical cult, however esoteric, however pure"—"can suffice to bridge the abyss between us and this Transcendent Creator of all Being" (*BW*, 35).

In his discussion of the psalms, written just after he announced, for the second time, his adieu to poetry writing, Merton declares that the psalms aim to fulfill a single purpose: "to awaken all the deepest powers of our being and raise us up to God" (117). Given such a criterion, little wonder that Merton developed a profoundly skeptical attitude about his own ability to negotiate, through poetry, that mystical leap implied in Paul's phrase: "the letter killeth but the spirit giveth life." "The 'letter' kills us," Merton writes, "not only by tempting us to miss a meaning. Even when the meaning (whether literal or spiritual) is abundantly clear, even when we fully grasp its implications, it 'kills' us if we get no further than *knowledge* of what it means." Language hamstrings the contemplative to processes of natural cognition, thereby preventing a supra-rational penetration into the mysteries of "Infinite Being"—just as poems, as Merton protested in "The Poet, To His Book," block "my gate to white eternity." One transcends that natural order only through an experience of grace. "Without grace, the 'letter'. . . serves only to condemn us." Since the mystical experience of grace passes human understanding, even human intuition, Merton created what amounts to an epistemological conundrum in his examination of the psalms and, by extension, in his own poetry writing. "The deep contemplative penetration of the Psalms" can only be achieved by those who have liberated themselves from the bondage of language. Language, like "Laws, rules, and methods [,] are for those who seek to get something for themselves. They therefore savor of this earth and of its slavery." So, he concludes, "the true meaning of the psalms is most fully apprehended by those who have been swept, by an experience of God's mercy, beyond the reach of any rule or any method" (121–22).

Merton argued, then, that the psalms are the foundation of the liturgical life of prayer, but they have, as such, no aesthetic value. While the psalms stand as the greatest religious poetry ever written, Merton insisted that they cannot be read or meditated upon as poems *per se*. To attach any aesthetic significance to the psalms tempts the contemplative to cling only to their literal or spiritual meaning and prevents a "deep contemplative penetration" beyond the letter of religious verse. The speculative realm of language, art, and aesthetic pleasure are, as Merton elsewhere maintains, "potential source[s] of unrest and dissatisfaction" for "the monk who really enters into the full meaning of his vocation." It is in this sense, Merton argued, that art, literature, and poetry in particular "can come to seem particularly shabby and unsubstantial—or else they become a lure and a temptation," especially "when a man lives in the naked depths of an impoverished spirit, face to face with nothing but spiritual realities for year after year" (i). To achieve what Merton called "infused contemplation," the highest degree of self-transcendence into which the monk enters deeply into the incommunicable mysteries of God, he says: "the only way in which we can at last enter into the possession of these realities, which lie at the very roots of our monastic existence, is to stop talking about them and lay our hands on them by living them out in the work of our contemplative vocation" (4). The logic is remorseless. "The desire for contemplation has nothing essential to do with art or with the aesthetic sense. It cannot be satisfied by poetry, any more than it can by philosophy, or music, or ceremonies, or biblical speculation." The monk cannot perfect his union with God through aesthetic experience, "not merely by faith," Merton continues, "not by theological speculation, but by intimate and incommunicable experience" (6).

Merton acknowledged, however, that the psalms do have a literal and comprehensible meaning. All of the battles, triumphs, agonies and didactic allegories depicted in the psalms have provided, he grants, "the constant basic spiritual nourishment of Catholic mysticism." But he was far more determined to stress the mystical dimension in which the "glorious, sometimes bloody and sometimes simply sensible and prosaic" aspects of the psalms, taken literally, serve only as "an outer shell." "The 'real' meaning of the psalms," then, "is held to be a spiritual kernel which must be arrived at by penetration of the 'letter.' To cling to the literal meaning alone is, according to this line of thought, to miss the whole significance of the Psalms, for 'the letter killeth'" (20).

Nowhere was Merton's renunciation of the artistic sensibility more dramatic and forthright than in his essay, "Poetry and the Contemplative Life" which appeared in *The Commonweal* in 1947. Since it treated the "esthetic instinct" as a handicap to contemplation, Merton also appended the essay to *Figures for an Apocalypse* as a sort of apologia to explain the difficulties the contemplative faces when writing poems. Speaking as a contemplative whose life is "entirely occupied with

God," Merton centers his argument on a progression between three degrees of contemplation. He first describes "natural contemplation"—a more or less instinctual appreciation of the beauty and perfection of creation. This is the level of consciousness achieved by the artist, the philosopher, and practitioner of "the most advanced pagan religions." "Active contemplation" follows; this is the mode of contemplation experienced by the "baptized Christian" who is lifted to a higher level of spiritual awareness through participation in the sacramental life of the church. But active contemplation, like natural contemplation, is still an inferior contemplative mode because "much of the initiative," Merton explains, "belongs to our own powers." Each degree of contemplation, in other words, is rendered insufficient because of persistent attachments to self-will. To liberate himself from such attachments, the active contemplative (who in Merton's lexicon is the Christian poet) must take the final plunge into "contemplation properly so-called: the life of *infused* or *passive* or *mystical* contemplation" (*FA*, 96).

The infused mystic transcends the experiential boundaries of the self. He lives "on the desire of God alone." His "mind [is] divested of all earthly things and united, insofar as human weakness permits, with Christ." Sounding as if he were giving some critical justification for the anti-secular mentality and apocalyptic imagery reflected in his own poems, Merton further claims that the infused mystic, having "tasted" and "possessed" God's goodness in the depths of the soul, will "rise up in judgment against our generation which refuses the treasures of infused wisdom, preferring the far lesser riches of worldly wisdom and philosophy." He will also rebel against "comfort-loving American materialism" and "insatiable emotional vulgarity" and "the pious 'art' that infects the atmosphere of the Church." And he will also rise above the inferior claims of poets who "prefer to struggle along in the wake of indifferent and mediocre secular models . . . of which even the children of our modern world have long since grown tired."

Just as he had offered a proviso in his study of the psalms, Merton argued that poetry still has a place in this progression through the three degrees of contemplation. Christian poets—Catholic poets in particular—are naturally disposed toward the ascent to infused contemplation. No Christian poetry, Merton demurs, "has been written by anyone who was not in some degree a contemplative." As far as

natural contemplative poets are concerned, their "technique will remain barren" without the liturgical and sacramental gifts of the (Catholic) church. With no little religiocentric bias, Merton argues that
modern poets must cast off secular prosodic and thematic models inherited from a corrupt past; they must no longer sing "the same old
cracked tune that Georgians inherited from Tennyson and Swin-
burne." In a word, poets must become baptized Catholics and active
contemplatives. "Therefore, it would seem fairly evident that the one
thing that will most contribute to the perfection of Catholic literature
in general and poetry in particular will be for our writers and poets to
start leading lives of active contemplation" (*FA*, 100).

Merton felt that this was an efficacious progression through the
first two degrees of contemplation and sufficient preparation for
"contemplation properly so-called." The active contemplative poet,
he decided, will quickly learn to "not shrink from . . . penance and
sacrifice." He will "seek them." The Christian poet will be naturally
inclined toward a life of infused contemplation. But here is the rub: "It
is obvious, then, that [active] contemplation has much to offer poetry.
But can poetry offer anything, in return, to contemplation? Can the
poetic sense help us toward infused contemplation, and, if so, how
far along the way?" (101).

Merton no doubt wanted to answer those questions affirmatively.
Judging from the basis of his own scenario, he himself had already
passed from the natural into the active contemplative mode; he had
just written a dramatic account of that progression in a forthcoming
autobiography. As he stood at the gates of infused contemplation,
surely he must have questioned—as he had in the epilogue to *The
Seven Storey Mountain*—whether he needed to surrender his poetic
sensibilities in order to gain entrance. In "Poetry and the Contemplative Life" Merton confronted again a central question that preoccupied, almost to neurotic proportions, the first ten years of his monastic life—the same question he encountered in his autobiography
and his in-progress diary, as well as in *Figures for an Apocalypse, The
Tears of the Blind Lions,* and *Bread in the Wilderness.*

In "Poetry and the Contemplative Life," Merton answers that question in no uncertain terms. The would-be mystic, he insists, will remain "utterly incapable of apprehending . . . the obscure light of infused contemplation" unless his soul "is suitably purified of images
and attachments to sensible things." The poet and artist must divest

themselves of "feeling and emotionalism" lest their art degenerate into sentimentality and attendant "evils that tend to corrupt religious experience before it has a chance to take root and grow in the soul." Merton hedges slightly by admitting that "the genuine aesthetic experience" is "a very high gift," one of "essential dignity." The resemblance between the aesthetic experience and that of infused contemplation may seem so close indeed because each is a "supra-rational intuition of the latent perfection of things." Nonetheless, even a poet like William Blake, Merton argues, "could almost confuse the two and make them merge into one another as if they belonged to the same order of things." Merton follows with the linchpin of his entire argument: "And yet there is an abyss between them."

It seems incredible indeed that Merton could come so close to re-solving, if only tentatively, the dilemma of art and spirituality and yet with such determination return to the conclusion that art is the one big obstacle to infused contemplation, the very pinnacle of religious life. Granting earlier in the essay the essential dignity of the aesthetic experience, Merton betrays that proviso with an ultimate disclaimer: instead of being a precious gift, art becomes a *"fatal handicap."* The danger is precisely this: "if the mystic happens to be, at the same time, an artist, when prayer calls him within himself to the secrecy of God's presence, his art will be tempted to start working and produc-ing and studying the 'creative' possibilities of this experience. And therefore immediately the whole thing runs the risk of being frus-trated and destroyed" (108). In a statement that clearly captures the spirit of denial that Merton turned against his own self-image as poet as well as the dogmatic sacred/secular polarity that fueled his denial, he concludes: "there is only one course for the poet to take, for his own individual sanctification: *the ruthless and complete sacrifice of his art.* This is the simplest and safest and the most obvious way—and one which will only appal someone who does not realize the infinite dis-tance between the gifts of nature and those of grace, between the natural and the supernatural order, time and eternity, man and God" (110). The above text, incidentally, is taken from "Poetry and the Con-templative Life" as it appears in *Figures for an Apocalypse.* In the *Com-monweal* version, the key phrase "will only *appal* someone" reads as "will only *appeal* to someone."[2] Such a misprint was either a colossal typo or the work of a devious copy editor, for there is little doubt which meaning Merton intended.

— 4 —

Just as Merton had tried to recoup the cold and unfeeling demeanor in his diary account of the Louisville trip discussed earlier, so too did he later atone for the excesses of his dogmatic stance on art and spirituality. It would be a simple matter, then, to turn directly to Merton's revisionary essay on poetry and contemplation which, like its prototype discussed above, appeared in the company of another volume of poems. Although Merton wrote "Poetry and Contemplation: A Reappraisal" as an appendix for *Selected Poems,* edited and introduced by his Columbia University mentor and good friend Mark Van Doren and published in 1959, Merton arranged for the essay's publication first (once again like its prototype) in *Commonweal* a few months earlier, in October 1958. While it may be purely coincidental, there is nonetheless a marked dramatic quality and appeal to the similar ways in which Merton announced the death of the poet in 1947 and, eleven years later, broadcast, somewhat belatedly, the story of his resurrection.

In 1947, Merton publicly renounced poetry in the pages of the popular Catholic press, a touching appeal to a mass audience. Here was a relatively unknown but promising young monk—a poet by nature—who was so dedicated to the monastic life that he was willing to sacrifice his art in order to perfect his spirituality. It was entirely appropriate that Merton should include his farewell address in what was surely to be his last volume of poems, *Figures for an Apocalypse,* published in March 1948, just a few months after the essay's first appearance in *Commonweal.* Poetry readers, a far narrower audience, were, after all, reading poems in *Figures* which raised themselves up as barriers to the poet who wrote them and at the same time wished to escape from them. The last poem in *Figures,* for example, merged so perfectly with the sentiment of sacrifice and renunciation at the heart of "Poetry and the Contemplative Life" that the poem read almost like an epigraph to the essay that followed on its heels. "Now is the day of our farewell in fear, lean pages," Merton wrote in "The Poet, to His Book." Calling his poetry a "thirsty traitor in my Trappist mornings," Merton moved from one image of accusation to the next, claiming that poetry blocked the gate to "white eternity," upset his silence, dirtied his clean hands, and hung "Around my mad ribs like a shirt of flame" (*CP,* 192).

Ironically, however, Merton could never break free from that burning armor, despite persistent disclaimers to the contrary. In fact, while readers of *Commonweal* were being touched by Merton's prose elegy to his poetry career, Merton's new literary agent was busy not only negotiating a contract for the forthcoming *Figures* with James Laughlin, the publisher of New Directions, but also drafting another contract for *A Man in the Divided Sea*, an earlier volume of verse New Directions had issued, without a contract, in 1946. That Merton enlisted the aid of a literary agent in April 1947 to help him with a budding literary career is a fact in itself that raises some interesting questions about his poetic farewell in *Commonweal* the following month. Moreover, in March 1947 Merton encouraged his agent to continue sending his novel, *Journal of My Escape from the Nazis* (published shortly after Merton's death as *My Argument with the Gestapo*), around to publishers, although she dampened his enthusiasm and felt it was not a good idea to publish the novel at that time, an opinion shared by editors at six publishing houses who had already rejected the manuscript. And when *Figures* appeared in March 1948, Merton quickly wrote to Laughlin and asked that he forward review copies to several people, including Robert Giroux, Merton's new editor at Harcourt, Brace, who had just sent Merton the page proofs of *The Seven Storey Mountain*. A comment Merton made to Mark Van Doren further compromised the strategy of denials announced in the original *Commonweal* essay. He wrote Van Doren less than a year after the essay's publication and told him that he still held "to everything I said in the article about the nature of the problem [of art and contemplation] itself." But he equivocated by explaining that "the problem is a fearful one [only] as it stands on paper—and *in the abstract.*" He noted apologetically that "it doesn't make so much sense anymore to be planning to either renounce or to adopt whole 'blocks' of activity—cutting out 'all' writing or 'going into solitude for good' (as I would like to)—the thing is to take a new line and let everything be determined by immediate circumstances"[3]—circumstances which included the meteoric rise of his autobiography on the best sellers list only a year after he had apparently surrendered his ambitions as a writer in the *Commonweal* article.

So, at a time when Merton was stressing the theme of the sacrifice of art in the popular Catholic press—a small price to pay, he said, for the fruits of true contemplation, "this pearl of great price"—he was

privately engaged in dealings with literary agents, editors and publishers, all in an effort, it would seem, to accelerate his literary career.
He often set a pace which frustrated his agent and created headaches
and contractual difficulties not only for his principal publishers, Harcourt, Brace and New Directions, but for a secondary contingent of
magazine publishers, foreign presses and publishing firms anxious to
buy up translation, paperback, reprint, and book club rights for
Mountain and *Waters of Siloe,* Merton's history of the Trappists, as well
as numerous pamphlets, essays, and poems which had lapsed out of
print. Even the appearance of *Figures,* with its "stubborn talker" vowing to withdraw from "the loud world's corner," did not slow the appearance of more new poems. Within two months Merton was placing poems in such prestigious periodicals as *The Partisan Review, The
Atlantic Monthly, Poetry* (Chicago), *The Hudson Review,* even *Commonweal;* all the new poetry would be collected and published in *The Tears
of the Blind Lions* the following winter of 1949.

While unfair, it is nevertheless tempting to argue that this inconsistency between Janus-faced personae—a pious young monk publicly
sacrificing his art and an eager young writer privately orchestrating a
formidable literary machine—amounted to an exercise in hypocrisy
on Thomas Merton's part. As the complex dynamics of his creative
drives are more fully revealed, we will be better equipped to explain
and accept the ambivalences and equivocations which marked Merton's attitude toward his self-image as a writer during the late forties
and early fifties. We will learn to see how crucial it was for Merton to
position himself in conditions which, paradoxically enough, threatened both his creativity and his monastic spirituality. If the soul of the
contemplative is, as Merton was fond of saying, like an athlete, so too
is the heart of the artist. Both monk and artist need worthy oppo-
nents, as we shall see, to test and try out and push and extend the full
potential of their powers, even while those powers were locked in an
often acrimonious conflict during Merton's formative middle years.

But for now, many troublesome questions could be dodged by turning directly to the apologetics of 1958 and reassessing the problem of
art and contemplation in the same revisionary spirit that Merton himself used in "Poetry and Contemplation: A Reappraisal": namely, that
the solution of sacrificing art as a means to "contemplation properly
so-called" was little more than an overly confident pronouncement of
an exceptionally enthusiastic young monk—in fact, no solution (in-

deed, not even a problem) at all, but rather an illusion created by a defect in logic. Simply put, Merton discounted the 1947 essay as full of "wrong-headed propositions." "The earlier problem," Merton explains, "was, largely, an illusion, created by this division of life into formally separate compartments of 'action' and 'contemplation.' But because this crude division was stated so forcefully and so frequently in my earlier writings, I feel that it is most necessary now to try to do something to heal this wound and draw together the two sides of this unfortunate fissure" (*LE,* 339). That "crude division" accounts as well for the dogmatic sacred/secular polarity that also informs much of his earlier writings, prompting his often dispassionate world-denials. While I will have more to say about Merton's "Reappraisal" later on, it will not suffice, for the time being, simply to turn to the renovated aesthetic that emerged in 1958. The inconsistencies, the contradictions, the kind of gamesmanship that Merton indulged in during these earlier years cannot be so easily dismissed, either by examining his later apologetics or indeed by pressing into use the famous cliché of Merton scholarship—that he was a prophet travelling toward his destiny in the belly of a paradox. I do not believe that the same claim can be made for Merton that he himself, in his master's thesis, made for William Blake—that "Children and Saints can believe two contrary things at the same time."

Questions, as interesting as they are troublesome, persist.

Did Thomas Merton announce his sacrifice of art in 1947 to guarantee a sympathetic readership at a time when his literary career was finally starting to take shape? Robert Speaight, in his foreword to an early English edition of Merton's *Selected Poems,* 1950, captured just such a note of intrigue when he wrote: "Thousands of Thomas Merton's readers in Britain will be eager . . . to savor for themselves the talent which he would be glad to sacrifice. They will wonder perhaps why the poet has not disappeared into the silence and anonymity where the Cistercian finds his soul" (*SP,* xii). Or did Merton use his renunciation of art—a dictum that stressed the ultimate, pandemic failure of art—to shield himself from the lukewarm, frequently adverse criticism his poetry was drawing from the critical quarters? Or was he struggling with the cause of a propagandist, cleaving tenaciously to his logic of denial, and trying to prove that art—especially as his contemporaries, the modernists, were defining it—was in league with modern life (which Merton described in *The Seven Storey*

Mountain as "that empty temple full of dust and rubbish") and that art, *ipso facto*, had to be renounced along with modern life as he converted his manners and took up residence in the monastery? And how did Merton feel, knowing that while he renounced art along with "my own disgusting century" he was participating simultaneously in the birth of James Laughlin's New Directions enterprise, the most significant avant-garde movement of the century, the very oracle of modernism? Or, to put it bluntly, was there a briar-patch mentality operating in Merton's position on art and writing? If he could go public with his desire to stop writing, would his superiors recognize in Merton's need to renounce art precisely that Cross that God intended him to bear? Merton flatly states in the epilogue to *Mountain* that "this shadow, this double, this writer" who dogged him into the cloister "has my superiors on his side. They won't kick him out. I can't get rid of him. . . . This is a situation," Merton continues, "in which . . . my enemy, Thomas Merton, the old man of the sea, has things in his favor. If he thinks up poems to be printed and published, his thoughts are listened to. If he suggests books about the Order his suggestions are heard. There seems to be no reason why he should not write for magazines" (412). And in an unpublished section of the epilogue Merton writes: "The most peculiar thing of all is this: the most unexpected Cross seems to be, in my case, that one that should have been the most obvious from the start. . . . [I]t seems that God has decided so far to operate on me in the way that I thought had to be renounced. The method I feared was the wrong one is one that He has chosen. And so far, at any rate, it has been God's will that I seek Him, not by *not* writing, but by writing."[4] Was Merton's desire to mortify himself through the exercise of that activity he most enjoyed and was most suited for an irony, or perhaps a strategy designed to guarantee that his superiors would exile him to a briar patch where he was, after all, most comfortable?

Finally, Merton's public sacrifice of his art brought him the kind of sympathy that counterbalanced the very unsympathetic, austere environment of the monastery during the forties, in the same way that *Mountain* brought him fame and identity, a similar compensation for the anonymity of his life at Gethsemani. When Mark Van Doren received his review copy of *Figures* with its note on contemplation, he wrote Merton immediately to tell him how deeply moved he was. "Nothing has ever touched me more deeply than the problem you posed." He urged Merton, "for the good of *other* souls," to refuse "to sacrifice the poet's art."[5] Merton replied by thanking Van Doren above all for "your kindness and deep understanding,"[6] and even noted in his diary that "Mark Van Doren wrote a beautiful letter about *Figures for an Apocalypse,* full of sympathy for the problem of poetry vs. contemplation . . . [and] wrote another, with the same sympathy for the problem of solitude" (*SJ,* 94–95). Merton drew a similar sympathetic response a few years earlier from Catherine Doherty when he wrote to tell her of his struggle with his identity as a writer. "Tom, oh Tom," she replied, "you will become so very small that your writing will be like fire, and sparks of the Holy Ghost lightening [sic] little torches everywhere to illuminate our terrific modern darkness"; she urged him "to write for the masses."[7] Sister Therese Lentfoehr, who was to become an avid and influential popularizer of Merton's poetry, was similarly moved by Merton's dilemma over art and contemplation— so moved, in fact, that she arranged for the publication of an unpublished section of *Mountain* where Merton offered a provisional reconciliation of the conflict between poetry and contemplation. "As for his friends the poets," Sister Therese wrote in her sanguine editorial note to the excerpt, "it is salutary indeed to have been told these things: made aware of the possible conflict between poetry and contemplation, and been allowed to observe at close range its resolution in the life of one of their own."[8]

I wouldn't be asking such questions nor raising such unflattering issues if I felt Thomas Merton could not bear up under their scrutiny. I have purposely tried to shed some light on a darker side of Merton, a side just as much subject to possible misinterpretation as, I think, the more popular mythic view of Merton as a paradoxical traveller inching toward his destiny in the belly of a whale. The fact is that Merton was a exceptionally complex man. He was constantly erecting barriers, mortared by the greatest dogmatism, both to his writing and to his progress in the spiritual life, only to surmount such barriers and erect others. He needed, it would seem, frustration, dilemma, and crisis to propel his growth and maturity as a writer as well as a monk. Crisis in Merton's life, as Erik Erikson has said of Martin Luther's, always anticipated and accompanied creative breakthrough. Thomas Merton thrived, in short, on the creative tensions engendered by his art of denial.

2

The Art of Denial, I

To those people who formed an inner literary circle around Thomas Merton in the late forties and early fifties—his agent, Naomi Burton Stone, Robert Giroux, and James Laughlin—the notion of Merton denying his art and flirting with a decision to cease all writing projects might seem odd, if not absurd.

While Mrs. Stone, for example, was always sensitive to the primary importance of Merton's spiritual life at Gethsemani, there were times when she wished Merton himself would just stress the affairs of his religious life and ignore the business details of his literary career. Her job as Merton's agent would have been much easier had Merton simply been an antiworldly monk who routinely forwarded all business letters to her office. But her job was complicated by Merton's penchant for getting involved in the affairs of his literary enterprises, by his breezy inattention to the language of contracts, by his great literary charity and indifference to matters such as royalty negotiations and copyrights. A good case in point occurred in July 1952, when Merton took it upon himself to give a Spanish publishing firm, Rialp, the translation rights for *Seeds of Contemplation, The Waters of Siloe, The Ascent to Truth,* and his poems, an authorization that violated a translation agreement Mrs. Stone's agency had with the publisher Sudamerica in Argentina. Writing to Merton, Mrs. Stone gently reminded him of the legal consequences of violating such agreements, then encouraged him, as she had done on numerous occasions before, to send all requests from publishers and editors along to the agency. "Clearly you are already involved with a good deal of correspondence which shouldn't take up your time. That is what we are for," she wrote. "I simply can't believe that your time is best employed in handling what amounts to business detail and I have asked you, begged you, to send on all business letters to us and let us save you that time."[1] Merton apologized with boyish indifference. He qualified his business error by admitting that he was more interested in getting his books into readers' hands than in royalties, agreements, or contracts. He jumped, it would seem, at the chance to garner an international audience.

I haven't chosen the affairs of July 1952 at random. While Merton was violating a contractual agreement in an effort to reach a wider audience for his writings, he was at the same time working on the final pages of his journal, *The Sign of Jonas*. "Fire Watch, July 4, 1952"—the epilogue to *Jonas*—is, as Jacques Maritain noted in his appeal to the Cistercian Abbot General to overrule the censors' objections to the journal's publication, the most beautiful and fully resonant piece Merton ever wrote on the freedom, joy, and abandonment he experienced in the grip of total silence and solitude. The beauty of "Fire Watch" rests as much in its language as in its thematic content. Yet there is a powerful tension between its theme of the exquisite joy and pristine innocence of silence and the perfection of the language— the *art*—that is communicating that theme. "I sit in human silence," Merton writes. "Then I begin to hear the eloquent night, the night of wet trees, with moonlight sliding over the shoulder of the church in a haze of dampness and subsiding heat." In the epilogue Merton shuffles through the Abbey, wearing a pair of communal sneakers, with the time clock of the night watchman slung over his shoulder. His progress through the stations of the fire watch—from the Abbey basement to the steeple of the sanctuary—becomes a symbolic journey through the degrees of contemplation he wrote about exactly five years earlier, on July 4, 1947, in his essay renouncing art. The problem of the epilogue, however, is that the fire watch also becomes the odyssey of an artist who was able, perhaps for the very first time, to keep pace with the contemplative during the ascent to true contemplation.

"When prayer calls [the mystic] within himself to the secrecy of

God's presence," Merton wrote in 1947, "his art will be tempted to start working and producing and studying the 'creative' possibilities of this experience. And therefore immediately the whole thing runs the risk of being frustrated and destroyed" (*FA*, 106). But as a more mature writer, working on the creative possibilities of the "Fire Watch" five years later, Merton began to discover that instead of frustrating and destroying the experience of contemplation and solitude, the writer was able to capture and perfect it through the beauty and subtle grace of his language, his art. This must have been a deeply troublesome realization for Merton. It exacerbated the dilemma of art and contemplation and foiled the strategy of renunciation which had seemed, five years earlier, the only path to true contemplation. The innocence which the artist in Merton helped him to recover, as he says in "Fire Watch," "has nothing reassuring about it. The very silence is a reproach. The emptiness itself is my most terrible question. If I have broken this silence, and if I have been to blame for talking so much about this emptiness [in *The Seven Storey Mountain*] that it came to be filled with people, who am I to praise the silence any more? Who am I to publicize this emptiness?" (357). That "most terrible question" can be rephrased to read: Would the incommunicable spiritual reality that Merton discovered in the heart of silence be deepened and purified by surrendering the language and art that tried to contain it? If so, how would Merton reconcile his other discovery—embodied in the very perfection and exquisite prose mastery of "Fire Watch"—that the closer he got to ultimate silence the more powerful and resonant his art and language became?

Having just touched the apex of aesthetic perfection in the pages of the "Fire Watch," Merton's otherwise unbusinesslike efforts to reach a broader audience were certainly justified, at least from an artistic point of view. There might not be such a clear-cut contradiction, then, between the writer who was violating terms of a business contract in July 1952, anxious to get his books into wider circulation, and the contemplative who climbed the vertiginous heights of the Abbey steeple that dark night in July, the contemplative who discovered the power of the writer's words but could not free himself as yet from a logic of denial that stressed the futility of those words. There is, rather, a dialogue taking shape in the pages of *Jonas*, a dialogue propelled by powerful ambivalences: a dialogue between a monk for whom "silence shall be my answer" and a writer who discovered that "what was fragile has become powerful." This dialogue, spurred by creative tensions, inspired *Jonas'* introspective style and its principal motifs. It was a dialogue that made *The Sign of Jonas* the journal of Merton's missing years and showed that his maturity as a writer was nourished, paradoxically enough, by his disavowal of the power and utility of language in the same ironic way that the contemplative's quest for a wordless, timeless eternity was nourished by a central symbol of time itself: that time clock which hung around Merton's neck like an albatross during his triumphant journey on the Fire Watch.

— 2 —

Merton strongly identified his situation as a monk headed for priestly ordination with the predicament of Jonas, the Old Testament prophet. "I feel that my own life is especially sealed with this great sign [of Jonas the prophet]," Merton writes in a prologue to the journal spanning his advancement to sacred Orders. Merton's assimilation of Jonas' story, as a kind of spiritual template as well as a compelling psychological narrative, is revealed through numerous striking parallels. In the biblical account, for example, the period during which Jonas finds himself entrapped in the belly of a great fish is a time of distress and intense self-scrutiny, an interregnum when Jonas confronts self-doubt. Merton's own diary is shot through with such encounters; his self-scrutiny is brought to bear on his self-image both as a writer and as a Trappist priest, something that may account for the Cistercian censors' initial objections to the journal's publication. Written during a time when he ached for a solitude more thoroughgoing than that available in the communitarian life at Gethsemani, Merton's misgivings over his vocation as Trappist also paralleled, in his mind, the situation of Jonas on the ship to Tharsis. Since he had publicized and romanticized the monastic life in *The Seven Storey Mountain*, hundreds of new postulants had flocked to Gethsemani, creating what Merton sensed as "the supreme spiritual risk" of "two hundred and seventy lovers of silence and solitude . . . all packed into a building that was built for seventy" (*SJ*, 5). As Jonas was an archetypal portent of bad luck, Merton questioned his own presence at Gethsemani as a cause of disruption which threatened to ruffle the monastic calm.

Thus he willed himself, in a manner of speaking, to be cast overboard in order to save Gethsemani from storms of disruption for which he was largely responsible while, at the same time, freeing himself for the life of *perfect* solitude as he continued to seek transfer to an eremitical religious order.

Above all, Merton internalized Jonas' mythic struggle between self-will and destiny. Throughout the pages of *Jonas* Merton grapples with two factional self-images. One is rooted in his own desires; it is a self-willed calling which he announced with dramatic understatement in *The Seven Storey Mountain* when he exclaimed to a friend, "I want to be a Saint." The other self-image points to a conflicting destiny from which Merton, like Jonas, sought escape. Merton finds himself fighting courageously against cross-currents of identity: one—his ideal hermit image—beckoning him to disengage and retreat further into the life of total solitude; the other—his shadow image—calling him to his destiny as a writer. I would suggest, then, that the power and dynamics of *The Sign of Jonas* obtain from a compelling psychological prototype revealed to Merton through his identification with the predicament of the Old Testament prophet: Merton's "Tharsis" is the contemplative life; his "Nineveh," the life of a writer. "Like the prophet Jonas, whom God ordered to go to Nineveh, I found myself," Merton writes in a reflective prologue, "with an almost uncontrollable desire to go in the opposite direction. God pointed one way and all my 'ideals' pointed in the other. It was when Jonas was traveling as fast as he could away from Nineveh, toward Tharsis, that he was thrown overboard, and swallowed by a whale who took him where God wanted him to go" (10–11).

It is important to note, however, that, with the possible exception of the "Fire Watch" epilogue, Merton does not, throughout the seven years covered by his diary, come to reconcile himself fully to his destiny as a writer. He follows the journey of Jonas who, although quick to obey God after his trauma at sea, remains displeased and angry when God sees fit not to destroy Nineveh. Resigned to obedience, Jonas nonetheless succumbs to the fears which drove him to escape to Tharsis in the first place. He is never completely liberated, that is to say, from self-will, just as Merton never fully surrenders those "ideals" which pointed him toward another destiny in a different religious order. Merton is not prepared yet to accept with much conviction what he claims years later: "It is possible to doubt whether I have become a monk (a doubt I have to live with), but it is not possible to doubt that I am a writer, that I was born one and will most probably die as one. Disconcerting, disedifying as it is, this seems to be my lot and my vocation" (*TMR*, 17). *Jonas* is not a journal of ultimate liberation, but one of ongoing struggle. For the first time, however, Merton endeavors to entertain doubts over his calling as a hermit/saint—in a way that he never could in *The Seven Storey Mountain*—as well as his instincts as a writer. In a telling moment just one day before his ordination on 26 May 1949, for example, he confesses uncertainty at that juncture and admits "the truth is, I am far from being the monk or cleric that I ought to be. My life is a great mess and tangle of half-conscious subterfuges to evade grace and duty. I have done all things badly. I have thrown away great opportunities. My infidelity to Christ, instead of making me sick with despair, drives me to throw myself all the more blindly into the arms of His mercy." This confessional mode gives *Jonas* its almost painfully ingenuous qualities as a frank, candid, and honest exploration of Merton's uncertainties. Given the strengths of his new journal as a searching psychological inventory, Merton's much more popular autobiography pales in comparison as a mere catalogue of assaults on the philistinism of secular culture.

Throughout *Jonas*, Merton frequently returns to the familiar theme of writing as a monumental distraction to the contemplative life. His quarrel with "the old man of the sea" persists. It nearly brackets the entire chronology of the journal, from December 1946 when he prays himself into silence and solitude, buoyed by the hope that writing will not harm his recollection, to March 1951 and the by-now tiresome plaint, "How weary I am of being a writer." A comment Merton makes midstream may suffice to summarize a motif that surfaces, according to my reading index, in at least sixty-six entries during the intervening five years: simply put, "since I have become a great success in the book business," Merton writes on 31 July 1949, "I have been becoming more and more of a failure in my vocation."

Although Merton had ample evidence of his stunning success in "the book business," he was less chary in his assessment of how good a writer he was and, by subtle extension, how good a writer he wanted to be. In keeping with his calculus of denials, Merton professed the dictum that literary instincts frustrate spiritual progress. Yet there is an underlying concern, often subject to evasions on Merton's part, which hints more at his low self-esteem as a writer. One is not entirely sure if he is lashing out at the writer's shadow because it stands in the way of Father Louis' spiritual evolution or betraying a deeper-seated fear that he has failed as a writer according to more rigorous self-imposed standards that cannot be measured by public acclaim. Even as early as 1951, for example, Merton discounted the public clamor over *The Seven Storey Mountain;* he became suspicious of its success in the marketplace of public opinion and, in a series of self-deprecating remarks, complains that its literary value was seriously compromised by youthful enthusiasm, rhetorical excess, and an absence of maturity and wisdom in both its vision and execution. When reading the proofs of a French translation, Merton notes in *The Sign of Jonas,* 13 June 1951, that he "might as well have been a proofreader working for a publisher and going over the galleys of somebody else's book. . . . *The Seven Storey Mountain* is a work of a man I never even heard of."

Merton distanced himself from other books as well. When correcting proofs of *Figures for an Apocalypse,* he simply exclaimed "I am disgusted with it." *The Ascent to Truth,* which Merton was working on throughout much of the latter half of the period covered by *Jonas,* bore the brunt of his literary frustrations and dissatisfaction. The many hours of heated effort Merton expended on his only theological work did not seem so much a distraction from his monastic agenda as they were hours of ill-spent and unprofitable literary labor. "I had been worrying and bothering for two months," he writes on 15 February 1949, "about being unable to get anywhere with this new book, *The Cloud and the Fire* [the original title of *The Ascent to Truth*]. There were some forty pages of it, written mostly in blood . . . . And they were terrible—great confusion. Too long-winded, involved, badly written, badly thought out and with great torture too." The fear of the manuscript going badly is heightened as Merton contrasts it with a prefatory note he had just written for *The Waters of Siloe* which "went like a breeze." Two months later he confesses to a certain terror over the project. "I sit at the typewriter with my fingers all wound up in a cat's cradle of strings, overwhelmed with a sense of my own stupidity, and surrounded by not one but a multitude of literary dilemmas."

This does not exactly sound like a monk who was goading his superiors to demand that he stop writing. This is the voice rather of a writer who encounters the unthinkable horror of a writing block. In a revealing headnote to Part Three of *Jonas*, Merton begins to reevaluate the nature of his writing crisis as "a state of intellectual siege." At a time, he writes, when "my mind was occupied with the last and most important steps in my progress toward the priesthood . . . [,] I [became aware] that my writing, which had once been a source of imaginary problems, was now becoming a real problem and that problem was reaching a crisis." Merton's distinction between writing as "an imaginary problem" and "a real crisis" is an important one. It suggests that if his innate drives as a writer spelled crisis in his life, it was a crisis not of distraction but one of inspiration. He continues: "I suddenly discovered that I was scarcely able to write at all. It takes more than good will to write a book. What you write has to come up out of the depths of your being and if, in those depths, the instinct for self-expression has dried up or become paralyzed, there is no way of writing a book" (125).

Fortunately, Merton found a spontaneity, joy, and lucidity in the pages of his diary which more than compensated for the frightful paralysis brought on by *The Ascent to Truth*. Even while he continued to affect an attitude of denial toward his writing throughout *Jonas*, there are nonetheless frequent flashes of sheer prose beauty. The poems he wrote during this time were stunted by a poetics of negation, so, interestingly enough, the strongest poetry of the period surfaced in the diary. The most poetic moments come when Merton liberates himself from trials of introspection. If the centripetal forces of introspection compel him inward to search himself and agonize over questions of self-doubt, centrifugal forces turn him outward where he engages with renewed enthusiasm and vigor the beauty of creation reflected especially in nature's handiwork: "an unspeakable reverence," as he says, "for the holiness of created things." During such moments of temporary detachment, Merton discovers great tranquility as he is absorbed into the landscape of Gethsemani's surrounding woods. This shift in Merton's vision often accompanies a change in the actual settings where he conducts his writing sessions. Usually he writes in an old vault converted to office space, a venue itself symbolic of introspection and conducive to feelings of "fear, dejection, non-existence" which crowd in on him. It is in the vault where Merton wrestles with *The Ascent to Truth* and its paralysis of inspiration and where he finds the futility of literary effort closing in on him like "a big wave of darkness [coming] up from inside me somewhere." After spending two claustrophobic hours shut in the vault, he "came out with the conclusion that writing is something very low and insignificant, and that I, who seem to have become identified with writing, am also low and insignificant" (14 April 1949). Yet he discovers another place to write in the loft of an old dilapidated garden shed. He often returns there to clamor up a broken ladder and sit in a rickety chair amid a clutter of strawberry boxes and rusted buckets and peer through "a beautiful small rectangular window which faces south over the valley—the outside orchard, St. Joseph's field, the distant line of hills." It is almost as if that window inspires a new vision of untroubled extrospection and calls Merton out of himself into "deep peace . . . and happiness" (250). It is here, amid the lovely old junk, that Merton crafts the poetry of *The Sign of Jonas*. This extrospective angle of vision inspires stretches of prose which resonate with the sights, sounds, and subtle textures of nature proliferating in the woods. Such blocks of descriptive prose poetry punctuate the diary and counterpoise its recurrent cycles of introspection. During such moments Merton is also able to experiment with the "creative possibilities" of narrative story telling. After making his usual trek to the garden house after dinner one evening, for example, Merton witnesses a hawk swooping down on a flock of starlings. He links the "terrible and yet beautiful thing, that lightning flight, straight as an arrow, that killed the slowest bird" to his own artistic flights. Reflecting on the power, grace, and sure aim of the hawk, Merton wonders "if my admiration for you gives me an affinity for you, artist! I wonder if there will ever be something connatural between us, between your flight and my heart stirred in hiding" (*SJ*, 275). On another occasion Merton strikes a less serious note when he transforms the scene of two hunters and their dog into a Chaplinesque episode. As one hunter, "White Pants," climbs atop the enclosure wall, Merton ponders an unlikely denouement. "The whole universe knew that as soon as he fired the gun he would fall off the wall backwards inside the enclosure, perhaps into the dirty old bathtub full of rain water and spring water and green weeds which is placed there as a horse trough. Then he would have to become a monk" (265).

In these entries Merton becomes a writer celebrating the possibilities of language, not a poet/monk denigrating its limits. The two contextual vantage points from which the narrative of *Jonas* issues— the vault and the attic in the garden shed—are symbolic, then, of the powerful ambivalences tearing at Merton during the late forties and early fifties. Father Louis, caught in the belly of the vault, submits to an "abysmal testing and disintegration of my spirit." Thomas Merton, gazing through the loft window, discovers "a new spring of life, a peace and happiness that I had never known before and which subsisted in the face of nameless, interior terror" (238).

The centrifugal impetus in *Jonas* that guides Merton to an appreciation of the natural world also prompts a new tolerance toward American social institutions and generally a more thoughtful and studied compassion toward other human beings. Merton still indulges in moments of indignation toward contemporary American culture, but in his new journal, indictments of secular culture are not nearly as sustained or self-conscious as in *The Seven Storey Mountain*. The more broad-minded, open, and accepting temperament reflected in *Jonas* owes much, I would suggest, to Merton's identification with the journal's biblical namesake. Jonas' story is one of intense self-scrutiny, but his lesson is ultimately one of compassion, tolerance, and deliverance. The reason, we may recall, that Jonas fled God's call to Nineveh was that he feared God would show compassion and not visit ruin on the wicked city. Once the citizens repent, God spares them the disaster He had threatened. Despairing of God's graciousness and compassion, Jonas wills that his life be taken, to which God counters by reminding Jonas of His tolerance for merely human faults and weaknesses.

Jonas' legalistic self-righteousness is mirrored in the reactionary attitudes Merton takes toward the unconditional apostasies of secular life in *The Seven Storey Mountain*, whereas the nascent humanism of *Jonas* suggests that Merton began to find some tolerance and compassion for human foibles and naiveté. He is able to admit, for example, that "My complaints about the world in the *Mountain* and in some poems are perhaps a weakness. . . . It is impure. The world I am sore at on paper is perhaps a figment of my own imagination. The business is a psychological game I have been playing since I was ten" (20 February 1949). The arrival of a copy of *Seeds of Contemplation* on the 6th of March, 1949 gives Merton further occasion to question his lack of "warmth and human affection": "I find in myself an underlying pride that I thought was all gone, but it is still there, bad as ever."

"What is my new desert?" Merton asks. "The name of it is *compassion*." Two signal episodes helped lead Merton to that renaming: tak-

ing the oath of American citizenship and his appointment as Master
of Scholastics, both of which occurred in June 1951. Although he anticipated the prospect of American citizenship with some trepidation,
"in the end," he writes after much reflection, "I have come to the
conclusion that I can't kid myself that it is as important a step as
religious profession or taking the habit of novice and it is useless to
try to act as if it were" (330). Accepting himself as a part of and not
alien to "my country" brought him a warm sense of belonging as he
passed through the secular ritual of naturalization. When named
Master of Scholastics, Merton felt a similar sense of altruistic integration into collective life. He remarked that his new responsibilities as
spiritual director of the young professed monks helped resolve his
struggles with stability which, during the previous years, had led him
to view himself as an outsider in the community life at Gethsemani.
As we shall see, any apparent solution to the problem of stability was
short-lived, but for "now I know that the reason why I had to resist
the temptation to become a Carthusian was in order to learn how to
help all the other ones who would be in one way or another tempted
to leave the monastery" (329). Both of these incidents summoned
Merton from the isolation of his self-searching and brought him,
"sometime in June [of 1951]," he recalls, to "stand on the threshold of
a new existence." Although still uncertain of what lay ahead, he was
convinced that

> I have become very different from what I used to be. The Man who
> began this journal [five years ago] is dead, just as the man who finished
> *The Seven Storey Mountain* when this journal began was also dead, and
> what is more the man who was the central figure in *The Seven Storey
> Mountain* was dead over and over. . . . Consequently, *The Seven Storey
> Mountain* is the work of a man I never even heard of. And this journal is
> getting to be the production of somebody to whom I have never had the
> dishonor of an introduction. (328)

Everything that Merton implied about his evolution over the five
years covered by *Jonas* was brilliantly synthesized in the "Fire Watch"
epilogue. As I mentioned earlier, the epilogue is empowered by Merton's integration of his long-conflicting monk and writer personae. As

a result, the epilogue may indeed bear the praise Jacques Maritain showered upon it as the finest piece of spiritual prose written in the twentieth century. Not only is it a finely crafted narrative journey from the Abbey cellar to the belfry high above the sanctuary; the epilogue attains a depth and symbolic resonance as an autobiographical journey. As Merton punches the time clock at the key stations along the watch route, he simultaneously unlocks crucial junctions in his own personal history. "The fire watch," as he says, "is an examination of conscience in which your task as Watchman suddenly appears in its true light: a pretext devised by God to isolate you, and to search your soul with lamps and questions, in the heart of darkness." From the damp earth of the cellar floor, Merton advances through the choir novitiate—"suddenly haunted by my first days in religion, the freezing tough winter when I first received the habit and always had a cold"—then on through the novitiate chapel, the brothers' washroom, the ceramic studio, and the second and third floor dormitories. Finally he climbs the twisted stairs to the belfry. And "a huge chorus of living beings rises up out of the world beneath my feet: life singing in the watercourses, throbbing in the creeks and the fields and the trees, choirs of millions and millions of jumping and flying and creeping things. And far above me the cool sky opens upon the frozen distance of stars." This is a moment of oneness and unity when "The Father and I are One," a contemplative still point to which the course of Merton's monastic life had been set. *Yet in that moment the Trappist is not rendered speechless.* On the contrary, the Fire Watch culminates in the most gracefully understated and elegant line of prose that Merton ever wrote: "There are drops of dew that show like sapphires in the grass as soon as the great sun appears, and leaves stir behind the hushed flight of an escaping dove" (362).

The sheer prose beauty of "Fire Watch" suggests that eventually the fructifying tensions which nurtured Merton's growth as a contemplative and his maturity as a writer may have indeed served him well. But such tensions created difficulties for Merton's superiors, responsible for the spiritual life of Father Louis, and for his literary circle, responsible for the dispensation of the writings of a best-selling author. Nowhere are these difficulties and frustrations more pronounced than in the relationship between the two dominant motifs of *The Sign of Jonas* and the story of its troublesome birth as one of Merton's most highly praised works.

Two parallel compulsions dominate *Jonas* up to that point in June 1951 when Merton found himself on the threshold of a new existence: the renunciation of his natural literary bent and the anguish he experienced over the problem of stability. "[F]or me," he says in the prologue, "the vow of stability has been the belly of the whale." Merton's rapt attraction to the life of perfect solitude compelled him to question the viability of Cistercian monasticism. This drive for an unconditional solitude, not readily available in Cistercian communitarianism, must be seen from the perspective of its relationship to Merton's desire to quit writing. Just as he flirted with a renunciation of art in an effort, ultimately, to perfect it, so too did he seriously consider leaving the Cistercians in an effort to perfect his spirituality. Both drives are parallel and intimate. They spring from the same posture of denials that dominate Merton's middle years. Moreover, Merton's problem with stability, like his struggle over the business of writing, is entangled with ambivalences. At a time, as we shall see, when Merton was tendering a formal petition to transfer to the Carthusians—an eremitical order that stressed a life of total solitude—he was beginning to shoulder enthusiastically more of the important *community* responsibilities of life at Gethsemani as Master of Novices. Similarly, while Merton explored the option of ceasing all writing activity in the pages of *Jonas* he was simultaneously, and with equal enthusiasm, sending his agent pages of the manuscript as they poured daily from his typewriter and receiving, almost daily in return, responses such as "it is exciting to read something that knocks sparks out of the tired old brain" and "let me have more Journal. . . . I am so proud of you and so grateful for you."[2] After Robert Giroux read a section of the Journal-in-progress where Merton meditates on the great joy he feels in the presence of the phrase, "I am finished as a writer," Giroux wrote to Merton: "I think it is magnificent! We must publish it. . . . It may be your most important book. . . . We can get the text into proofs in the next few weeks."[3] ("Nothing," Merton writes, "seems so foolish as to go on writing.")

There is an almost perfect symmetry of ambivalences, in other words, in these tandem motifs of denial. And they derive their power, furthermore, from the bearing they have on the solemnity embodied in Merton's vows as a priest. If Merton continued writing (and the pitch, pace, and quantity always quickened in the wake of these spells to abandon it), he would come dangerously close to compromising the vow of silence, if not in a legal at least in a psychological sense. If Merton toyed with the idea of joining another religious order, he would come dangerously close to violating his consecrated vow of stability. Both strategies suggest a compulsive, but nonetheless fascinating psychological positioning on Merton's part: his need to be constantly acting out the drama of a man violating the inviolable, without quite advancing beyond the edge into a tragic denouement.

Of course publicly, in the pages of *Jonas* when it was finally published in 1953, Merton had to manipulate his need for a deeper solitude quite carefully, for it amounted to a critique of the Cistercian way of life that would not set well with the Trappist censors. Any public pronouncements concerning his dissatisfactions with the Cistercians were in fact blunted by the censors, who worked over the manuscript ruthlessly. Few entries dealing with Merton's "instability" escaped their blue pencils. One censor, who insisted on deleting certain passages he called "mere drivel" and "the ravings of a crazy man"—and others, like "the greatest part of this is mildly insane"—concluded: "with self-revelation as intimate as that contained in this 'journal,' [it] seems to this censor a matter of questionable prudence [to publish it at this time]—a sort of canonization ante mortem."[4] Besides, Merton had a reputation to protect, a reputation which may have seemed more important to his superiors than to Merton himself. He was already a public figure of no little influence; his transfer to another order could have been viewed publicly as a defection.

So Merton had to camouflage his criticism of the Trappists in *Jonas* by pointing, for example, to the dangers inherent in the phenomenal growth of the monastic community during the postwar years, especially at Gethsemani, whose population in 1952 skyrocketed. Merton sensed a "supreme spiritual risk" in the overcrowding at Gethsemani, with its cacophony of machines and bustling activity which threatened his passionate drive for a deeper silence and solitude. "The young monk who makes his vows at Gethsemani in this unusual moment of crisis and transition," he warned in the prologue, "is exposing himself to something far more than the ordinary vicissitudes of a Trappist monastery. He is walking into a furnace of ambivalence which nobody in the monastery can fully account for and which is designed, I think, to serve as a sign and portent to modern America." One ironic aspect of Gethsemani's swelling population was that Merton-the-contemplative was trying to escape from a problem created, in large part, by Merton-the-writer. As Louis Lekai says in his historical study of the Cistercians in the twentieth century, Merton himself "was undoubtedly the magnet which attracted hundreds [of postulants] to one or another of the mushrooming Trappist communities."

If Merton made it sound as if "the ordinary vicissitudes of a Trappist monastery" during the pre-boom years were enough to satisfy his demands for the silent life, he was taking a far different slant in his private correspondence. As early as 1950, Merton was sending strong signals of his dissatisfactions to Dom Jean Leclercq, a Benedictine monk whose writings on the eremitical life had greatly influenced Merton. He sensed in Dom Jean an ally, and would capitalize on that allegiance five years later when the question of his transfer to an order of hermits was officially broached. In a comment to Dom Jean about the Cistercian reformers De l'Estrange and De Rance (whose strict reformist principles were in the ascendency at Gethsemani at the time), Merton noted in October 1950: "To my mind the most regrettable thing about both of them was their exaggeration of externals, their ponderous emphasis on 'exercises' and things to be done."[5] In keeping with the pattern of dual motifs which dominated the journal Merton was then working on, he later told Dom Jean, "I hope to withdraw from the field of professional writing," and begged Dom Jean's prayers that "God may deign to open to us here in America the ways of solitude. . . . This, I think, is much more important than any books."[6] It might have seemed to Merton that his prayers to be "an eremitical son of St. Benedict" were soon answered when he found out that the Carthusians had established a monastery in America.

— 4 —

Merton's restlessness with the Cistercian way of life continued to fester until it became an all-consuming preoccupation. I quote at length from a letter Merton wrote to Father Barnabas Ahern, a Passionist priest from Chicago, in December 1952:

> I have been fretting over this question [of transferring to another order] for some nine years. . . . I have never really succeeded in quite believing

that the ordinary routine of Trappist life is exactly what I am called to do. It is just "not it." With me it does not *work*. . . . It produces effects in me which are more or less opposite to what it produces in those who are really called to it. . . . The perpetual motion of exterior exercises, the constant presence of a lot of people . . . , instead of helping me to pray and liberating me from myself, tends to get me tied up in myself to a point that it is really harmful. To be alone, with real silence, real solitude without material responsibilities straightens everything out.

Merton told Father Barnabas that a decision to enter another order was "close to the heart of the matter" but that

such a step might possibly be regarded by many as a kind of 'defection,' a retreat from duty, a concession to self-will and human weakness, an eccentricity. . . . One of the things that I think I must face and work out. It may well be a temptation, but the refusal to face it, the fear of it, has been making a mess of my interior life. . . . What I find in solitude is so worthwhile, so truly the thing I am *really called to* and so much the real reason for my existence on earth, that it is worth facing the accusation of defection in order to get it. Such accusations might occur. Let them, then. . . . Frankly I don't think there will be any but pharisaic scandal at what I hope to do in the future. . . . I hope in the future to live completely as a hermit.

This was a familiar posture for Merton. In facing accusations and creating scandal he would once again be courting the inviolable, a courtship which would also require him, of course, to sacrifice his identity as a writer. "In the most complete possible solitude," he concluded in his letter to Father Barnabas, "I will be doing a work more pleasing to our Lord . . . than if I wrote many books."[7]

Clearly, the combined force of his need to surrender all writing activity and his decision to leave the Cistercians created tremendous inner turmoil for Merton during these years. This period of conflicting renunciations accounted for what both Merton's biographers agree was a time of major crisis in his life: "the personal anguish," as Merton said to Father Barnabas, "of travelling a road on which there is great danger of illusion and on which I will undoubtedly meet many critics and many obstacles." Father Barnabas' prescription to ease that anguish was certainly well intended. "My advice," he wrote, " is to take a full sabbatical year, by giving yourself to Trappist life as the ordinary monk lives it. Follow the monastery horarium to the letter, work in the fields, eat well; if you write anything—poetry or prose—

do so as a congenial form of self-expression. Forget publishers and articles entirely. Do not pressure yourself to turn out notes for the students. Live the quiet, leisurely, and peaceful life of the ordinary religious at Gethsemani. For the past nine years," Father Barnabas continued, "you have been living under constant *tension*. No man could have written as much as you have done . . . without pressure pain. Your mental powers have been constantly taxed. Eat a few beef steaks and sleep in for Matins!"[8] This was probably just what Merton needed, but held in the powerful grip of ambivalences, he could never express himself congenially, much less surrender all thoughts of publishers or give himself over to the life of an ordinary monk at Gethsemani.

Merton's anxious fretting over a decision to enter another order and the private anguish he must have felt over the thought of giving up all writing activity had to reach a flash point eventually. As Merton's Abbot said in a letter to Dom Jean, "Father Louis . . . has worked himself into a great brain fever, and he is blaming everyone else and his surroundings for his lack of peace—which is common to neurotics."[9]

Merton finally set in motion what promised to be a catharsis when he applied to Rome for an official "transitus" to a small order of Italian hermits in May 1955. Although Merton's Abbot was opposed to the idea of his leaving Gethsemani—ostensibly because of the possible scandal Merton's "defection" might excite—"one thing," as Merton explained to Dom Jean, "is certain, everyone more and more seems to agree that I should not stay in the precise situation in which I find myself at the moment. I honestly believe, and so do my directors, that being a cenobite is no longer the thing I need." If the plan to join the Italian hermits failed, Merton hatched an alternative scheme, which he shared with Dom Jean, to "secretly enter a hermitage of Monte Corona, and live there unknown without writing or publication, as a true solitary. . . . I think . . . that I could leave secretly enough to keep . . . comment at a minimum. It would never be more than a rumor, and there have been so many rumors before that people would not pay much attention, until it was all forgotten."[10]

A slight note of paranoia accompanied these scenarios. Instead of easing tensions, Merton's restive planning seemed only to excite them. The closer he got to the *reality* of being a hermit and the closer he came to the ultimate anonymity of no longer being a writer the more uncertain he became. Although the conventional view is that Merton's Abbot only aggravated and prolonged such painful uncertainties by handling Merton cruelly, in the manner of a drill sergeant, it strikes me that the Abbot, on the contrary, seemed to be the only person who really understood the confusing ambivalences resting at the heart of Merton's decision to leave Gethsemani and quit writing. "Can [Father Louis] actually give up writing completely?" the Abbot asked rhetorically.

> The more I think of it . . . the more I seem to see in Father Louis just a lot of poetical fancy and imaginings.
>
> He never struck me as being destined for the eremitical life, and I feel, in conscience, that if he were to leave here, for [Italy], for example, he would not stay there very long either. Some new wild idea would hit him and off he would go. He would be a roamer, a gypsy.
>
> Yet because of his reputation as a writer and his most skillful use of words, he could convince almost anyone who does not know him.[11]

So the Abbot, in direct consultation with Merton himself, posed a compromise scheme in June 1955, an alternative to the transfer to an order of obscure Italian hermits or the dramatic, surreptitious flight to Monte Corona. Merton explained his Abbot's compromise plan to Dom Jean.

> At the moment, it does seem that there is a real chance of my being allowed to live in solitude *here*. . . . On the material side, the way seems to be preparing itself. The State Forestry Department is erecting a fire tower on one of our big hills . . . and they are going to erect a small cabin there, in which one might conceivably live. It will be an austere and primitive kind of hermitage, if I ever get to live in it. . . . I think I can count on a semi-solitary life for part of the year as the Watchman on this fire tower.[12]

This seemed like a splendid plan. Merton could be a hermit in residence at Gethsemani. There would be no scandal stirred up by rumors of defection. Merton could climb up the ladder of the fire tower, slam the trap door of the little cabin behind him and lock himself away into the obscurity he so passionately desired. And he could also expel the writer up there. "I intend to renounce [writing] for good, if I can live in solitude" in the fire tower, he promised Dom Jean in the same letter where he detailed the Abbot's new plan. Merton continued:

I realize that I have perhaps suffered more than I knew from this "writing career." Writing is deep in my nature, and I cannot deceive myself that it will be easy for me to do without it. At least I can get along without the public and without my reputation! The whole business tends to corrupt the purity of one's spirit of faith. It obscures the clarity of one's view of God and divine things. It vitiates one's sense of spiritual reality.[13]

Should the Abbot's plan materialize, Merton had to start making preparations for his new life as Gethsemani's fire tower hermit, which brought him to "the main purpose" of his effervescent letter to Dom Jean. "I am clearing out my files." In the same way that he had burned his manuscripts fourteen years earlier when he entered Gethsemani, Merton now needed a similar ritual sacrifice to purge him of the writer's shadow. But there was one last manuscript (just as there had been in 1941!) which Merton decided to rescue from the flames, the swan song of the writer. "There is one manuscript which I think ought to interest you for your Tradition Monastique" (a series of monographs under Dom Jean's general editorship). "It is a short, simple collection of meditations on solitude . . . , worth sending to you. They will make a small volume, better I think than *Seeds of Contemplation* and more unified. The manuscript is being typed. Let me know if you are interested, and when it is finished I shall be sending it to you."[14] It would seem that while Father Louis was immolating the writer, Thomas Merton, the writer, was rising from the flames and peddling one of his books. Recalling the words of Merton's Abbot, "Can he actually give up writing completely?"

The Abbot did not have the authority to permit Merton immediate access to the fire tower, but he promised Merton he would bring the matter to the attention of the Abbot General during the General Chapter meeting in France, scheduled for September 1955. The Abbot recalled the events surrounding his return to Kentucky in an essay he wrote for a collection of tributes prepared in honor of Merton after his death.

> At the Chapter [meeting], I explained the situation to the General. He said: "O.K., but with this condition, that Fr. Louis be 100% hermit—that is, not be a cenobite in the morning and a hermit only in the afternoon."
>
> On my return from the General Chapter, Fr. Louis came at once to see me.
>
> "The General says O.K.—provided it is a full-time life as a hermit."

Fr. Louis was radiant. "Terrific—Terrific," he said. "I never expected it." Although his expressions of gratitude and delight were quite prolific, I seemed to sense that, now he was actually confronted with the reality of living alone in the tower, he was a little hesitant. . . . Now it was up to him.[15]

There was another stipulation that the Abbot didn't mention in his essay: he and the Abbot General decided that if Merton set up a hermitage in the fire tower he would not be allowed to write. He had to give up all contact with publishers, editors, and agents for at least five years. Merton's enthusiasm for joining the Italian hermits had cooled considerably when he found out that under no circumstances would a hermit be permitted to publish his thoughts. How would he react now, knowing that the path had been cleared to the fire tower but that his notebooks and typewriter had to be left behind?

— 5 —

If Merton had given Dom Jean the impression that only one small pamphlet of meditations on solitude would survive in the wake of his departure to the fire tower, he was taking a far different and more ambitious tack with his literary agent. Just a week before he posted his letter to Dom Jean, Merton wrote his agent and listed for her the literary "line-up that, I think, includes everything. It is all that will be left after I dive into the bushes and disappear."[16] He catalogued the following manuscripts: *The Living Bread* (one of four books he was under contract to deliver to Harcourt, Brace); *Silence in Heaven* (later published as *The Silent Life*, 1957); *Solitude* (which became *Thoughts in Solitude*, issued by Farrar, Straus and Cudahy; it never appeared in Dom Jean's *Tradition Monastique*); and *Tower of Babel*, Merton's versified morality play later published by New Directions in an exquisite limited edition on handmade paper, a gem of typography and book design that would bloat the pride of any author. (Merton told his agent "I hope [New Directions] can give me a good looking book without having to go through outlandish contortions to do it.") These manuscripts were ready for publication. Others were on the drawing boards: *Praying the Psalms, Christmas Sermons of Guerric of Igny,* and *What Is Meditation?*. As a footnote to this formidable bibliography, Merton squeezed in the following request to his agent: "In a last paroxysm of vanity and ambition I dreamed for a moment of getting a poem in something called *Botteghe Oscure*. Have you any contacts with them—must be in Italy. As I read over that last paragraph I say to myself, more realistically, 'What do you mean *last* paroxysm of etc.?'" Moreover, two weeks before Merton petitioned for his transfer to the Italian hermits, his literary coterie was encountering enormous censorship difficulties with the second edition of *The Sign of Jonas* because Merton had failed (or refused) to make some of the changes the censors had insisted on after their review of the first edition, which had barely made it into print over the censors' initial objections. A letter from Merton's agent summed up the pitch of activity surrounding Merton's literary career at a time when he was making feverish plans to abandon that career for a life in the fire tower.

> from now on we are going to move at a more leisurely pace, believe me, and no more dashing into print before [the censor] has had his say. . . . The strange thing is I was going over an old T. Merton file this morning . . . and it's clear that there's an aura of—what? frenzy isn't quite the right word, but we've had our fair share of troubles and impasses. . . . Certainly the frenzy is all caused in the outside world. . . . I do have to smile a bit when people assume that being the agent for one Trappist monk must be child's play.[17]

When confronted with the Abbot's stipulations for the hermitage project in the fire tower, no wonder Merton seemed a bit hesitant. How could he write all these books when locked up in the fire tower without a typewriter? Without access to publishers for five years? How could he read proof? Would he be allowed to see that handsome edition of *Tower of Babel* with its woodcuts and tooled ivory spine and its gold lettering? Would he be able to sign the colophon pages when they arrived from the famous German typographer whom Laughlin had hired to print the book on handmade paper? Such questions must have been on Merton's mind when he sat in conference with his Abbot that afternoon late in 1955. Judging from his letters to his literary agent, Merton had good reason to be hesitant. His hand had been forced. He could no longer retreat into a strategy of equivocations, either with himself, his Abbot, or his literary circle. Interestingly enough, five years earlier Merton recorded a dream in his journal that foreshadowed the waking dilemma he now faced. In his dream, he is granted permission to visit Haiti, and he confronts the same impasse posed by the circumstances presently surrounding the fire tower plan. "I kept debating in my mind," Merton remembers, "whether God wanted me to take back my request [to visit Haiti] and just stay at home. I dreamt of many factors in the problem and finally asked Reverend Father what I should do and he said he wished I would just make up my mind once and for all" (*SJ*, 278). Five years later, however, Merton was not accorded the luxury of decisions postponed by waking from a dream. It was either a 100 percent life as hermit with his literary instincts banished from the scene, or time for compromise and reconciliation.

The possibility of just such a compromise appeared immediately on the scene with the kind of timing that defies mere coincidence. On the same day the Abbot returned from France and negotiated with Merton the terms of the hermitage deal, Gethsemani's Master of Novices left Kentucky for a position in another monastery. Merton's Abbot recalled, "Three days after my previous conversation with Fr. Louis about his 'Fire Tower' hermitage life he came in again to see me. 'Reverend Father,' he said, 'you have need of a new Father Master of Novices. I've been giving it deep and prayerful thought. If you so judge, I'll be willing to take the job, and thus help you out.'" Although the Abbot's heart immediately "leapt with joy," he let Merton stew for three days while he thought the offer over. "In three days Fr. Louis returned. 'It's all right to be Father Master,' I said, 'but only on two conditions. One, that you'll keep the job for three years, and two, that you'll give no conferences on becoming hermits!' At this he laughed and laughed. I laughed, also. He knew what I meant. 'Don't make me take any vows on this,' he said, 'I've enough now.' This appointment seemed to lift a tremendous load off his heart."[18] Nothing could be as far removed from the life of a hermit as that of Novice Master. It was probably the most important communitarian job in the monastery. Instead of finalizing those plans he had initiated just weeks earlier to leave Gethsemani—either secretly or through an official *transitus*—he assumed, in a blinding turnabout, the responsibility of maintaining the continuity of Trappist traditions by becoming the spiritual director of Gethsemani's future monks. Besides, there were perquisites to the new position which probably appealed to Merton. As Novice Master he would be able to sleep in his own little room apart from the monk's dormitory. He would spend most of his time in the novitiate, reading, teaching, and conducting the kind of research crucial to his work as a writer. He would have a private office where he could prepare his notes for the novices and, as time permitted, work on his own manuscripts which the novices could type for circulation to publishers.

— 6 —

The events which transpired during the latter half of 1955 were crucial for Thomas Merton. By all accounts, these months were a pivotal period in his life. Biographical interpretations, however, differ. Michael Mott, for example, explains Merton's hesitancy as a matter of Merton's own realization that he was not as yet fully prepared for the spiritual and psychological rigors of the hermit's life. Monica Furlong argues that this was a ruefully sad time for Merton, that the Abbot's conditions for the fire tower project were extreme, even cruel and a bit spiteful. She writes of Merton's frenzied and half-baked plans to become a hermit as "a brave struggle to attain the kind of life he needed." While acknowledging that Merton "had . . . serious doubts about continuing as a writer," she sees nonetheless "a cruelty in the [writing] ban that had no relevance to the issue under discussion and had therefore a suggestion of spite about it."[19] This line of interpretation fashions an exterior drama which capitalizes on Merton's heroic efforts to conquer the heights of his own spirituality. Such a position stresses the image of Merton's spiritual ascent as being tragically blocked by the power politics of an institution bent on holding him in check. Merton did, it is true, sound sad and depressed when he wrote to Dom Jean to announce the failure of the hermitage project and his appointment as Novice Master. "I care very little what I do now," he said dejectedly. "My only task now is to remain quiet, abandoned, and in the hands of God."[20] But his depression was short-lived, or so at least it seemed in an effervescent letter he sent to Mark Van Doren the same month. "You don't know, do you," Merton wrote, "that I am now master of the novices—a much more responsible and occupying job than the other one [as Master of Scholastics]. I have practically a small kingdom of my own, a wing of the monastery in which Canon Law says I am the boss. . . . The best of it is that the [novitiate] is quiet, and we have our own garden and chapel, and also the job is not too plaguing. In fact I find that if I overcome a little

of my selfishness it is quite pleasant." Reflecting on his "awful wrestling" with the question of solitude, Merton concluded that "it sounds
silly but I had to go through with it."[21]

Judging from Merton's comments to Dom Jean, the pivotal events
of 1955 were the source of great emotional trauma and depression.
The Abbot's version stressed the theme of catharsis and resolution, as
if the Novice Mastership lifted a great burden from Merton's heart.
Merton's letter to Van Doren seemed to suggest that the events leading up to 1955 were just a passing folly. All three versions point the
way into a cul-de-sac of contradictions.

Viewed from the perspective of an interior drama, however, a different scenario emerges. This is the drama of a man, not cowed by his
superior's will to power, but suffering rather from deep misgivings
over his own decisions, misgivings powerful enough to prompt self-
deceptions and manipulations in his dealings with his abbot and
friends: a man, as we have seen, paralyzed by ambivalences. It is a
drama driven by internal conflicts between Merton's rival personae,
not between Merton and his Abbot. And the struggle that enlivens
the dramatic line is not Thomas Merton's battle to attain the kind of
life he needed; it is the struggle of Thomas Merton deciding on what
kind of life he *wanted*.

What sort of life did Merton envision up there in the fire tower? He
had said to Father Barnabas that "as far as writing goes, I do not feel
that I will ever write anything worthwhile if I cannot have access to
the depths which solitude alone seems able to lay open to me."[22] And
while he seemed to imply to Dom Jean that he was clearing out his
files, the letters to Mrs. Stone show, on the contrary, that Merton was
organizing his files in preparation for the move to the fire tower.
Perhaps life in the fire tower would not free him from the writer's
shadow after all. Perhaps it would liberate him instead from the "perpetual motion of exterior exercises" that punctuated the monotony of
daily life down at the Abbey and excuse him from "material responsibilities" and cut him loose from the drudgery of the monastery
horarium. Maybe Merton had visions of the hermitage being an ideal
writing studio, far better than the vault or the tool shed adjacent to
the Abbey machine shop where he worked on his manuscripts for
only two or three hours a day. Maybe that "semi-solitary" life as a
hermit in the fire tower he had described to Dom Jean might have
become a semi-solitary life as a part-time writer in the fire tower, with

its magnificent 360-degree view of the surrounding countryside. Merton might even have been trying to recapture the symmetry of that moment he had briefly experienced three years earlier on his "Fire Watch." The parallels are striking. In the fire tower, as on the Fire Watch, he would not be bothered by the other monks. The writer would be invited to follow the saint up the ladder to the fire tower, in the same way he had during the ascent into the Abbey belfry.

The conditions, however, would not be those proscribed by Merton's Abbot. While the Abbot's stipulations may seem dogmatic, there was nonetheless a touch of therapeutic common sense to them. The very fact that Merton opted out of the fire tower project when confronted with such stipulations suggests that he had no intention of giving up his writing projects. In actively lobbying for the Novice Mastership one has to question too the strength of Merton's resolve to live as a hermit. The Abbot's decision meant only that Merton had to make a decision of his own. He could no longer rely on ambivalent denials which only shielded him from making a painful decision about what kind of life he really wanted.

3

The Art of Denial, II

Among the many complex factors contributing to Thomas Merton's renunciation of art during the missing years, perhaps the most obvious was the influence of the monastic tradition he entered into in 1941 and embraced, at least during his early years as a monk, with such enthusiasm and totality of commitment. The Cistercian spirit of simplicity and ideal of poverty were so deeply ingrained in the traditions of the Order that art, almost by definition, seemed suspect and superfluous to a religious life stripped down to only the barest necessities. A rigorous asceticism left little room for artistic expression. The historical record suggests, in fact, that the Cistercian Order was established partly as a reaction to the material ornamentation and gaudy Romanesque artistic excesses gradually infiltrating the medieval church. St. Bernard, the eleventh-century founder of the Order, had insisted, in his seminal *Apologia*, that artistic ornamentation aroused devotion in carnal people incapable of living a truly spiritual life. "For monks," says the Cistercian historian Louis Lekai, "whose devotion must be formed through contemplation, every external impulse was, in Bernard's mind, necessarily more distracting than inspiring."[1] Since Merton was reading St. Bernard studiously as a young scholastic at Gethsemani, it seems plausible that Merton's abnegation of art derived from the influence of Bernard coupled with the severe asceticism of life at Gethsemani in the early forties.

But there is considerable disagreement among art historians over this perhaps too simplistic equation of Cistercian asceticism and the radical devaluation of the practice and function of art. One noted historian of Gothic architecture—Otto von Simson, in *The Gothic Cathedral*—has argued that St. Bernard's active role in redefining the design of Cistercian architecture inspired the new Gothic style of the thirteenth century.[2] Merton arrived at the same conclusion in *The Waters of Siloe* (1949), his history of the Cistercians. While acknowledging that the Cistercian founders rebelled against "sensible beauty as an aid to devotion," Merton pointed to the paradox nonetheless that "it was the Cistercians who, in the long run, made the more lasting contribution to Christian art." Cistercian architecture, Merton cited as an example, "is famous for its energy and simplicity and purity, for its originality and technical brilliance." It was the Cistercians who effected the transition from the massive, ponderous Norman style to the thirteenth-century Gothic, with its genius for poising masses of stone, as it were, in mid-air, and making masonry seem to fly and hover over the earth with the self-assurance of an angel" (*WS*, 14).

Although the Cistercians have always stressed the primacy of contemplation in the spiritual life, they have never, even during periods of their strictest renewal, insisted on the total sacrifice of artistic expression as a means to their spiritual ends. They have developed instead a fully organic aesthetic, one characterized by great simplicity, purity, and, in their architecture, a lean cleanliness of line—an aesthetic, in other words, *responsive* to their spiritual ideals and very much in step with the quiet dignity of their daily lives.

The apparent anti-art mentality of the Trappists, then, is too problematic to serve as anything but a minor footnote in Merton's forceful denial of art. I doubt, in fact, that Cistercian aesthetics contributed much of anything either to the growing conflict between art and contemplation he experienced during the early forties or indeed to the poems Merton wrote at that time. If he had incorporated the spirit of simplicity, originality and inostentatious technical brilliance that he praised in Cistercian architecture into his early poems, Merton might well have emerged as a better poet. That the early poems were ponderous and cluttered, that they owed their form to borrowed prosodic models—particularly bothersome to Robert Lowell in his unkind review of Merton's poems in 1945—suggests that Merton was oddly oblivious to the possibilities of Cistercian aesthetics as he persisted in pressing his case against the efficacy of artistic expression. Besides, Merton's superiors never demanded that he sacrifice his own art purely for the sake of his interior growth; his Abbots, especially Dom Frederick, encouraged Merton to write and to use his art in the service of his faith.

Perhaps a potential conflict between art and Christian morality that Merton encountered when he gave himself over to the church after his conversion contributed more to his logic of denial. The view of artistic expression as an end in itself is, after all, anathema to Catholic moral theology. Any work of art must be responsive ultimately to final causes embodied in moral dogma. Accordingly, the artistic experience, cut off from its roots in moral orthodoxy, threatens to degenerate into an exercise of mere sensual aesthetic pleasure. By his own accounts, Merton viewed his preconversion years as a young bohemian novelist and would-be Marxist intellectual as a time of sensual indulgence. Given a new moral perspective, perhaps Merton came to associate the apparent debauchery of his younger years with the life of an artist worshipping art and aesthetic pleasure only for their own sake. Since his religious conversion was so all-encompassing, he may have felt a compelling need to surrender his art, just as he felt compelled to renounce his former lifestyle. Merton's burning of his manuscripts shortly before joining the monks of Gethsemani dramatically underscored the connection he made between his writing and the hedonism that characterized his former life as a bar- and bed-hopping undergraduate at Cambridge University and Columbia.

Merton's sacrifice of his art on such moral grounds might be tenable if his early artistic endeavors were inspired by such pleasure-seeking imprudences. But there is little indication that much of what he wrote before entering Gethsemani was in the least sense libido-driven. Although Merton led readers of *The Seven Storey Mountain* and *My Argument with the Gestapo* (an early autobiographical novel not published until after his death) to believe that his early life was lived in a fog of sensual indulgences, he used such titillating references to his past life, it seems to me, more as dramatic counterpoints to heighten the drama of his conversion, more as literary devices, I believe, than as straight autobiographical facts. In no sense was Merton the "godless artist," the *poète maudit* whom he wrote about years later when the editors of *The New Catholic Encyclopedia* asked him to contribute a definitive essay on "Art and Morality." The pre-Gethsemani Merton reflects little fidelity to the portrait of "the accursed poet" whom Merton sketched in that essay, using Rimbaud as his model—the poet who substituted art for religion and morality, and worshipped "the cult of art as an end in itself."

> The . . . accursed poet or saint in reverse lives as an outcast [Merton writes] and delivers himself up unresistingly to every passion and new experiment. Refusing no drug or perversion, he makes it a point of honor to shun nothing except conventional morality and becomes the hero of decadent romanticism. He becomes the symbol and embodiment of the desire to be without limitation, to escape from the tyranny of norms and rules.[3]

Had Merton been a young poet of such temperament, he would have had compelling reasons to denounce art after his conversion. But the image of the young Merton as a "hero of decadent romanticism" is, by any account (even Merton's own in *Mountain*), a grossly exaggerated one. The determination with which Merton pursued his decision to become a priest and his single-minded, fitful search to find a religious order that would take him suggest, on the contrary, the image of a young man in need of conventions, norms and rules, not an accursed poet driven to rebel against conventional moral standards.

An episode worth mentioning in connection with this innocuous conflict between art and Catholic morality occurred early in 1951 and concerned Merton's relationship with New Directions. By the early fifties Merton had established a solid reputation as a best-selling author. His habit of promising and delivering manuscripts to a variety of publishers created chaos in the business affairs of his literary life. In an effort to eliminate confusion, Robert Giroux, with the support of Merton's agent, proposed to Merton and the Abbot of Gethsemani that Harcourt, Brace act as the exclusive publisher of Merton's work in America. Giroux felt that such a plan made sound business sense and was, after all, accepted practice in the publishing industry. The proposition forced Merton to reassess his relationship with James Laughlin of New Directions, who had published all of Merton's poetry. Giroux's proposal bothered Merton because, as he said in a letter to his agent, "it seems too bad to slam the door of the monastery in [Laughlin's] face, which is practically what would result from our dropping all contact with him." Because of Merton's great respect and admiration for Laughlin and his New Directions enterprise, Merton could not, in good conscience, go along with the arrangement proposed by Giroux. The only thing, as Merton explained to his agent, that would force him to cut all ties with New Directions was a "moral question which would confront me if I were found to be actively cooperating in the production of books by other people ([Laughlin's] protégés) who write what might be considered as morally undesirable material."[4]

Merton had a good point. At a time when New Directions was publishing the poems of a cloistered religious, it was also issuing titles from the work of other authors like Henry Miller, whose books were headed to the Supreme Court in a landmark pornography case. The second edition of Kenneth Patchen's *The Journal of Albion Moonlight* appeared under the New Directions imprint the same year Laughlin published Merton's own first volume of poetry. Patchen's journal, to put it mildly, was baldly irreverent in its treatment of traditional Christian moral concerns. The jacket blurb, for instance, proudly announced "an allegorical journey . . . in which the far boundaries of love and murder, madness and sex are sensually explored." Nothing would have seemed a better example of a literature that worshipped itself than *Moonlight*—except, that is, *A Season in Hell*, written by the poet Merton would later call "the accursed poet or saint in reverse," Arthur Rimbaud, whose masterpiece of decadent romanticism was published by New Directions shortly before Merton's second volume of poems.

Merton was not blind to the existence of such books. They confronted him, in fact, with a far more substantive conflict between art and Christian morality than those dramatic allusions he made in *Mountain* and *Gestapo* to the comparatively inoffensive "immorality" of his pre-Gethsemani days. If his high moral standards with respect to art forced him to renounce anything, perhaps he should have gone along with Giroux's proposal and severed his ties with New Directions. Giroux's scheme could have been a relatively painless solution to a real moral dilemma for Merton. After all, it was more than a matter of Merton appearing to the reading public in the company of writers like Miller, Patchen, and Rimbaud. Merton, in effect, was subsidizing the publication of their "morally undesirable" work, since Laughlin used the profits from the sales of books by profitable authors—Merton, Tennessee Williams, William Carlos Williams, for a while, and others—to fund the work of notoriously unprofitable writers like Patchen. From a business standpoint, this arrangement made good sense, but for Merton it established a tacit link to an art that violated Catholic moral doctrine. "I know it is all 'art,'" Merton explained to his agent, "but it might accidentally have a bad effect. . . . I would not be concerned . . . with the character of this material, except for the very important fact that [Laughlin] uses the profits of my stuff to publish these other books. This is a matter of conscience. If . . . I am actively cooperating in the publication of morally undesirable books . . . then I have to pull out—or [Laughlin] has to drop half his authors."[5] If it was indeed a matter of conscience, as Merton seemed to indicate—a matter, that is, at the heart of the relationship between art and Christian morality—then Merton, bound as he appeared to be to his moral convictions, would have only one course to take. He would *have* to pull out because Laughlin, in spite of his great dedication to Merton, would never have dropped half his authors for the sake of keeping Thomas Merton's name on the New Directions list, and Merton knew this too.

Although Merton promised his agent that he would "thrash out this moral angle" with Laughlin, no such thrashing ever took place. I can find no reference in the voluminous correspondence between Laughlin and Merton which even hinted at Merton's moral qualms over the books that New Directions published. Their literary as well as personal relationship never broke stride over the issue of art and Christian morals. If Merton experienced a conflict between art and morality *vis à vis* his relationship with New Directions, it certainly was a benign one which made inconsequential demands on his conscience.

The arguable anti-art sensibility of the Trappists and the innocuous conflict between art and Catholic morality cannot adequately account for the compulsive denials Merton brought to bear on his self-image as writer. Nor can such institutional factors sufficiently explain the ambivalent maneuverings which further complicate Merton's renunciations. We must move beyond these institutional rationalizations, then, and trace the vulnerability and self-doubt Merton associated, perhaps unconsciously, with his identity as a writer to more vestigial sources rooted in Merton's life well before he joined the monks of Gethsemani in 1941. To that end, we must inevitably turn, it seems to me, to Merton's relationship with his father, the artist Owen Merton, and, to a lesser extent, with his mother Ruth.

— 2 —

Ruth Jenkins Merton's cool intellectuality sharply contrasted the volatile emotionalism of Merton's father, Owen. She is described by Merton's biographers as a perfectionist whose maternal affect reflected an odd combination of fawning devotion and clinical detachment. Before the birth of Merton's brother, for example, Ruth ministered to the slightest detail of her infant son's behavior, noting down every fragment of his development in a journal she called "Tom's Book"—his vocabulary, the songs he sang, updates on the status of his baby teeth, descriptive scenes of his infrequent interaction with other children, and so forth, the kind of developmental minutiae one might find in an ethnographer's field notes. Such attention was inevitably deflected to the Merton's new son, John Paul, something that occasioned fits of jealousy and temper tantrums on the young Merton's part. As a result, "his mother's discipline grew harsher," Michael Mott writes, "yet it was probably her changed attitude, rather than the individual acts of discipline, that left such an impression that Merton would feel compelled to tell others about it thirty and forty years later as if it were a recent hurt. Love, with both encouragement and correction, had been replaced by cold, intellectual criticism, making the three-year-old afraid."[6] Monica Furlong also describes Ruth as a perfectionist who showed at times a degree of "slightly chilling detachment" toward her first born. "Ruth's high expectations [for her boy]," Ms. Furlong comments, "seem to have taken from Merton that sense of total acceptance, that conviction of being a deeply good and satisfactory person, that children of less critical mothers enjoy."[7]

Perhaps Ruth's "chilling, intellectual criticism" was unconsciously extrapolated by her young son, as Merton's biographers suggest, as a maternal indifference which inhibited her full, nurturing acceptance of the young Merton. Perhaps too Ruth's supercritical perfectionism, especially when trained on her expectations for the boy, carry over into Merton's later incessant questioning of his talent as a poet and his overly sensitive reactions to such things as rejection slips as a young writer. In *The Seven Storey Mountain* Merton commented, in a vaguely circumspect sort of way, on these two hallmarks of Ruth's maternalism: her predilection for distance in interpersonal affairs and, in particular, her high standards of achievement, which left her young son vulnerable to low self-esteem and self-doubt. "Mother must have been," Merton recalled, "a person full of insatiable dreams and of great ambitions after perfection: perfection in art, in interior decoration, in dancing, in housekeeping, in raising children. Maybe that is why I remember her mostly as worried: since the imperfections of myself, her first son, had been a great deception" (*SSM*, 5). We might be able to discern at least the faint outlines of a psychological analogue here between Merton's latter ambivalent denials of his self-image as writer and his relationship with Ruth. A boy's fear of failure triggered by his mother's expectations of infallibility plays itself out years later in the central inner conflict of Merton's middle years. Just as the mother spurned a son for his imperfections, so too would the monk, questing for an uncompromised spiritual perfection, snub a writer for the imperfections and shortcomings of his art. From his infancy Merton was imbued, it would seem, with a habitual propensity to devalue his achievements and overvalue the risks of intimacy in interpersonal relationships. Solitude, for such a boy, would become a natural haven.

Ruth's penchant for detachment in interpersonal relationships and the painful consequences it must have had for Merton are nowhere better illustrated than in the events surrounding her death when Merton was just six years old. Dying of stomach cancer, Ruth eventually had to leave the household for extended care in a hospital. She insisted that her son must be spared the sight of her suffering, so Merton was not permitted to visit her. Not only was his mother's absence unexplained, but shortly after Ruth left for the hospital, Owen Merton moved his young son into Ruth's parents' house, yet another of the many moves Merton experienced as a young boy. It was there, in the wake of another domestic displacement, that Merton learned of the impending death of his mother. Characteristically, there was an absence of intimacy in the manner in which Ruth informed her perplexed son of her terminal illness: she posted, through Merton's father, a letter for Merton to read. "Mother was informing me, by mail," Merton recalled in his autobiography, "that she was about to die, and would never see me again."

This chilling memorandum and the event which it inevitably foretold meant that Merton had no choice except to transfer to his father the role of nurturing acceptance that his mother could no longer fulfill. With the death of Ruth and the added insecurity of being simultaneously uprooted, Merton surely must have turned to his father for comfort, protection, compensatory love. He must have yearned as well for a secure and stable home environment. Both needs, however, would be left unmet. "Mother's death had made one thing evident," Merton remembered. "Father now did not have to do anything but paint. He was not tied down to any one place. He could go where ever he needed to go, to find subjects and get ideas, and I was old enough to go with him" (16).

Merton did accompany his father on the first of many odysseys in search of artistic inspiration—this time, shortly after Ruth's death, to the budding art colony of Provincetown. But the romance of Provincetown quickly wore off and Owen returned Merton to his maternal grandparents on Long Island where, he later said with a touch of irony, "I went back to the rickety grey annex of the Public School for a couple of weeks—not for longer. Because Father had found a new place where he wanted to go and paint pictures, and having found it, came back to get his drawing boards and me, and there we went together. It was Bermuda" (17). But the lure of the Caribbean also wore off and Owen repeated, once again, a pattern of domestic instability that would continue to set the rhythm of Thomas Merton's life for the next twenty years, a pattern broken only by Merton's entrance into a Cistercian monastery and his somewhat shaky embrace of the vow of stability solemnly sworn by a monk.

After Bermuda, Owen deposited Merton with his grandparents again and left for two years, painting his way across the Atlantic, through France, along the Mediterranean shore, and eventually into Africa. "But then something happened, and we got a letter from one of [father's] friends, telling us that he was seriously ill. He was, in fact, dying." It had only been two years since Merton had learned of the imminent death of his mother through the impersonal means of her death memorandum; now he confronted the impending death of his artist/father through tactics equally depersonalized. "I was old enough to understand what [the letter] meant, and I was profoundly affected, filled with sorrow and with fear. Was I ever to see my father again? This could not happen" (27).

Fortunately, it turned out that Owen had only suffered a nervous breakdown resulting from the strain of his newly-adopted bohemian life-style. He eventually recovered from the episode, returned to Long Island, and announced to his son, "We are going to France." "[B]y now," Merton writes, "having become more or less acclimatized to [Long Island], after the unusual experience of remaining some two years in the same place, I was glad to be there, and liked my friends, and liked to go swimming in the bay. 'France,' I said, in astonishment. 'Why should anybody want to go to France?' " (28).

So they went to France where Merton, now eleven years old, lived with Owen for a year until he left on another art trip. Merton was shuttled to a French boarding school for two years, then, in 1929, moved to England where he attended another boarding school for another two years.

It was while on vacation from the English school, with his uncle in Scotland, that Merton encountered once again the crushing announcement of death linked to detachment, loneliness, the absence of intimacy. Owen lay in a delirium in a London hospital. Mentally unhinged by a brain tumor, he sent his son a strange telegram: "Entering New York harbor. All well." Perhaps there was a deeper significance to Owen's otherwise delirious message, as if he was trying to comfort his son and compensate somehow for his absence, as if he was saying to his boy, "I am finally coming home." With the intuition of a sixteen-year-old, Merton knew what it all meant:

> the bottom dropped out of my stomach. I walked up and down in the silent and empty house. I sat in the smoking room. There was nobody there. There was nobody in the whole huge house.
>
> I sat there in the dark, unhappy room, unable to think, unable to move, with all the innumerable elements of my isolation crowding in on me from every side: without a house, without a family, without a country, without a father, apparently without any friends, without any interior peace or confidence or light or understanding of my own (71).

Merton immediately returned to London where he stayed with his godfather to be near Owen. Merton's recollections in *Mountain* of the hospital scenes at his father's bedside are deeply touching and carry a heavy burden of isolation, loneliness, pain, and powerlessness.

> I said: "How are you, Father?"
> He looked at me and put forth his hand, in a confused and unhappy way, and I realized that he could no longer even speak. But at the same time, you could see that he knew us, and knew what was going on, and that his mind was clear, and that he understood everything.
> But the sorrow of his great helplessness suddenly fell upon me like a mountain. I was crushed by it. The tears sprang to my eyes. Nobody said anything more.

I hid my face in the blanket and cried. And poor Father wept, too. The others stood by. It was excruciatingly sad. We were completely helpless. There was nothing anyone could do (82).

As if to compensate for the painful estrangement he suffered during his mother's lingering illness, Merton returned daily to his father's bedside. Merton's great devotion to Owen during these final days was broken, however, by another of the episodic displacements that had marked their relationship for the past sixteen years. The summer had ended; after a final visit to the hospital, Merton returned to his boarding school where, barely a week after his arrival for the beginning of the Fall term, he was called into the headmaster's office and handed another of those cold and distant announcements of death. "The Headmaster . . . gave me a telegram which said that Father was dead. The sorry business was all over. . . . Here was a man with a wonderful mind and a great talent and a great heart: and, what was more, he was the man who had brought me into the world, and had nourished me and cared for me and had shaped my soul and to whom I was bound by every possible bond of affection and attachment and admiration and reverence: killed by a growth on his brain" (84).

It is as interesting as it is revealing to explore the ways Thomas Merton recreated the portraits of his parents when, as a thirty-one-year-old monk cloistered in a monastery, he was hard at work on his autobiography sixteen years after his father's slow, agonizing death. Not surprisingly, Merton's comments about his mother were spare in *The Seven Storey Mountain*. Aside from remembering her as somewhat of a worry-wart and attributing to her his own "dissatisfaction with the mess the world is in," Ruth emerged from the autobiography only as a minor figure in Merton's recollections of his youth. The thinness of Ruth's portrait might be a result of the natural amnesia of a thirty-one-year-old man trying to remember the events of his first six years of life. Or Merton's reticence with respect to his mother may be attributable more to the psychomechanics of repression, as if, through his relative silence, Merton betrayed the hostility he harbored toward Ruth's detached intellectuality. Whatever the case, Merton's relationship with his mother would remain problematical throughout the balance of his life. The reticences would persist even into the late sixties when Merton was undergoing psychotherapy with a Louisville psychiatrist and corresponding regularly with a woman who, like Ruth, was an intellectual, capable and willing, as Ruth had been, of pointing out and questioning Merton's imperfections and inconsistencies. Merton recognized the parallels in the two relationships. But even with the help of analysis, he could still only question why, as he wrote to his female correspondent, "you frighten me so"—and answer, only provisionally and in parentheses, that "you are 'cerebral' and I probably . . . resent my mother's intellectuality."[8]

But if Merton was reluctant in the pages of *Mountain* to engage Ruth, he spared no detail in his portrait of Owen. If Ruth emerged only in outline, Owen loomed forth in near-Herculean proportions. Merton inflated the image of his father well beyond, as we shall see, any dimensions which Owen realistically deserved. And Merton exalted his father's character on two quite specific accounts, each of which have a crucial bearing on the central conflict Merton suffered during the missing years: Owen as artist and saint.

Merton spoke of Owen's talent as an artist with great admiration and respect. He lifted his father to the ranks of greatness by comparing him favorably, for example, to the most famous of Owen's contemporaries.

> My father painted like Cézanne and understood the southern French landscape the way Cézanne did. His vision of the world was sane, full of balance, full of veneration for structure, for the relations of masses and for all the circumstances that impress an individual identity on each created thing. His vision was religious and clean, and therefore his paintings were without decoration or superfluous comment, since a religious man respects the power of God's creation to bear witness for itself. My father was a very good artist (*SSM*, 3).

And, by Merton's account, a successful artist as well. He remembered Owen's return to New York, after his nervous breakdown in Europe, as a triumphant one. Merton further embellished the details of his father's success in the art world by citing Owen's election to a British art society ("so that he could write F.R.B.A. after his name"), the inclusion of his father's name in *Who's Who*, and a successful exhibition of his watercolors held at a reputable London gallery. "He had gained," Merton specifically noted, "the attention and respect of such an important and venerable critic as Roger Fry, and the admiration of people who not only knew what a good painting was, but had some money with which to buy one." Measured against such carefully chosen standards, Owen was, one might suppose, a success. He was a salon artist. His works sold. His name appeared in the standard registers. And he had received the imprimatur of one of the most famous art critics of his day.

As Merton reconstructed his early years in *The Seven Storey Mountain*, however, he surely had little, if any, awareness of a mood of dark sadness that entered his father's painting and caused Owen to question his talent—in much the same way, interestingly enough, that Merton himself would later be inclined to harsh self-criticism. Merton's ebullient and reverential descriptions of his father's paintings in the opening pages of *Mountain* as "sane and full of balance" and "religious and clean" counter Owen's less sanguine self-assessment as a watercolorist "who is the poorest colorist in the world." In a letter to a fellow New Zealand watercolorist named Esmond Atkinson, Owen described the agony of a creative dry spell. "I have lost the knack of seeing where color is vivid and where it is undercolored," he wrote. "My work has been for the past 18 months as black and triste, as any you ever saw. . . . [My] own feebleness is so apparent; I know where my own weakness lies only too well. . . . My weakness for the time being is that I am probably trying to fly somewhere, where I have no business at all."[9] It may not be entirely coincidental that Owen's confession of creative lassitude came one day after his eldest son's first birthday. The central conflict of Owen's life for the next fifteen years would be between his single-minded dedication to painting—"tantamount to 'monomania,'"[10] it has been said—and the more parochial, but no less demanding claims of paternal responsibility. Owen's admission of creative languor may be an early expression of the guilt he often felt as an artist/father throughout the balance of his life, an issue I will return to below.

At any rate, history has not served Owen Merton quite as well as one might expect from the effusive praise accorded his painting in his son's popular autobiography. I can find no mention of Owen Heathcote Grierson Merton in any of the standard art histories of the United States, Great Britain, or France. His name does appear, along with the reproduction of one of his early watercolors ("The Old Curiosity

Shop," painted in 1910), in Gordon Brown and Hamish Keith's *New Zealand Painting, 1839–1967* (the country of Owen's birth), but he is mentioned only in passing and numbered as one of the many talented expatriate artists who left New Zealand at the turn of the century for the more robust art climate of Europe. There is also a quick reference to Owen in a study of Percyval Tudor-Hart, Owen's mentor. In fairness, I should note that Owen's watercolors do reside in two permanent collections: the Witt Library of the Courtauld Institute of Art, London, and the New Zealand Academy. It is true too that an exhibit of Owen's paintings at the Leicester Galleries (London) in 1925—the show Merton had in mind when he spoke of his father's financial success in the art world—"gained [Owen Merton]," according to a Christchurch, New Zealand newspaper report, "honorable mention in English art circles";[11] of the sixty-one pieces exhibited, over half sold. More recently, in June, 1986, the periodical *Art in New Zealand* dedicated an entire issue to Owen's painting, suggesting perhaps some revival of interest in his work after many decades of relative neglect. Nonetheless, Owen's painting is not represented in any public collections in England (the country where he most frequently exhibited); to my knowledge, only one watercolor is held by a public museum in America (the Brooklyn City Museum). Critiques of Owen's paintings, moreover, were more uneven than Merton was willing to admit in *Mountain*. While Merton, for example, credited the influence of Cézanne favorably, one art critic complained that "the spell of Cézanne" had reduced Owen's watercolors of Provence and Algeria to "frail and airy things."[12] Another critic predicted that "Mr. Merton's art, which eschews pettiness in favor of simplification, will probably never appeal to the many."[13] Two dissimilar reviews of the successful Leicester exhibit best summarize the uneven response to Owen's paintings among his contemporaries.

> His palette is simple—stripped . . . of all the rhetorical glamour traditionally associated with his subjects. . . . [Due to] an absolute banishment of unnecessary detail[,] the impalpable vision always dominates.[14]

> [Owen Merton's] looseness of touch [wrote another reviewer] is not always discriminating . . . but [it gives] an illusion of spontaneity and buoyance of spirit. . . . Too many of the scenes seem to be dissolving or in a dynamic condition on the verge of chaos.[15]

I have to question gently, moreover, Owen's apparent financial success as an artist. Merton himself noted in tones romantic that all his father wanted to do was "paint, and live on practically nothing, because we had practically nothing to live on," especially during Merton's earliest childhood when Ruth and Owen frequently fell back on the financial support of Ruth's father, a wealthy publisher. Even after Owen began exhibiting and selling his works, it seems likely that he exhausted the modest profits on his frequent art trips, while Ruth's parents continued to pay the tuition bills at the private boarding schools where Merton was left behind. Moreover, Merton inherited little money, if any, after Owen died. The year after his father's death, Merton's graduation trip to Rome was financed by his uncle who, along with Ruth's parents, supplemented Merton's modest scholarship to Cambridge University and, later, his education at Columbia.

My point here is not to belittle Owen Merton as a second-rate artist whose work was and remains justifiably neglected. I am interested only in weighing Owen's modest success and talent as an artist in a more objective balance so that Merton's inflated image of his father falls into sharper relief. What is at issue is not Owen's talent *per se*, but the dynamics of veneration which inform Merton's recreation of his father-as-artist sixteen years after Owen's death.

The same motives of veneration entered into Merton's reconstruction of Owen's spirituality and the powers of his religious faith. Returning to Owen's last days in the London hospital, Merton recalled an interesting episode which immediately triggered a passage in *Mountain* testifying to the saint-like greatness of Owen's faith and the manner in which that faith was perfected by his great physical suffering. Merton remembered seeing Owen's "bed covered with little sheets of blue notepaper on which he had been drawing. And the drawings were real drawings . . . unlike anything he had ever done before—pictures of little Byzantine-looking saints with beards and great halos" (*SSM*, 83). We shall see in the next chapter that one of Merton's tentative resolutions of his dilemma over art and spirituality was to exalt Byzantine art and venerate the great Byzantine painters as the only artists who had successfully united aesthetics and spirituality into a truly iconographic art. It would seem that Merton was summoning a similiar calculus during the tragic moments of his father's debilitating decline. Most important, this passage launched Merton immediately into another in which Owen's physical suffering is transformed into a spiritual catharsis not unlike that of the Christian martyr/saints. Owen's intelligence, faith, and will, Merton believed, "were not hampered in any essential way by the partial obstruction of some of his senses." On the contrary, they "were turned to God," Merton writes, utilizing the same rhetorical superlatives he applied to Owen's accomplishments as an artist. On his deathbed, Owen

> communed with God Who was with him and in him, and Who gave to him, as I believe, light to understand and to make use of his suffering for his own good, and to perfect his soul. It was a great soul, large, full of natural charity. He was a man of exceptional intellectual honesty and sincerity and purity of understanding. And this affliction, this terrible and frightening illness which was relentlessly pressing him down even into the jaws of the tomb, was not destroying him after all (*SSM*, 83).

Owen's fight with the tumor, Merton continued, "was making him great. And I think God was already weighing out to him the weight of reality that was to be his reward. . . . His struggle was authentic, and not wasted or lost or thrown away."

Merton's efforts to transmute his father's suffering from a physical to a spiritual plane were not intended simply to cushion Merton from the painful memory of Owen's morbid decline. The dynamics of veneration were so compelling when Merton engaged the memory of his father that he seems to have abandoned autobiography altogether. He lapsed instead into hagiography. He *sainted* Owen. Interestingly, Merton had just finished writing *Exile Ends in Glory,* a hagiography of a Trappistine nun, Mother Mary Berchmans; in that book (which, years later, he rated as the worst book he had ever written) Merton spared little detail in his recreation of the ultimate spiritual profit derived from Mother Mary's great physical and emotional suffering. The motives of veneration and rhetorical excess which moved his life of Mother Mary were not unlike those which colored his portrait of Owen. What is more, even while working his way through the recollections of his own childhood in the manuscript of *Mountain,* Merton had laid plans for another hagiography, *What Are These Wounds?* (1950), whose title alone suggests a further preoccupation with suffering and pain. Coming at a time, then, when Merton was engrossed by the life stories of Christian martyrs—whose superhuman strength of faith provides more than sufficient dispensation for their abject human suffering—his hagiographical treatment of Owen's otherwise debilitating decline reveals a compelling need on Merton's part, I believe, to mitigate the ignobling decline of a failed artist/father.

By inflating the portrait of Owen as an exemplary artist and a man of extraordinary charity of spirit, Merton seemed to be internalizing a certain select image of his father and projecting that image as an endorsement of Merton's own lofty aspirations. Like his father, Merton wanted to be, in spite of his public protest to the contrary, a very good artist (writer), successful and recognized. Like Owen, Merton wished to have a "vision . . . religious and clean." He wanted to be, like his father, "a religious man [who] respects the power of God's creation to bear witness for itself" (*SSM,* 3), a desire made obvious enough by the extremity of Merton's commitment to the monastic life. In seeing himself reflected in the image he recreated of his father, Merton reached for the most powerful source a young man has to confirm his own identity: the acceptance and psychological imprimatur of the Father. The personal impact of Owen's image on Merton himself differed little from the effect Owen's portrait had on Merton's readers—readers like Henry Miller, who, years later, felt compelled to write Merton after finishing the first chapter of *Mountain* to tell him "how deeply moved I was when reading [about] . . . that wonderful father of yours!"[16]

If, however, a young man answers a powerful need to certify his own identity by mimicking the elements of his father's eminence, what happens to that identity when the father-image he re-enacts is, essentially, a fiction? In recreating a distorted father *imago,* might not a young man inevitably suffer ambivalences with respect to those aspects of his own identity based on the distorted father-image? What makes Merton's portrait of Owen in *The Seven Storey Mountain* as interesting as it is problematical is that Merton had to *create* a certain archetypal role for his father. We have seen how Merton lapsed into hagiography in his recollections of Owen as *homo religioso* and how Merton selectively manipulated facts concerning Owen as a successful, much admired artist. I would suggest provisionally, then, that the ambivalences and equivocations which characterize Merton's later renunciations of his self-image as a writer derive from internalizing the myth of his father's greatness. Merton's punishing travails over his literary ambitions are rooted in his refusal to accept his own father as a frustrated artist, as a man broken financially and emotionally, and, above all, as a failed father.

Frankly, I have difficulty identifying Merton's feelings for Owen *as father* in *The Seven Storey Mountain.* It may seem as though Owen was as exemplary a father as he was an artist and a man of faith. It may seem as though Merton was describing strong paternal traits in Owen when he spoke of his father's sincerity and purity of understanding and his "great heart," when he wrote of the strong feelings of affection, attachment, and reverence that he had for Owen. But the contexts in which Merton discusses such attachments reveal more Merton's admiration for Owen than an affective paternal bonding between a father and a son. Merton admired Owen, that is to say, not as a *father*, but as an artist who painted like Cézanne. He reverenced and venerated Owen not as a father, but as *homo religioso*, a man whose will, during the tragedy of his final hours, was turned not to his son, as his son said, but turned "to God . . . to perfect his soul."

What kind of father was Owen? Let's recall a five-year-old boy punished by his mother because he spelled "which" without the first "h"; a mother who modeled her son's early education after a progressive system she had read about in a popular magazine; a mother who routinely noted in her diary her son's height and weight and who catalogued his vocabulary and proudly recorded on his second birthday a working list of 160 words: a clinician, in other words, whose need for maintaining a comfortable distance in interpersonal relationships opened a void of intimacy that her six-year-old son had difficulty growing accustomed to. After her death, the boy naturally transferred his affections to his father, who had yielded to his wife the active parental role in his son's upbringing. The wife's death meant that the husband was now free to dedicate himself to his art. He was liberated from domestic responsibilities. He sensed a new lease on his creative aspirations which, since the birth of his two sons, had been held in check by certain obligatory distractions, such as playing the piano at the local movie house and gardening for the *nouveau riche* neighbors on Long Island. He could go anywhere he wanted to go to get inspiration and ideas: a landscape painter, as it were, set free in a global landscape. And he followed his art dream, frequently leaving his son behind in the care of a gallery of substitute fathers: an uncle, a godfather, a grandfather, a couple of headmasters. Sometimes the father would take his son along, but never for intervals of more than a year. Years later his son recorded a slight but telling detail in his autobiography: "[father] came back to get his drawing boards and me" (17).

Merton's syntax in that sentence from *Mountain* may seem of little significance to the trials of his youth. But his word order takes on the dimensions of metaphor when we consider that Owen's return on this occasion was not an isolated event; Owen's exits and returns formed the pattern of Merton's youth, the very geography of his adolescence. Owen's drawing boards, in short, had priority over his young son. Barely two years after Ruth's death, Owen, in a letter to a wealthy patroness, spoke with a conviction that leaves little doubt where his priorities lay: "If I don't get enough [money] to have at least a year of hard painting . . . —I shall not care what happens to me—I might as well take poison, but I cannot overcome the conviction that I am going to achieve all I wish, and soon."[17] This is the scenario of a young boy desperately in search of the acceptance of an otherwise loving father who was nonetheless more dedicated to his art than to the unmet needs of his son.

— 4 —

The years following his mother's death were woven with much complexity, both in actual circumstances and, more importantly, in psychological consequences for Thomas Merton. Much new evidence has recently surfaced concerning those years. Thanks to the investigations of such scholars as Arthur Callard, Robert Daggy, and Michael Mott,[18] we are able to piece together a fuller picture of what Merton himself later referred to as "a lost childhood" and, from that picture, empathize more deeply with "what a desperate, despairing childhood I had around the ages of seven—nine—ten."[19] And we are able to surmise with more certainty than ever before that the labyrinth of Merton's missing childhood prepared him for a lifelong quest to recover his youth, to "journey back," as Anthony Padovano has said, "to the home he never had as a child[,] . . . to be a child again, to begin the journey once more, to start out with people and God and do it better."[20] We now know that Merton navigated what has been appropriately described as "an unsettling, rootless, jarring and confusing period" after his mother's death—more unsettling than Merton was willing to admit in the somewhat sanitized version of those years told in *The Seven Storey Mountain*. The contrast between events as we now know they occurred and Merton's later retelling of them exposes the revisionary tactics that Merton employed as he sought to reconstruct and thus rediscover his lost childhood. Nowhere are such tactics more revealing than in Merton's treatment of his father. The Owen Merton who emerges from the newly documented historical record is a different, more complex, decidedly more human and, as it seems to me, much more interesting man than the artist/saint depicted in *Mountain:* a man variously described by his new lover Evelyn Scott (with whom Owen became entangled in a tempestuous affair just weeks after Ruth's death) as "obscene," "a lost soul," "naive," "weak . . . helpless . . . impressionable."

For purposes of brevity, I will follow Robert Daggy's probing essay "Birthday Theology: A Reflection on Thomas Merton and the Bermuda Menage" and his reconstruction of the key events largely responsible for Merton's "desperate, despairing childhood." Dr. Daggy speculates that Owen Merton met the novelist Evelyn Scott and her common-law husband, Cyril Kay Scott, before Ruth's death. By the end of 1922, Owen had assumed his position in a classic ménage à trois when he travelled to Bermuda, with his seven-year-old son in tow, and lived with the Scotts. Looking back, it is not hard to imagine a near-caricature of the bohemian expatriate ethos of the twenties lived out in the Scotts' dilapidated mansion in Somerset. Here was a life-style that seemed the very embodiment of that decadent cult of art Merton would later condemn with such indignation as flouting the norms and rules of conventional morality. It is said, for example, that Cyril hardly protested Evelyn's shift of affections to Owen. Her apparently equitable switch of partners to the recent widower, after all, had followed a string of infidelities which included trysts with such literary figures as William Carlos Williams, Waldo Frank, and Dudley Nichols. Kay Boyle (with whom, along with such period luminaries as Djuna Barnes, Jean Rhys, Lola Ridge, and the anarchist Emma Goldman, Evelyn maintained close ties) said of Evelyn's capacity for indulgence that "one was aware at every instant of the nervous complexities of Evelyn's marital, sexual, and professional lives."[21] "She seems to have been," according to Robert Daggy, "simply unable to exist without a man or more than one man in attendance upon her." Evelyn's appetite for excess, what Cyril called her "absolute lack of reserve," was fully expressed in her quintessentially modernist fiction. Of her novel *The Narrow House,* for example, D. H. Lawrence said: "Well, I think it's all vile, but true and therefore valuable. . . . I say this, *The Narrow House* made me hate the disease of love finally, for which, many thanks. . . . Why don't you just spit in the eye of the world and shit on the doorstep of the narrow house?"[22]

From 1922 to 1925, Merton would be buffeted by the stormy machinations of Owen's relationship with the volatile Evelyn. This was the period, immediately following his mother's death, when Merton saw little of his father, who, in the company of Evelyn and Cyril (until he left for a new mistress), journeyed on art excursions back to Long Island, then to Cape Cod, the South of France, and Algeria. The relationship—launched precariously amid what Evelyn described as "the brutal insanity which possessed [Owen] after Ruth's death"—was doomed to an uneasy denouement. "The end of the affair" in 1925, Dr. Daggy writes, "was wrenching, drawn-out and stormy. Misunderstanding developed on both sides though both tried in their letters not to blame the other while the letters are full of implicit reproaches. Owen, seemingly, tried to end the affair gradually, and, rather than making it easier, made it stunningly harder, convincing Evelyn that he was unbalanced. Since she apparently could never quite blame Owen entirely, she placed much of the blame for the relationship's collapse on Tom, a nine-year-old child." Ostensibly, the reason for Owen and Evelyn's parting company was that the Jenkinses, Ruth's wealthy parents, could no longer abide Evelyn; as long as she remained in the picture the Jenkinses threatened to cut off the regular stipends Owen depended upon to subsidize his painting. "If Tom is to live with [Owen]," Evelyn wrote to her confidant Lola Ridge, "he and I, living together, would need to marry at once. If we married at once there would be no help . . . from Jenkins." As Evelyn saw it, this issue of support was compounded by Owen's "terrific terror of repeating his life with Ruth and that disaster of poverty" the Mertons had lived before the Jenkins stepped into the financial breach. Yet for her part, Evelyn sensed an even more compelling explanation for her and Owen's "very queer and messed up and . . . ruined love." "[W]hat [O]wen has been through about Tom," she felt, "is as genuine as about me. Tom is a morbid and possessive kid and Owen is made morbid about Tom through various things that occurred in connection with Ruth. Tom is and will be until he is big enough to be set adrift a constant obstacle to peace of mind."[23] Clearly, the young boy detested Evelyn. Freshly wounded by the death of his mother, he acted out a powerful rejection of Owen's immediate choice of a surrogate, as if his father's affection for Evelyn was a betrayal of Ruth—even to the extent, according to Robert Daggy, that Merton successfully lobbied against Evelyn with the Jenkinses. Owen himself determined that, in the final analysis, his son's hatred was the principal cause of the "terrible catastrophe" of his break with Evelyn. "You will believe my own word on the Gospel," Owen wrote Lola Ridge, "that I know I could not have reconciled the children and the question of either living with or marrying Evelyn. Tom's jealousy and irreconcilableness are perfectly enormous. There was no choice except to leave the children altogether—and then every night for the rest of my life would have been hideous with repentance. Only I see now that for the last eighteen months I was with Evelyn I was in a violently hysterical condition, perhaps controlling it made it more violent."

Faced with the choices, then, between betraying his love for Evelyn, forgoing the financial support of the Jenkinses, or living with the crushing guilt of abandoning his sons, Owen opted to break off the affair with Evelyn and move to France with his eldest son. It is certainly understandable that Merton's descriptions in *The Seven Storey Mountain* of his new life in the village of St. Antonin are full of warmth, joy and renewed intimacy toward his father. Disemburdened of Evelyn's presence, Merton became the sole object of his father's affections.

It hardly requires much expertise in child psychology and development to calculate the effects these years of dislocation had on the young Merton. Perhaps the clearest picture we have of those effects comes from Evelyn Scott's son, Creighton, Merton's playmate during the time of the "Bermuda ménage," who lived as a child amid the same bohemian menagerie. In a never-published autobiography entitled *Confessions of an American Boy*, Creighton Scott writes:

> One may imagine, without understanding it, the plight of a boy bereaved of a mother whom he loved; whose father becomes entangled with someone else's mother, like mine. The ménage à trois is unnatural and repugnant, and my mother made it far worse in [Tom's] eyes than it would otherwise have been by arrogating to herself motherly duties she had no right to assume. Tom was punished by her, not by his father, who stood aside from disciplinary things when my mother was handy. . . . Since she lived by a logic deliberately intended to be different from that of everybody else, it must have seemed capricious and cruel; and I have never been at all certain that cruelty and caprice did not enter into what she did, the fact that she always had explicit reasons for everything being somewhat irrelevant. Tom used to grind his teeth in bed "British tooth-gritting" his father used to call it, half-jokingly; and as far as I can remember, it was always because of what my mother did to him or forced him to do.

. . . I can remember his being punished for crying—it may have been over bereavement for all that any of the rest of us knew—for losing his appetite, for being late to meals, and an infinite number of things that other children are reprimanded for but no more. . . . Quite apart from the actual deeds, there is something bestial, I think, in usurping the position of a dead mother by force majeur, over the anguished protests of the child, and punishing him for not liking it. She used to have tantrums behind his back, too, and I remember her screaming at [Owen] Merton, "I'm sick of his damned mother. Sick of her, sick of her, sick of her! I hate her, hate her, hate her, do you hear?" That was what mattered, not what Tom felt. This was a woman who sneered at jealousy and despised it as infantile. . . . In my late twenties, when she and I were still on speaking terms, her reminiscences about Tom's "badness" and intractability were all accompanied by little unctuous giggles, like that of a schoolgirl using a dirty word for the first time.[24]

Years later, in an unpublished segment of *The Seven Storey Mountain*, Merton, recalling his life on Bermuda, confessed that "that beautiful island fed me with more poisons than I have a mind to stop and count."[25]

— 5 —

Such evidence concerning Merton's vulnerable and uncertain childhood provide fascinating material for speculation, especially as one turns to examine the repercussions those self-described "poisons" of a lost childhood had in Merton's later life. The driving force behind Merton's idealized portrait of Owen in *The Seven Storey Mountain* is considerably clarified by the circumstances surrounding the so-called "Bermuda ménage." Moreover, a childhood Merton himself remembered as disordered and disfiguring sheds light on the two major themes which dominate Merton's probing and intense autobiographical reflections during the forties and early fifties: the acerbic condemnations of modernity in *Mountain* and Merton's denials of his self-image as writer in *The Sign of Jonas*.

As Michael Mott and Robert Daggy suggest, Merton certainly had much to forgive Owen for; "Forgiving our parents," writes Michael Mott, "is one of the most difficult lessons life gives many of us, often marking us forever. . . . Merton's father had such a strong, continuing influence on him precisely because his son felt there was something to forgive."[26] Dr. Daggy agrees: "Though some things may have continued to rankle, certainly by the time we reach the cut and edited version of *The Seven Storey Mountain*, he gives his father a full measure of forgiveness, a forgiveness which may have been the necessary antidote for the poisons of the Bermuda ménage."[27] Eulogizing Owen as an exemplary painter and a man of such extraordinary faith, and making it seem as though such qualities carried over into traits of Owen's paternal character, might be viewed, then, as an act of generous dispensation on Merton's part—his way of forgiving Owen for a wounded childhood. As Merton plumbed the travails of those few short years separating the deaths of his parents, he surely must have encountered much need to forgive himself as well. Even though Owen and Evelyn's relationship was marred by a fumbling condescension on Owen's part and, on Evelyn's, an abusiveness that bordered, at least according to her son Creighton, on emotional sadism, Owen nonetheless loved her. And Evelyn, unreconciled after the relationship ended, still remained "obsessed," as she explained to Lola Ridge, "[by] three years of the closest identity I ever had with any living creature."[28] Nor was it easy for Owen to break that close bond, for he too continued to "suffer the tortures of the damned, because I shall never see anyone else but Evelyn."[29] Since Tom's "possessiveness," and his "morbidity," "jealousy," "irreconcilableness," and "anguished protests" were the sole obstacle to Evelyn and Owen's relationship, Merton had compelling reasons to absolve himself for his role in Owen's unrequited love. Here again, perhaps the idealized gloss of his father in *Mountain* helped assuage some degree of guilt Merton still harbored, especially as he reconstructed the stirring deathbed scene and we recall that Owen's morbid physical decline began not long after his emotionally debilitating break with Evelyn.

Merton's panegyric on his father's greatness as artist and man of faith were compensations, I further believe, for Owen's failure as a father. The tactics of the eulogy deflected Merton from a painful rejection of his father. The veneration which moved his portrait of Owen served no doubt to shield Merton from the uncertainties, vulnerabilities, fears and erosion of self-esteem which derive from a young boy's powerful need to be accepted by his father and his father's failure to meet that need—a failure, in Owen's case, evidenced by his obvious priorities, his all-consuming dedication to painting, his frequent absences, his escapades with a woman Merton detested, and, ultimately, by his tragic death when Merton was sixteen years old, a death that ended Merton's search for a father who was, in both psychological and temporal senses, never really there.

Owen Merton's failure to serve as a stable source of acceptance for his son wounded the young Merton and left him with a lifelong sensitivity to nonacceptance. That sensitivity was ultimately expressed as a complex of persecution that marked certain passages in his autobiography as well as the last novel he wrote before entering Gethsemani. In *Mountain,* for example, Merton recalled the pitiful rejection he suffered when, shortly after he and Owen moved to St. Antonin, Merton entered a French lycée. His feelings of being surrounded by a vicious "wolf-pack" of boys at the boarding school were intensified by the most bruising of the many domestic dislocations he had already suffered, since it was in St. Antonin where Merton finally felt settled and at home with his father. Wrenched from the promise of some stability and briefly renewed paternal love, Merton's account of attending the new school is full of the pathos of rejection. He trembled under the glare of the strange boys' "fierce, cat-like faces, dark and morose"; he was scorched by "scores of pairs of glittering and hostile eyes." "They began to kick me and to pull and twist my ears," he writes, "and push me around, and shout various kinds of insults." Even the nerve-splitting syntax and high-strung diction of Merton's descriptions underscore his heightened sensitivity to rejection:

> when [the other boys] were all together there seemed to be some diabolical spirit of cruelty and viciousness and obscenity and blasphemy and envy and hatred that banded them together against all goodness and against one another in mockery and fierce cruelty and in vociferous, uninhibited filthiness. Contact with that wolf-pack felt very patently like contact with the mystical body of the devil: and, especially in the first days, the members of that body did not spare themselves in kicking me around without mercy (*SSM,* 50).

A similar climate of persecution entered into *My Argument with the Gestapo,* a largely autobiographical novel Merton wrote in 1941 while teaching at St. Bonaventure's. The novel is full of interrogation scenes in which the protagonist is grilled by gendarmes, British police, Gestapo agents, military police, and border guards—replays, one suspects, of the same sort of suspicion, fierce cruelty and rejection Merton suffered at the hands of those French boys and, in a deeper sense, as I have suggested, by the loss of self-confidence and security attributable to the absence of a father. In a rare moment many years later, Merton looked back at the "rejection and frustration" of his lost childhood lived as a virtual orphan. "As an orphan," he confessed to a correspondent, "I went through the business of being passed around from family to family, and being a 'ward,' and an 'object of charitable concern,' etc. etc. I know how inhuman and frustrating that can be— being treated as a thing and not as a person. And reacting against it with dreams that were sometimes shattered in a most inhuman way."[30]

There is sufficient reason to speculate further that Merton's renunciations of his own artistic instincts during his middle years, as well as his reactionary jeremiads against the evils of secular society, also derive from the shattered dreams of his lost childhood. Support for that latter point comes from the deleted sections of the original draft of *The Seven Storey Mountain*. Two sections, in particular, best illustrate how Merton depersonalized the private and specific suffering of his childhood by shifting blame to causes rooted in the abstract culture-at-large. By generalizing his plight to such things as modern systems of childrearing, Merton effectively alleviated any burden of fault from Owen.

"When I think of my own childhood," Merton writes in the first passage, "and of the love and conscientiousness of my Father, and his well-meaning desires to bring me up an intelligent and happy person: and when I think how completely impossible it was for him to succeed, under the circumstances in which he had placed himself and me, I cease to wonder at the wars and crimes that have filled this century with blood."[31] Instead of probing the specific circumstances of his own upbringing, Merton leaps immediately into monolithic crimes of the century; the circumstances in which Owen placed him are not responsible, that is to say, for his father's failure to provide Merton a happy childhood. In an extended digression, Merton directs the onus of blame instead to "grandiose, abstract systems": to "a world where states pass laws to take children away from their parents," to "fancy educational factor[ies]" where children are raised not with "love and the natural, organic needs of a human conscience . . . but according to charts and mathematical averages," such systems, we may remember, Ruth subscribed to from the pages of a progressive magazine. Merton lashes out, in short, at a "murderous and conceited century" where "millions of children . . . have grown up like weeds on any dung they could put their roots in!" And he adopts a similar strategy in another deleted passage; the intimate "fact[s] of being [raised] among strangers, and the feeling that I was unwanted and even disliked" are, once again, steered to "the modern world [which] seems to have forgotten about family life."[32] Such maneuvers clearly deflect Merton from the painfully concrete realities of his own upbringing. Other passages reflecting the same diversionary strategy survived the editing of the manuscript, while the spirit of *contemptus mundi* that accompanied such evasions would persist well into the mid-fifties when Merton finally made his peace with modernity.

Finally, the issue of Merton's persistent denials of his calling as a writer are connected as well to a childhood that imbued a young boy with a feeling of being rejected, "unwanted and even disliked." It may be too simplistic or naive merely to assume that Merton learned to associate the life-styles of artists with an endemic immorality, although, as we have seen, there was sufficient flaunting of conventional moral standards among the artists/writers who comprised the Bermuda ménage. As I argued earlier, such moral associations cannot adequately explain the relentless self-recriminations Merton foisted upon his inclinations as a writer. It is not so much a question of morality, I believe, as a matter of Merton's willingness, indeed courage, to assume the risky burdens of artistic commitment. Merton witnessed firsthand in his father a totality of dedication to art; as a young boy he may even have taken his father's desperate desire to paint, and the dislocations which inevitably followed, as both a sign of rejection and an act of punishment. For a boy who needed his father, Merton came to associate Owen's extraordinary commitment to paint with certain unacceptable costs: the impossibility, for example, of combining an artistic vocation with paternal responsibilities and, more generally, with human affection and love. Merton suffered from Owen's commitment, while Owen's failure to achieve a standard of success requisite to the degree of his dedication only exacerbated his son's suffering. With his father as an archetypal role model, Merton saw that the artistic temperament was patently self-centered and self-consuming, that the vocation of artist meant a surrender of intimacy, a willingness to forgo the comfort of secure interpersonal bonds for the alienation and the ever-tenuous rewards of artistic endeavor. By later denying his own self-image as writer, Merton was, in effect, renouncing the sort of commitment that ruined his father and devastated his childhood. I would concur, then, with a provocative assessment suggested in a question raised by Arthur Callard: "Did [Thomas Merton] fear that he, like his father, might grow up a fumbling, brutal and fragmentary man? In the extremity of his surrender to God, Thomas Merton must have hoped to reconcile the warring currents within himself, and so avoid the rocks upon which his father had been so mercilessly broken."[33]

4

The Art of the Sacred

On the last day of January 1915, under the sign of
the Water Bearer, in the year of a great war, and
down in the shadow of some French mountains on
the border of Spain, I came into the world. . . . That
world was the picture of Hell, full of men like
myself, loving God and yet hating Him; born to love
Him, living instead in fear and hopeless
self-contradictory hungers.

In the famous, often-quoted lines which begin *The Seven Storey Mountain*, Thomas Merton announced to his readers his entrance into a world that "was the picture of Hell." It was a world, Merton wrote from the vantage point of the monastery, where all men had surrendered their birthright of loving God and, in an apparent Faustian compact with modernity, now worshipped instead selfishness, hatred, fear, hopelessness and self-contradiction. And violence. "Not many hundreds of miles away from the house where I was born," Merton continued, "they were picking up men who rotted in the rainy ditches among the dead horses and the ruined seventy-fives, in a forest of trees without branches along the river Marne." The lassitude informing Merton's portrait of 1915 surely must have struck deep chords in the heart of his readers in 1948, a generation still binding the wounds of another great World War. The world of 1915 differed little, in fact, from the one which preoccupied Merton's own generation of writers and artists who, between the World Wars, shaped the modernist sensibility and whose poetry and art were saturated with an imagery characteristic of modernism: nature subdued and denuded by man, life lived "in rat's alley / Where the dead men lost their bones"[1]—an art and literature shot through with the psychological impress of nihilism, despair, and abandonment. On January 31, 1915, under the sign of the Water Bearer, in the year of a great conflagration and in the shadow of the Pyrenées, Thomas Merton came into the broken world of the Waste Land.

So, at least, it seemed from the perspective of high drama in "Prisoner's Base," Merton's title for the opening chapter of his autobiography. History certainly bears out Merton's description of 1915 as a time of unprecedented violence. But it was also, for the young Merton, a world immersed in art and lived in relative domestic tranquility. The simple two-story house that Merton's parents kept in Prades was organized in such a way as to suggest the two major preoccupations of the Merton household. Owen Merton used the ground floor as his painting studio. Upstairs, in the family living quarters, Ruth Merton spent her days caring for their infant son. Although Ruth rarely took Thomas out of the house, she set up a daily routine of putting him out on a balcony overlooking the quiet street below, where the days passed peacefully and precisely, undisturbed by any sign of a world war convulsing the landscape a few hundred kilometers to the north. Owen felt a touch of guilt over their being "out of all trouble," as he put it in a letter to his friend Esmond Atkinson. "We ourselves are some of the very few who are out of all trouble . . . and we are pretty selfish to be as we are, but we are selfish on account of little Tom, and so far I do think I am worth more to Ruth and him than to the armies."[2] Any disturbance which might have threatened the fine balance of life upstairs came not from the trenches along the Marne but, as we saw in the last chapter, from Owen's painting studio where he wrestled with the agony of a creative dry spell and began to question his talent.

Most important in the opening pages of *Mountain*, however, is the immediate equation Merton sets up there between the life of the artist, keyed on the models of Ruth and Owen, and the corrupting influences of modernity, that "picture of Hell" dramatically framed in by the horrors of World War I. In confronting the life of the artist with the moral depravations and atrocities of modern life in "Prisoner's Base," Merton began to pose powerful questions for himself, questions which had taken shape soon after Owen's death—when Merton felt he had become "a true citizen of my own disgusting century: a century of poison gas and Atomic bombs" (85)—questions which would preoccupy Merton throughout his early years as a monk. Could the artist, through exercising and perfecting his talent and shaping his vision, be delivered from the corruptions of modern life? Or was the artist inevitably corrupted by those corruptions? In a strange way, such questions collide in the standoff between Owen's depressing description of his paintings as "black and triste" and Merton's generous evaluation of his father's work as sane, full of balance and veneration, religious and, above all, "clean." After sketching in the horrible world of 1915, Merton moved quickly to note that his artist/parents were, like himself, "captives in that world, knowing," like himself, "they did not belong with it or in it, and yet," again like himself, "unable to get away from it." Merton tried desperately to deliver himself from that world through a "conversion of manners" to the monastic life. Could the artist do it through art? His parents "were in the world and not of it—not because they were saints, but in a different way: because they were artists. The integrity of an artist lifts a man above the level of the world without delivering him from it" (*SSM*, 3).

This was a frustrating and ambiguous answer that could not work because its central premises cancelled each other out. To be not *of* the world but still *in* it implied that the artist remained a captive of that world, a prisoner of its corrupting influences. This was really a nonanswer, then, and posed another central ambiguity of the missing years. The problem derived not from the saint's inability to liberate himself from the captivity of the temporal world and its inevitable corruptions, for the saint, like the monk, made a clean break from the world; he was no longer *in* it and no longer *of* it. The dilemma was created by Merton's need to establish a parallel between the experience of the artist and that of the monk. But that parallel served only to frustrate him, because the integrity of the artist, as Merton said, lifted him above the base morality of worldliness but could not deliver him from the world, while the monk's prime spiritual directive was total liberation from the exigencies of worldly life.

There was only one solution to the dilemma of how the artist, like the monk, could be liberated from modernity's corrupting influences. It was a solution quite obvious in Merton's portrait of his father in *The Seven Storey Mountain*, a solution evident as well in Merton's choice of a topic for his Master's thesis at Columbia, in the intellectual, literary, and spiritual role models he borrowed to shape his own identity during his formative years, and, most importantly, in a never-published manuscript he agonized over, with a devotion that verged on obsession, from 1953 to 1967. The artist and the monk could come together and achieve perfect equanimity and freedom from the corruptions of modern life only in the figure of the sacred iconographer. Only through the devotion to and the creation of sacred art could the spirituality of the monk be adequately reconciled to the drives of the artist; similarly, only through sacred art could the artist and religious be delivered from the modernist nightmare. This amalgamation of art and the sacred motivated Merton's portrait of Owen as painter/saint in *Mountain*. It also prompted Merton's treatment of William Blake as an exemplary Christian sacred artist in "Nature and Art in William Blake", Merton's thesis. It also helps to account for his early preference for writers and poets like St. John of the Cross, Gerald Manley Hopkins, Aldous Huxley, Jacques Maritain, Leon Bloy and others, writers whose basis of aesthetic, intellectual, and spiritual authority was mystical, trans-sensual, and sacred.

The most compelling evidence of Merton's attraction to sacred art as a potential bridge between art and spirituality is in his manuscript, *Art and Worship*. That study of sacred Christian art, which began with some rough conference notes Merton drafted early in 1954, can be viewed as his first effort to resolve the central conflict between art and spirituality that had prevailed throughout the just-published *Sign of Jonas*. The argument that the sacred artist embodied the perfect balance between an artistic vocation and a religious commitment must have seemed compelling to Merton. But the fact that his treatise on sacred art evolved only with extraordinary difficulty and passed through a number of unsuccessful revisions without ever being published suggests that its argument ultimately failed him.

The story of that failure will be traced in the balance of this chapter. It is important to note from the outset, however, that the ultimate untenability of sacred art as an efficacious aesthetic played an important role in the evolution of Thomas Merton's mature humanism during his later years. In a failed effort to integrate the conflicting identities of the artist and the monk *vis à vis* sacred art, Merton did succeed in freeing himself from that "Prisoner's Base" of modernity which held him captive as a young man. The breakdown of the internal logic of *Art and Worship* was one of the most compelling factors in Merton's growth from an embittered young man, bent on withdrawing from his own disgusting century and revolted by its picture of hell, to the compassionate, world-embracing humanist of the 1960s.

— 2 —

Thomas Merton never viewed the function and presence of art in human life with the eye of the dilettante. His disdain for the acquisitive mentality that treated art as a commodity subject to fashion remained constant throughout his life. Like Eric Gill, whom Merton considered one of the rare prophets of sacred art in the twentieth century, he insisted, with a dogmatism that frequently bordered on polemic, that art existed for the sake of life, not life for the sake of art. Merton's attitude toward both the artist's creation of a work of art and the individual's response in the presence of a product of the creative imagination, in other words, was deeply imbued with an experiential component. Art must not serve itself, he felt; it must remain subservient to higher ends. From the very moment of his initial conversion to Catholicism in 1933 to just a few days before his death in 1968, Merton considered those higher ends as essentially spiritual and largely liturgical.

A little more than a year after Owen's death, for example, Merton travelled to Rome, where a Byzantine mosaic in the apse of Sts. Cosmas and Damian descended upon him with such power that it triggered a religious conversion episode and established one of the first felt links between aesthetics and spirituality in Merton's life. Coming at a time when he considered himself nothing more than a dissolute and directionless eighteen-year-old driven by an unchecked adolescent libido, the effect of the mosaic hit him, as he wrote in his high-pitched autobiography, like a bolt of spiritual lightning:

> what a thing it was to come upon the genius of an art full of spiritual vitality and earnestness and power—an art that was tremendously serious and alive and eloquent and urgent in all that it had to say. And it was without pretentiousness, without fakery, and had nothing theatrical

about it. Its solemnity was made all the more astounding by its simplicity—and by the obscurity of the places where it lay hid, and by its
subservience to higher ends, architectural, liturgical and spiritual ends
which I could not even begin to understand, but which I could not avoid
guessing, since the nature of the mosaics themselves and their position
and everything about them proclaimed it aloud (108).

Merton was so fascinated by the mosaic that he sought out all the
Byzantine art he could find in Rome. He felt like a pilgrim searching
out the shrines, tombs, altars and arches where he could come under
the spell of sixth-century Christian art. His mood was as ecstatic as
the grandiloquent rhetoric which strained to contain his descriptions
of what he felt when visiting the churches that became "the refuge of
my mind." The art on the walls and the frescoes in the tombs of the
martyrs and the renderings of St. Peter in chains and the stiff, elon-
gated portrait of St. Lawrence burning on a gridiron— through these
works of Byzantine art, Merton's first "conception of Christ was
formed. . . . I first saw Him, Whom I now serve as my God and my
King, and Who owns and rules my life" (109).

If Merton "saw" Christ—"the Christ of the Apocalypse, the Christ
of the Martyrs"—beaming down upon him through the luminescent
imagery of these Byzantine icons, he also "saw" his father again. In
one of the most perplexing fragments of his autobiography, Merton
described a visionary encounter with Owen that occurred just after
his agitated discovery of Byzantine art and its deep spiritual vitality.
Although the religious art in Rome stirred him deeply and awakened
an interior peace he had never felt before, "still there had been no
deep movement of my will, nothing that amounted to a conversion."
But that was to come soon with the full force of a visionary crescendo
in his hotel room one night. "Suddenly it seemed to me that Father,
who had now been dead more than a year, was there with me. The
sense of his presence was as vivid and as real and as startling as if he
had touched my arm or spoken to me" (110). Using a language and
following a pattern consistent with descriptions of God-encounters in
Christian mystical literature, Merton wrote of the moral horror that
shuddered throughout his whole being, of how he was "pierced" to
the quick "with a sudden and profound insight into the corruption of
my own soul." His Owen-encounter was a visceral cleansing, a painful cathartic purgation which prepared the way for the "light [of] escape and liberation and freedom from . . . the thousand terrible
things that held my will in their slavery" (111).

Although it would be a few years before Merton entered a monastery, his vision of Owen in a Rome hotel room was the benchmark of his religious life. The necromantic overtones of the episode are, of course, of little significance and import. Most fascinating, however, are the interconnections between patterns of images that run together in the vision: the literal bonding of sacred art, Owen, Christian spirituality, and Merton's nascent attitudes toward modernity, and the psychological causalities which bring these together. Merton's powerful need to venerate his father must have provided a locus for Owen's entrance into the vision. The memory fragment of the sketches of little Byzantine visages strewn on Owen's deathbed and Merton's immersion in the Byzantine art of Rome set up another sequence of parallels which merge in the vision. Perhaps, too, the still-fresh pain that Merton felt over the loss of his father was eased by two other factors. First, Merton hesitates to claim that Owen came to him from Heaven; rather, "I should say it was 'as if' he had been sent to me out of Purgatory." Second, Merton had just fallen under the influence of Byzantine art and architecture; the Byzantine aesthetic stressed a totality of otherworldliness, depicting through its symbols a Heavenly Jerusalem or City of God where the material world was radically dematerialized and transformed into a luminescent, transcendent world of eternal life in the hereafter. Merton's joining of his father in Purgatory with the Byzantine aesthetic of otherworldliness may well have lifted Owen heavenward, or at least helped redress the still-vivid agony of his dying. Moreover, Byzantine depictions of, for example, the Christ of the Passion, scrupulously avoided any visual references to bodily pain, perhaps soothing even further the anguish Merton felt over Owen's physical suffering.

Most important, the combination of an episode of religious conversion, Byzantine icons, and the vision of his father fired Merton's antimodern convictions and stirred his revulsion for the secular and worldly. As if to prepare the way for his conversion, Merton had to purge himself first of all worldly attachments. Indicative of this purging was the sudden disgust he felt when reading, the night before Owen's visitation, the poems of the quintessential modernist D. H. Lawrence. Once one of his favorite authors, Lawrence now embodied all that was unholy, unclean, hideous, perverted, self-possessed, "personal and home-made." Intolerant of the "falseness and futility" of Lawrence's poetry, Merton tossed the poems violently aside and scolded himself for "wasting my time with a man of such unimportance as this." And then in a leap of questionable literary faith Merton concluded that Lawrence was "full of unearthly seeds, all ready to break forth into hideous plants like those that were germinating in Germany's unweeded garden, in the dark weather of Nazism." Pressing his excited logic further, Merton even felt compelled to deride one of the greatest works of High Renaissance sculpture, Michelangelo's "Moses," for its "horned and pop-eyed frown and . . . the crack in the knee" (110–11). Any work of art, Merton seemed to be saying, which hinted at the presence of human genius in its execution and form— whether a poem by Lawrence, a sculpture by Michelangelo, or the "heavy melodrama" of a Baroque painting—violated the higher ends to which the artist must be dedicated: those religious and liturgical ends Merton found only in the spiritual vitality, the understated mysticism and purity of Byzantine art. Thus the "modern" period in Merton's reading of art history began with the Renaissance, when individualism and humanism entered art, and when, as in the great Byzantine age of faith, art was no longer created in Heaven, but made on earth. Any art, in other words, which did not serve a liturgical purpose for an age of Christian faith, served only itself and was, as a consequence, pretentious, fake, and theatrical.

Thirty-five years later, less than a week before he died in Bangkok, Merton encountered other works of art which, like the Byzantine mosaics in Rome, descended upon him with the rush of an epiphany. Walking barefoot up a path leading to the colossal Buddhist rock sculptures at Polonnaruwa, Ceylon (the present-day Sri Lanka), Merton was "knocked over," as he had been when walking into the apse of Sts. Cosmas and Damian as an eighteen-year-old, when he saw the "huge and yet subtle" smiles of the great rock carvings and felt "the silence of the extraordinary faces." The fine passage from *The Asian Journal* is well worth quoting at length.

> Looking at these figures I was suddenly, almost forcibly, jerked clean out of the habitual, half-tied vision of things, and an inner clearness, clarity, as if exploding from the rocks themselves, became evident and obvious. The queer *evidence* of the reclining figure, the smile, the sad smile of Ananda standing with arms folded (much more "imperative" than Da Vinci's Mona Lisa because completely simple and straightforward). The thing about all this is that there is no puzzle, no problem, and

really no "mystery." All problems are resolved and everything is clear. All rock, all matter, all life, is charged with dharmakaya . . . everything is emptiness and everything is compassion. I don't know when in my life I have ever had such a sense of beauty and spiritual validity running together in one aesthetic illumination. . . . I mean I know and have seen what I was obscurely looking for. I don't know what else remains but I have now seen and have pierced through the surface and have got beyond the shadow and the disguise (*AJ*, 233–36).

The similarities between the Rome and Ceylon episodes are significant and obvious. They share an experiential vitality, as if the mosaics and rock sculptures drummed through to the core of Merton's being. Both were *felt* with a striking urgency far more immediate than anything that could be adequately contained by a mere intellectual response to the art works. On both occasions Merton felt charged by a sense of clarity and obviousness, simplicity and straightforwardness. Beauty and spirituality "ran together." Tensions were resolved, puzzles solved.

But the equally obvious differences between the two experiences suggest that Merton's views on art had undergone a significant evolution during those thirty-five years. The key to the change rests, certainly not in Owen's failure to reappear in Ceylon, but in the "higher ends" which the Byzantine mosaics and the Buddhist rock carvings served. Both remained subservient, to be sure, to a liturgical end, in the sense that they promoted and bore witness to the religious sensibilities of their creators. But the very shift in geography and culture—from Rome and Christianity to Ceylon and Buddhism—shows that Merton's doctrinal depth of field had broadened, to say the least, considerably. In *Mountain*, Merton had used the purity of Byzantine art as a foil to discredit the entire history of art after the great age of Christian faith. In *The Asian Journal*, Merton took pains to insist, in contrast, that the "essences" he discovered in the rock carvings could not be contained by *any* doctrine—aesthetic, religious, or otherwise. He even used the attitude of the Vicar General of the Asian Cistercians, who accompanied Merton up the path to Polonnaruwa, to contrast with his own, noting that the Vicar General hung back, "shying away from 'paganism,'" while Merton padded, barefoot and reverent, toward the huge, smiling faces. What he saw was "filled with every possibility, questioning nothing, knowing everything, rejecting nothing." He felt the peace of *sunyata*, of an emptiness interior to any category of thought or any doctrine "that has seen through every question without trying to discredit anyone or anything—*without refutation*—without establishing some other argument. For the doctrinaire, the mind that needs well-established positions, such peace, such silence, can be frightening" (233).

The eighteen-year-old, seeking so desperately the Christian art of Rome as "the refuge of my mind," was just such a doctrinaire mind with an appetite for well-established positions, bent on discrediting some arguments, while establishing and refuting others. The teenager, emerging tentatively from adolescence, may indeed have been frightened then by the kind of peace he would discover on another continent halfway around the world thirty-five years later. At any rate, an important change took place during these intervening years, a change only framed in by these two episodes. It was a change born out of struggle and crisis. And its story is best chronicled in the pages of Merton's manuscript, *Art and Worship.*

Before delving into *Art and Worship*, it may be useful to consider briefly Merton's earlier writings on art—especially his Master's thesis which clearly anticipates some of the ideas developed later in his treatise on sacred art. In fact, "Nature and Art in William Blake" (1939), like *Art and Worship*, is an intellectual and interpretive treatment of that experiential discovery Merton made in Rome in 1933: when the tension between art and spirituality is resolved *vis à vis* sacred art, inevitably the sacred artist, it follows, finds himself at odds with the material world, which Merton identified in his youth with the moral corruptions of modernity. Merton's treatment of William Blake as a Christian sacred artist became, like *Art and Worship*, a scholarly vindication of antimaterialism and antinaturalism in art and, by extension, in the religious life.

Merton used in his thesis a combination of Thomist theology and the aesthetics of the Christian scholar Jacques Maritain (whose *Art and Scholasticism* had a profound influence on Merton during his years at Columbia) as a basis of his argument that naturalism in art is tantamount to idolatry for the Christian artist. Quoting Maritain, Merton wrote, "the Thomist point of view is, 'Nature concerns the artist simply because it is a derivation from the divine art in things. . . .' Pure naturalism, on the other hand, aims to yield," citing the Hindu iconographer A. K. Coomaraswamy's *Transformation of Nature in Art*, "'sensations as nearly as possible identical with those aroused by the model itself.'" Merton's conclusion: "This, however, is idolatrous, for idolatry is the love of creatures as they are in themselves and not as they are in God" (*LE*, 437). The entire thrust of the thesis aimed to show that Blake reacted against such idolatry in his poetry and etchings. Merton positioned Blake, that is to say, directly in line with the history of Christian art first perfected in sixth century Byzantium.

"Everything," Blake says, "is atheism which assumes the reality of the natural and Unspiritual world." (*LE*, 437)

As an artist, Blake found in art a way of knowing and loving the principle of all Being. (430)

Blake . . . has forgotten all intellectual distinctions, all labels and categories, in the ecstasy of the mystic who surely knows God, and is dazzled by the glory of all his attributes at once. (446)

[O]nce nature had been assimilated and transformed by [Blake's] imagination, it blazed before him in a vision fired with the glory of God. (451)

These fragments capture the general contours of the argument in Merton's thesis. They reflect, as well, certain signs that Merton was using the thesis to bolster his own nascent identity as artist and mystic with the rather narrowly sketched portrait of Blake that emerged in an argument somewhat reductionist and reactionary. Intent on revealing Blake as an exemplary Christian sacred artist, Merton largely discounted, for example, Blake's visionary pantheism, in much the same way, as we shall see later, that Merton effectively dismissed Albert Camus' atheism by stressing instead Camus' essentially Christian vision of social witness. Merton projected himself into William Blake in much the same way he later would in his selectively-crafted caricature of Owen as painter/saint in *Mountain*. The autobiographical resonances in the thesis are numerous. For example, in his efforts to prove that Blake "hated naturalism" and "pure sensuousness," Merton emphasized that Blake—like Merton himself during the years clustering around his entrance into the monastery—rebelled against "the turmoil and blindness of a changing, contingent world," a world where money-making and commercialism threatened to corrupt the artist and turn him away, as in Blake's case, from his "unprofitable poems or . . . incomprehensible mystical drawings." Like the young Merton (especially of *Mountain*), Blake "despised the 'vegetable' universe or the world of perishing, blind, created things." Merton fashioned for Blake a brand of mysticism suitable then to Merton himself, a mysticism that "despises the world and believes that man by God's good grace, and Free Will, can transcend the material world, with its confusion and deceits, and rise into a visionary supernatural world of True Being and unity" (424). Like Merton, "Blake believed living according to the evidence of the senses alone was living in darkness and illusion, cut off from God and 'reality'" (430). Writing at a time when he had already unsuccessfully petitioned for entry into the Franciscan Order, Merton argued that Blake was essentially a contemplative and an ascetic who had deliberately chosen, in good Franciscan fashion, the "sacrifice of immediate physical goods for the good of the spirit [and] for the success of the work of art" (448). "Blake chose poverty as deliberately as any Franciscan brother," Merton wrote, citing in his concluding remarks Blake's encomium:

> Prayer is the study of Art
> Praise is the practice of Art
> Fasting etc all relate to Art
> The outward ceremony is antichrist.
>
> (449)

Finally, the key to Merton's attraction to and treatment of William Blake lies in Merton's identifying in the life of Blake the same dialectical conflict that would assail Merton himself during the missing years. Blake "always deals with the fall into a violent, tragic conflict of ideas, and the subsequent regeneration into spiritual . . . harmony. This is the drama which mystics understand to underly the whole of human life" (410). It was just this sort of drama of conflict that would spark the journal of Merton's missing years and account for its argumentative dialogue between the monk and his shadow-double, the poet. Sounding very much like an entry in *The Sign of Jonas*, Merton wrote of Blake in the thesis that, once his struggle over art and mysticism was over, "he hardly wrote anything more." Reborn as mystic/saint, Blake realized that "long poems growing out of [the conflict] were unnecessary, and he deliberately gave up writing them. Now, too, he realized that it was useless to try and become a popular or successful artist: not that it was impossible for him, but because it involved too great a sacrifice and too much suffering" (410).

"Nature and Art in William Blake" is important, then, for two reasons. It foreshadowed the struggle between art and the contemplative life that would occupy Merton throughout the first half of his monastic experience. And it was really the first treatment of a potential resolution of that conflict, a treatment that Merton would return to nearly twenty years later when he set about to write the first draft of *Art and Worship* in 1958. Interestingly, the Columbia thesis anticipated, too, the seeds of another dilemma that Merton would wrestle with in his study of sacred art. If the identity of the sacred artist appealed to Merton because it reconciled the conflicting identities of monk and artist within him, it also forced him to accept the limitations of an antinaturalistic aesthetic and to adopt a profoundly critical sensibility not only about art since the Renaissance but about the very conditions of life in his own century. Merton could willingly embrace this antimodernism in 1939. He could say of himself what he claimed for William Blake: that Blake did not belong to his century, that he lived instead "in the same kind of intellectual climate as a Saint Thomas, or a Saint Augustine, or a Saint Francis." But as Merton's social conscience began to mature in the late fifties, he was forced to reconsider the reactionary antimodernism of his middle years because it conflicted with a compassion for humanity and an embrace of life in the modern world that were rising within him. Merton eventually came to realize, in other words, that, *unlike* William Blake, he was a man very much *of* his own century. He came to realize that he did not live in an intellectual climate of medieval saints, but in a world of Marxist philosophers like Herbert Marcuse, existential novelists like Albert Camus, radical Protestant theologians like Dietrich Bonhoeffer, social critics and modernist writers like Boris Pasternak and James Joyce, and poet/musicians like Bob Dylan. Once Merton grew to accept his position *in* the world, many significant and meaningful changes would take place. Among those changes, he decided to abandon the years of effort he had put into writing a book on sacred art, a book he eventually called, in a letter to his friend, the abstract expressionist Ad Reinhardt, "a bucket of schmalz . . . a great book of horrors which I have despised and do recant."[3]

— 4 —

To summarize briefly, Thomas Merton's interest in the art of the sacred derived from the experiential epiphany that swept him off his secular feet in 1933. Six years later, his Master's thesis provided a margin of intellectual credibility to his fascination with sacred art. Numerous passages in *The Secular Journal,* which traced Merton's life from Columbia University to his arrival at Gethsemani in 1941, showed him still very much attentive to the liturgical power of religious art—especially in the Cuba sequence, where the church architecture in Havana inspired some of Merton's best early poetry, notably "Song for Our Lady of Cobre." And Merton reaffirmed both the experiential and intellectual dimensions of his interest in sacred art in his 1948 autobiography.

This line of development came to fruition in a full-fledged and ambitious study of sacred art begun in September, 1954, when Merton sketched an outline for the first draft of *Art and Worship,* written in 1958. That original manuscript underwent at least six substantial revisions between 1958 and 1964. Although it is clear that by 1964 Merton had little active interest in still publishing the book, he nevertheless clung to it with a stubborn hope that, with more work, it might be published some day. The very fact that Merton asked his editor in 1967 not to send the manuscript to the archives at Bellarmine College (the official repository of Merton's manuscripts) but to forward it directly to Gethsemani instead, suggests that Merton still had plans to rework the manuscript again. And when he journeyed to Asia in 1968 he included *Art and Worship* on a list of manuscripts left in the care of his secretary, books either awaiting publication or in progress at the time. On a cover-sheet of the heavily reworked manuscript at the Thomas Merton Studies Center there is a notation in Merton's own hand: "a book on Sacred Art—still awaiting publication." Clearly, Merton's interest in sacred art spanned his entire adult life.

The devotion so apparent in Merton's decade-long effort to publish his study of sacred art reaches the pitch of obsession when one considers that, quite frankly, *Art and Worship* is a mediocre book, falling well short of the standard of Merton's writing, especially after 1958. The book's failure resulted from Merton's inability to extricate himself from certain rock-bottom tenets of the argument worked into the original 1958 draft. As Merton's temperament and perspectives evolved and changed over the years, he could never adequately compensate, in spite of numerous insertions and deletions, for the dogmatic premises which held the original argument together.

But the reasons accounting for the failure of *Art and Worship* are also good evidence for the critical importance of the manuscript in understanding the life of Merton's mind. Nothing else he wrote evolved over such a long period as *Art and Worship*. No other book was subject to such a plethora of revisions and rewritings. Once the chronological sequence of revisions can be established, *Art and Worship* becomes an accurate measure of Merton's evolving attitudes and ideas, especially during and after the pivotal years between 1954 and 1958. The manuscript reveals Merton as a revisionary tactician constantly in dialogue with himself over the years, growing and maturing through the dynamic dialectical interplay of changing voices and evolving identities. This same revisionary process is evident in some of Merton's other writing: between the text and headnotes, for example, of *The Sign of Jonas*, or between the original version of "Poetry and the Contemplative Life" (1947) and its 1958 revision "Poetry and the Contemplative Life: A Reappraisal," or, most notably, between the first edition of *Seeds of Contemplation* (1949), its "Revised Edition" of 1950, and the thoroughly reworked version of *New Seeds of Contemplation* (1962).[4] But no other manuscript, not even the seminal *Conjectures of a Guilty Bystander*, captures Merton's growth with the same clarity, economy, and focus as *Art and Worship*. No other book reveals better one of the most fascinating things about Merton: that if the outward appearances of his life between 1941 and 1968 underwent such little change, the inward journeys of his mind covered a vast and constantly changing terrain.

The trail-head of at least one of those journeys began in April of 1958 when Merton completed the original typescript of his book on sacred art. The book was originally intended as a discussion, pitched to seminarians, of the role of sacred art in religious education. It also promised to be an expensive book to produce because Merton planned to illustrate its text with photographic reproductions of paintings, sculptural works, and architectural details. For these two reasons, Merton's Abbot decided that the book should be published under Gethsemani's own imprint and printed at its own expense. So the original 1958 typescript, with Merton's very minor holographic corrections in black ink, was given to a Louisville typographer named

Terrell Dickey, who set the text in an oversize format and returned to Merton, in the Autumn of 1958, what can be called the "galley draft" of *Art and Worship*.

Merton must have been impressed with Dickey's galley draft. He immediately decided to include *Art and Worship* as one of the four books he was under contract to write for his principal New York publisher. He mailed the galley draft to his agent. She, in turn, forwarded it to Robert Giroux, who quickly read the draft and wrote back to Merton: "I like the text of *Art and Worship* enormously, and we certainly want to explore the book possibilities thoroughly. It would make an ideal gift book for Christmas 1959 publication."[5] Giroux explained to Merton's agent that it would take time to work out the production schedule and calculate costs for such an elaborate book, but "from the editorial point of view . . . it's a lovely book," which Giroux compared favorably to Andre Malraux's popular *Museum Without Walls*.[6]

For reasons explored in more detail below, however, *Art and Worship* would not appear by Christmas, 1959. Instead, Merton continued to rework the galley draft for the next seven years, even though an imprimatur was granted in June of 1958. The first substantial revision came early in 1959 when Merton worked over the second section of the galley draft—"The Importance of Sacred Art"—with heavy deletions and the addition of a two-thousand-word typescript insert. Merton returned to the galley draft again in 1962 and virtually rewrote the entire third section, "Sacred and Profane," adding two more sizable typescript inserts. Another flurry of major changes occurred in 1964; Merton deleted three entire sections, collapsed three others under a single subhead, and rewrote, from top to bottom, section VII, "Changing Notions of Art" (originally titled "What Is Art?"), Merton's history of sacred art. 1964 was a busy year; Merton had to adjust the argument to accommodate the new documents coming out of Vatican II. He worked through the entire manuscript two more times and made significant changes holographically, first in red ink and later in blue. Many of these later holographic additions stretched to over one thousand words, often crowded between lines of the previous typescript inserts, wedged in the margins of what remained of the original galley draft, or connected with a blizzard of arrows to the verso of the preceding manuscript leaf. After Merton died, an ambitious and patient monk at Gethsemani prepared a clean typescript of the gutted document: a 25,000-word manuscript, not counting the cut lines Merton wrote for the illustrations.

Merton published seven articles on art and the sacred between March of 1954 and the winter of 1964—articles extracted verbatim from either the original galley draft of *Art and Worship*, its prototype scenario of 1954, or one of the later variant drafts. The first, actually an excerpt from *No Man Is an Island* (1955), appeared as "Reality, Art, and Prayer" in a March, 1955 number of *The Commonweal*; Merton drew a few verbatim fragments for this piece from "Notes on Sacred Art," his lecture outline for a series of conferences given to the scholastics at Gethsemani during October and November, 1954, but the *Commonweal* piece was comprised largely of germs of ideas Merton would develop later in the original draft of *Art and Worship*.

In November 1956 Merton's "Notes on Sacred and Profane Art" appeared in the left-leaning Catholic periodical *Jubilee*, edited by Merton's good friend Ed Rice, who was later hired by Robert Giroux to handle the layout of *Art and Worship* and to produce a working dummy. The *Jubilee* article, a verbatim extract from the 1954 conference notes, was significant for a number of reasons. It showed Merton on the attack, trying, almost single-handedly, to spark a revival of interest in serious church art. In fact, Robert Giroux criticized the piece because it read too much like a manifesto, a point well taken especially in light of Rice's layout. With its huge block type and oversize shaded cutlines chopping up the text, the emphatic typography assaulted the eye. Also, Merton stressed in the article that sacred art must adhere as much to qualities of "good" art as to orthodox religious dogma, and he worked exclusively within the Catholic tradition in his efforts to cinch the argument—two points which would later create logistical problems in the evolving argument of *Art and Worship*. The logic of the manifesto, moreover, backed Merton into another tactical corner that would cause him difficulty later: he was obliged to argue that true sacred art was virtually impossible in the context of a spiritually anemic modern age. Finally, Merton chose Cézanne, interestingly enough, as a prototype of an artist who had successfully united qualities of art and sacredness in his paintings—a particularly fascinating choice considering Merton's earlier treatment of his father and Cézanne as exemplary painter/saints in *Mountain*.

Briefly, five other articles appeared after the *Jubilee* manifesto. Two were published in *Sponsa Regis* in 1957 and 1959, the second lifted verbatim from the first typescript insert of *Art and Worship*. Merton revised two more sections, each published separately as articles, and included them as essays in *Disputed Questions* (1960): "Sacred Art and the Spiritual Life" and "Absurdity in Sacred Decoration." Four years later, "Seven Qualities of the Sacred," section IV of the final draft of *Art and Worship,* appeared in *Good Work.* The two essays in *Disputed Questions* were important because they anticipated new developments in the argument of *Art and Worship* itself. They indicated as well a new voice beginning to take shape within Merton, the voice of a more compassionate and flexible social critic unlike the unceremoniously blunt speaker of the *Jubilee* manifesto, and showed that Merton's study of sacred art contributed to the evolution of that voice. Within the pages of *Art and Worship* itself and the articles spun off from it, then, a new man began to emerge from the shell of the old misanthrope, a man germinating in the post-1960 revisions of *Art and Worship.*

— 5 —

The central purpose of Merton's study of sacred art, announced in the preface and reaffirmed in his concluding remarks, was essentially threefold. He set about to define Christian sacred art within the parameters of its historical development, to explore "the traditional Christian expression of the Mystery of Faith in art." He wished also to clarify and revive the function of sacred art for the modern church. And he wanted to equip his readers with the ability "to distinguish between what is genuine and what is faked in modern sacred art." The ostensible purpose of the book was, then, largely educational.

One of the major reasons for the book's failure, however, was that Merton's pedagogical purpose was too frequently compromised by his lapses into sheer polemic. The post-1960 Merton tried to tone down the anger of the embittered younger man who had originally set up his discussion of sacred art as a springboard for attacking the spiritual bankruptcy and crude vulgarities of his own age. But Merton could never successfully disengage himself from the logic of the original argument, a logic which relied upon a rigid polarity between sacredness and modernity, the sacred and the profane.

For example, in a 1961 revision Merton marked "omit" the following passage from the original galley draft.

1

[T]he progressive secularization and paganization of artistic taste—
due in large part to commercialism and materialism—should really be
regarded as a grave menace to the purity of Christian worship. . . .

Sacred art cannot flourish where money, worldly display, and the worship of business hold sway. In other words, sacred art and commercialism are mutually exclusive of one another for the simple fact that no man
can serve two masters and both the artist and the worshipper must make
their choice between God and Mammon.

This was terribly watertight. It held rigorously that the secularization
of modern culture corrupted artistic taste and fouled—"paganized"—
the purity of Christian worship and faith. It meant, by simple extension, that sacred art was anathema to modernity, thereby directly violating one of the announced purposes of the entire book. In an effort
to soften the logic and rescue the modern sacred artist from the obliv-
ion to which he was consigned in the passage quoted above, Merton
wrote a large typescript insert, excerpted as follows:

2

[S]acred art is [not] sacred in so far as it represents sacred events in a
manner traditionally accepted by the church as fitting and proper. . . .

3

[R]eligious insight is really irrelevant in a good artist: he may be a sinner
and still paint a magnificent picture of Christ. This requires qualification.
It is true that morality is not relevant to art as such, and we do not have
to demand that an artist, before attempting a sacred subject, present a
certificate that he has been to confession. . . . What is necessary . . . is
that the artist, whoever he may be, and whatever may be his condition,
should be able to present himself before God as he is and acknowledge
the truth of his own being and his own state. . . . [H]e must somehow, at
least implicitly, recognize his relationship to God as sinner and prodigal. . . . But the demonic self-complacency of an artist obsessed with his
own talent can never paint a Christ that is truly sacred. . . .

4

[I]t happens that sometimes the very art which claims to be sacred,
and which supports its claims with intolerable gestures of pharisaical
prudery, is in fact the most basely and shamelessly secular. For . . . the
"profane" in art is that which, completely empty of any artistic quality or
form, serves as a tool or device for getting money, or for producing some
useless and mereticulous kind of satisfaction. . . . Pseudo sacred art . . .

makes the crudest and most shoddy pretense at "realism" that can be
effected by economical means of production from a cheap mold. . . .

5

If it be urged that such unspeakable vulgarities are permissible because "they help some people to pray," the only possible answer is that
then the meaning of prayer and indeed the whole meaning of religion
itself has been forgotten. . . .

6

[T]he great problem [for the church today] is the complete and unruffled philistinism of many of those members of the Church whether
clergy or laity, who even for a moment consider the idea of making the
house of God beautiful with works of art. This is not their fault but the
fault of the society to which they belong, in which patronage of or taste
for "the fine arts"—modern or otherwise—is considered a sign of "status." What pastor would hesitate to put Matisse all over the walls of his
sanctuary if he were really certain that this would make his Church as
respectable and as "significant" as the local steel company in the eyes of
his fellow citizens?

Merton began this rewrite in a strong revisionary spirit. His disclaimer that the sacred artist need not adhere to church conventions,
nor even present his credentials as a practicing Christian, certainly
helped to broaden the range of possibilities for modern sacred art, so
severely restricted by the choice between God and Mammon Merton
had offered modern artists in the original version. But Merton's disclaimer was, in effect, rendered moot when he backpedaled, in [3],
and insisted that the artist *must* nevertheless acknowledge his relationship to God as sinner and prodigal returning to the fold of the
faithful, lest he fall victim to the pride—"the demonic self-complacency"—of his own talent. Note too how Merton merely shifted, in
excerpt [4], the burden of proving the corrupting influences of secularization from modern culture at large—as in [1]—to evidence
of "pseudo sacred art"—the waxworks aesthetic of the dashboard
Jesus—that had crept shamefully into the modern church. Merton's
revision still hung upon a logical split between the sacred and profane
(which he persisted in identifying dogmatically with traditional and
modern), a split that continued to compromise the viability of sacred
art in the modern context. Merton could not, in short, reconcile the
progressive secularization of modern culture—flowering, to be sure,
in the plethora of counter-religious "movements" in modern art—and

the conditions of faith and spiritual vitality and commitment necessary for the creation and appreciation of sacred art.

He tried. And his efforts resulted in some promising overtures to compromise. For example, when Merton rewrote, in 1964, section 7—"Changing Notions of Art," his history of sacred art—he made a noble effort to accommodate what he called the traditional gospel of Christian hope and the avant-garde gospel of Bohemian despair. But the thrust of his historical analysis continued to render that union too fragile and weak and ultimately ineffectual.

In his reading of the history of sacred art, Merton naturally established medieval Christian art as his controlling paradigm. Byzantine art became the aesthetic bench mark to which all historical developments in art had to refer, for Byzantine artists had perfected "a hieratic and noble style which affirmed triumphantly the Church's belief in the sovereignty of Christ." Byzantine art was "dominated," Merton believed, by a single aesthetic mandate: "by art, as by contemplation, man recovered something of the purity of vision and the selfless simplicity before God, which had belonged to Adam in paradise." The end of the Middle Ages was marked, according to Merton's argument, by the emergence of "pre-Renaissance humanism," "the threshold of a more modern, individualistic and subjective view of both art and religion." In Merton's view, a historical chain reaction followed, from "the degeneracy of art in the late Middle Ages" and its "adulteration of genuine worship by superstition and vain observance," to the reaction of the Renaissance.

7

The Renaissance sought to restore art to life, and succeeded. But this was a different kind of life,—not so much in the depths of the spirit as in the enlightened imagination and senses. Where the ancient tradition had been rich in *spiritual understanding* the new artists cultivated the refinements of *aesthetic pleasure.* . . .

8

From then on, art was involved in a confusion of secondary and accidental elements, cultural and psychological by-products. . . . Art then gradually lost its life and character and became a dead thing. . . .

9

The Renaissance decayed into the official pomposities of *Baroque* and *Roccoco:* a court art. . . . This operatic and inherently mendacious art was bound to exercise a bad effect on religious sentiment. . . . The German slang word *kitsch* expresses this condition better than any other: it suggests all that is trivial, absurd, false, facile, sentimental and vulgar in art or music. . . .

10

Meanwhile, in reaction against official and operatic court classicism, more genuine artists took flight into Romanticism, seeking to recover their spontaneity, their freedom, and their true creative power. But they sought this creativity most of all in the cultivation of aesthetic feeling. Confusing this aesthetic experience with life in its deepest and most spiritual roots, the Romantics (and modern impressionists, post impressionists, expressionists, surrealists, action painters, etc. are heirs of the Romantic movement) ended in a Bohemian cult of art as a special way of life.

Thus art entered the modern age in a flush of narcissism, and the predictable result, Merton continues, is that

11

the intelligentsia elevate the artist and poet to the level once occupied by the saint, the seer, the prophet and the shaman. In the secularized modern world, the poet and artist have inherited the mantle of a discredited priesthood. . . . *The man who is not afraid of the most powerful drives hidden in his psyche,* has earned the awestruck though grudging respect of massmen and acquires the right to speak as a prophet. . . .

12

[T]his myth of the artist . . . is full of ruinous ambiguities. In the first place, all the attention is transferred from the *work of art* (which according to the ancient norms is the true object of the artist's concerns) to "art" as such and above all to "the artist." [What matters is] *the artist's own life, considered as an ikon of himself . . . .*

In this way the modern world finds the only kind of saint (apart from the spaceman) in which it can be fully interested. He is, like Gaugin, Van Gogh, Jackson Pollock, Rimbaud, Hart Crane, Bix Beiderbecke, Charlie Parker, Bessie Smith, the martyr of his gift.

Swept away in the strong current of his own historical analysis, Merton tried to accommodate the indisputable reputations of these artists and poets to his discussion of modern art. In a waffling rhetoric characteristic of the entire manuscript—a rhetoric in which an assertion was tripped up by a strong qualifying clause—Merton noted that "the integrity associated with some of these names is incontestably pure. But to interpret this integrity as equivalent to religious purity and mystical union is a fatal step into puerile fiction." He went on,

13

Let me say . . . that the work of these artists is sometimes of very great significance . . . at least as prophetic witness of the world's alienation in our own time. There is in my mind no question that these artists and poets have voices that ought to be heard . . . even . . . in the Churches. But under what conditions can this become possible? Obviously, the gospel of despair has got to try somewhere along the line to meet the gospel of hope, and perhaps the two are not as far apart as sedate and bourgeois Christians may imagine. . . . If there is to be a meeting, the artist must be able to see the element of true hope that is hidden in his despair, but the complacent Christian must also learn, from people like Kierkegaard, to admit that perhaps his hope is more fallacious than he realizes and that though his formulas may be correct, they may conceal what is, in his life itself, a real despair.

But, by and large, the qualifications Merton had to apply to artists like Van Gogh and Pollock and poets like Rimbaud and Hart Crane—artists, in Merton's mind, whose "absurd destruction of life in the name of life is also the destruction of [their] art"—severely constricted his discussion of sacred art in the modern context and limited the range of artists he could include in that discussion. He did see some possibilities for an earlier generation of artists. "Chagall, for one, has manifested a most extraordinary creativeness . . . in all his work." "Then . . . there is Rounault with his dark, compassionate scenes of sorrow, his Christs in heavy black lines. . . ." He saw hopeful signs of sacredness in the work of the Mexican revolutionary muralists José Clemente Orozco and Diego Rivera. But as Merton scanned the horizon of modern art, he considered the lion's share of artists "more prone to the comforts of a facile and dionysian way," "caught in the web of effete dilettantism and experimentation" and held in "the stifling and deadly embrace of the academies."

14

Modern art . . . has tried to live up to its vocation to spirituality by liberating itself from representation. But in order to be free of matter the artist must be a spiritual man. Now in some modern artists who have not generally painted "religious" subjects at all, there can be found a deep and original spiritual quality: for example in Cézanne's landscapes, or in Paul Klee's mysterious and cult-like symbols, or in the painstaking dreamlike evocations of the jungle by Le Douanier Rousseau.

In spite of this, modern art remains to a great extent frustrated in its search for valid symbols, because it is out of touch with the Logos Who gives meaning as well as existence both to the world of images and to the world of things.

Not surprisingly, then, the most "modern" example of sacred art that Merton selected for the appendix of illustrations for *Art and Worship* was El Greco's sixteenth-century "Agony in the Garden." Merton even deleted the modern artist Lambert Rucki's "Good Shepherd." He saw no reason to include the "psychological . . . waxworks representations" of Dali. And he brushed off the Catholic Catalan architect Gaudi as "a purveyor of interesting curiosities."

If Merton succeeded in anything throughout the trial of revisions of *Art and Worship* it was in his ability to shift his voice from that of a reactionary proselyte to that of a more broad-minded critic of the modern church and modern culture. But since he was handcuffed by a logic which guaranteed tension between the sacred (traditional) and profane (modern) he could never deliver on his promise to discuss sacred art in the modern context and, above all, revive it. The same thing could be said of modern sacred art that Merton claimed for the efficacy of modern worship:

15
In the 13th century, the age of the Gothic cathedrals, it was considerably easier for the average man to be a believing Christian than it is in the age of Atomic War.

Marred by its polemical tone and frustrated by a logic that only defeated its announced purposes, *Art and Worship* was further compromised by Merton's inflexible definition of sacred art and the conditions imposed on the sacred artist deriving from that definition. "For there to be a genuinely sacred art," he argued, "two things are absolutely necessary: the work of the artist must conform to certain norms of *sacredness* and to norms of *art*." He pulled back slightly and admitted that such norms were relative and could not be adequately contained by a juridical code and that art, in particular, "has its own laws

. . . not written in books." Nevertheless, he remained trapped by an ironclad syllogism that rendered his doctrinaire definition of sacred art inflexible and dogmatic. He further strengthened the premises of that syllogism by reaffirming elsewhere:

> 16
> There are *two things* above all that make art
> "sacred":
>   1. It bears the mark of divine
> transcendence. (*religious fervor*)
>   2. It is really alive, creative, universal.
> (*creative fervor*)

To complicate matters further, Merton devoted two middle sections of *Art and Worship* to a detailed catalogue of the precise qualities of religious and creative fervor which, according to his definition, had to meet in a work of "genuine" sacred art. So not only did the sacred artist have to forge a union of spirituality and creativity in his art; he was also instructed to adhere to a cluster of fourteen distinct qualities as he perfected that union: "Seven Qualities of the Sacred" and "Seven Qualities of Art." The sacred artist had then to be a man of deep, abiding and fervent religious faith *and* a practioner, a "maker" of the highest calibre.

One of the reasons, no doubt, for Merton's failure to handle sacred art in the modern context adequately was the reified conditions he imposed on the modern sacred artist. The contemporary Church artists responsible, for example, for "a rosary permanently encased in plastic and designed to clip on the gear shift lever of one's car" or "a Rhodium finish crucifix prayer book sparkling with hand-set imported rhinestones" may have been moved by religious fervor, but they were third-rate artists. Similarly, the great twentieth-century artists might have succeeded in meeting Merton's demands for great art, but they were spiritually impoverished, subject, in fact, to "the subtle intrusion of a demonic element into art, by reason of the fact that a pagan world has bewitched the artist into an unconscious cult of his own 'creative powers.'"

The insularity and tight contextual specificity of conditions and terms he imposed on sacred art certainly compromised the quality of Merton's analysis and hampered his ability to allow for what even the finest contemporary artists could achieve in actual practice. Quite possibly, however, Merton was not setting out to write the definitive text on sacred art, for the tension between art and spirituality in *Art and Worship* pointed to a more private and much deeper dialectical tension in Merton's own evolving personae. If *Art and Worship* failed, in other words, as an art book, it succeeded as autobiography: it gave Merton an opportunity to explore, on a different level than *The Sign of Jonas* and from a more intellectual perspective, the crisis of his own middle years. The frustrations the potential sacred artist encountered in the argument of *Art and Worship* were precisely the same frustrations Merton himself experienced during the missing years: the tension and conflict between his natural instincts and training as artist and the demands and rigors of his monastic commitment. The monk—a man of religious fervor—and the poet—a man of creative fervor—met again in the pages of an unpublishable art book where each detailed for the other his specific needs.

Those specific qualities of "sacredness" and "art" that Merton worked into the middle sections of *Art and Worship* read like a psychological profile of the Merton of the missing years. Briefly, "sacredness" (religious fervor) was encompassed by the following prescriptions, which I quote as actually outlined in the manuscript:

1. Hieratic
2. Traditional
3. Living
4. Sincere
5. Reverent
6. Spiritual
7. Pure

And Merton's qualities of art ranged as follows:

1. Original
2. Creative
3. Spontaneous
4. Intellectual
5. Inspiring
6. Competent
7. Pure

Through the figure of the sacred iconographer, Merton sought, within the pages of *Art and Worship*, "an integrated, living, creative unity" between these aesthetic and religious parameters, just as he had

struggled, in *The Sign of Jonas,* for some equanimity between his conflicting vocations as writer and monk. But the terms he employed in
his art book were antinomies, ultimately as irreconcilable as Merton's
monastic and literary agendas. "Intellectual" was inconsistent with
"spiritual" and "hieratic"; "original" was inconsistent with "traditional"; and "competency," especially in light of Merton's unkind
treatment of trends in modern art, was inconsistent with "reverence."
Interestingly enough, the only common denominator was "purity" in
both religion and art, the single quality Merton had reserved to praise
exclusively in the work and life of his father and Cézanne. In art, such
purity, however, could only be found in the religious art of the Great
Age of Christian Faith. In religion, such purity, in the modern age,
could be found only in medieval monasticism. And in both art and
religion, such a demand for purity inevitably foisted upon Merton a
righteous antimodern sensibility that, as he admits in *Jonas,* only
made his complaints about the world "impure," and that, as he eventually discovered in *Art and Worship,* only crippled his discussion of
modern sacred art.

— 6 —

Merton knew that his art book was weak in the modern period, a
weakness readily acknowledged by his editor who wrote Merton in
November 1959 and asked him to expand the section on modern religious art "which is almost perfunctory. There is so much interest
in this that it ought to be dealt with more fully (which is what we
hope you will agree to) or be dropped altogether, which would be
regrettable."[7] Merton replied by return post. *Art and Worship* would
just have to wait, he said, "above all as I am in no mood to do any
work on modern sacred art now, since I know too little about it. About
how many more pages do you want? Can you send me something to
look at?"[8]

Other factors held up presswork on *Art and Worship.* Robert Giroux
knew that the book, unlike anything Merton had written before under a commercial imprint, would have to sell on the highly specialized
and risky art book market. Giroux's immediate concern, then, was to
make *Art and Worship* "a more attractive and saleable book." Much
attention would have to be given to design and layout, especially in

light of the fact that Giroux rejected the original design—the Terrell Dickey galley draft—because the layout and type were "too thin and oversized." "The other first reaction," he objected, "is that this layout does not give full value to the artwork, bunching it together in one section."[9] Considering Giroux's objections, there was enough evidence to suggest that Merton and his publishers were probably working at cross purposes almost from the very moment the manuscript arrived at Farrar, Straus, and Cudahy. The original design, laid out according to Merton's own directions, showed that he was far more interested in the text of *Art and Worship* than in its possibilities as an art book; after all, he relegated just a few illustrations to an appendix. Giroux, on the other hand, probably had great misgivings about the quality of the text (perhaps sensing already that the book was an anti-modern polemic masking as a text on religious art) and felt that *Art and Worship* had to make it on the art book market, or perhaps not make it at all.

This latter problem—how to make *Art and Worship* into a viable art book—was addressed late in 1959 when Giroux hired Ed Rice to re-design the book. Although Giroux counseled patience in his letters to Merton, noting frequently that "the press work and manufacture of *Art and Worship* is [sic] going to take time and care," Merton grew increasingly restless over delays. Giroux and Rice even travelled to Gethsemani with prototypes of a new design. But Merton still chafed over delays, especially during the latter half of 1959 and early 1960 when he pestered his agent to the extent that she finally wrote: "This seems to me like a victrola record, but I have been told all along that the art book would be quite slow. I know Ed Rice has been working on the layout, and I can only assume that they have not yet reached a point where they should be in touch with you."[10]

The other problem with *Art and Worship*—how to strengthen its coverage of modern sacred art—was more difficult to solve. Although he told his editor that he did not know enough about the modern period to handle it adequately, Merton nonetheless dutifully revised a few sections and added more references to modern art and architecture. Recognizing the inadequacy of his revisions, Merton defended himself against polite objections by frequently noting in his letters that a cloistered monk just did not have the kind of access to museums and galleries necessary for the task. A more likely reason, however, for Merton's reluctance to extend his coverage of modern sacred art was his own growing realization that the original argument was seriously flawed by its antimodern biases. How could he bolster his discussion of sacred art in the modern period when handcuffed by a logic which held sacredness and modernness as mutually exclusive?

Giroux grew a bit impatient. He must have decided that the fate of the book hinged on whether its weakness in the modern period could be redressed. Realizing that Merton himself could not be moved to the task, Giroux arranged for the outside assistance of an art historian named Eloise Spaeth. After notifying Merton, Giroux gave Mrs. Spaeth the manuscript and asked her to write a report detailing her professional opinions, especially with respect to the section on modern art.

In July 1960 Mrs. Spaeth confirmed in her report to Giroux that *Art and Worship* was indeed too thin in its use of examples of contemporary art. She offered many useful suggestions to add to the original groupings of illustrations, all "examples of contemporary art where the artist has drawn on a traditional theme but worked in new materials." Although she politely "quarrelled with Father Louis" over a few key points in the text itself, she ultimately tempered her objections with the most effusive praise of the book. "Father Louis has established a pattern throughout the book that is so concise and clear that I think the average layman will have a better understanding of the subject than if tomes had been written about it."[11] Giroux was delighted. He asked Mrs. Spaeth to contact Merton directly and proposed to Merton that "if your exchanges develop into a real collaboration as far as the modern section goes, I am going to propose that she receive a small royalty."[12] As Mrs. Spaeth continued to work on the book during the early sixties (she travelled to Gethsemani in February 1964), Giroux eventually considered an equitable split of the royalties between her and Merton and a sharing of the byline.

Merton's reception of Mrs. Spaeth's collaboration was cool but cordial. He was not used to sharing bylines. But since he was "paralyzed," as he said in a letter to Mrs. Spaeth, over the modern art section and growing more impatient and "sick of the whole thing," he welcomed Mrs. Spaeth and issued her a carte blanche "to dig up anything and everything you think we agree on and let me have a good lot to choose from. And please feel free to make all the suggestions you like, though I may not be able to follow them always."[13]

Mrs. Spaeth's contributions to *Art and Worship* promised to move the book off dead center. But in one of the many twists which foiled the ill-fated project, her collaboration ultimately set the seal on the book's unpublishability.

Although she praised the manuscript, with only minor reservations, in her memo to Giroux and her letters to Merton were always upbeat and supportive, Mrs. Spaeth's cordiality masked her deeper misgivings over the text of *Art and Worship*. She never shared with Merton the irritated comments and questions she penned into the margins of her copy of the manuscript. Prompted by her private misgivings, Mrs. Spaeth sought another opinion of Merton's manuscript. She asked a close friend, an art historian and critic, to review the text and pass along his assessments. It is difficult to identify Mrs. Spaeth's correspondent because the only copy of his letter to her in the Merton archives is an undated and unsigned carbon of the original. But his response—critical in no uncertain terms—was the first time that anyone had addressed, with forthrightness and reasoned clarity, the unevenness of *Art and Worship* and its hopeless antimodern biases.

> Dear Eloise,
>
> I have read Merton's manuscript three times now and it is my best advice that you have nothing to do with it. The text is obscure where it should be clear, irritated where it should be passionate. In all its parts it is simply incredibly naive—as you well know and expressed in your own rather irritated marginal comments and queries. It is based entirely on the author's reading and meditation on theological writings, not at all on his ever having looked at an individual work of art.
>
> Specifically, the opening 16 or 17 pages are pure adolescent-Catholic raving at the modern world and seem rather pointless. . . . The subsequent presumed analytical description of the properties of sacred art (I agree [sic] you wholeheartedly about the "sacred artist" who keeps creeping in with his frightful icons or ikons) is a masterpiece of theological tautology. . . . After three readings I am still without a clue as to what he can conceivably mean by "hieratic," which is certainly his key word. Art is legitimately called sacred art when it is hieratic and it is hieratic because it is sacred. Here and practically everywhere else, Merton is continually turning in back upon his own muddled thought. . . .
>
> His tired old thesis on the corruption of Renaissance art doesn't really merit discussion at all; it has been worked to death by every cleric who has ever interested himself in the question; it saves them all the trouble of having to go to the Met . . . and actually looking at the art they are dismissing so loftily. . . .

The "history" loses itself completely in the modern period, failing to make the most obvious distinctions within 19th and early 20th century art . . . without actually examining a single picture. The text ends as it began in a cluster of tautology, unjustified irritation with the modern world, intolerable self-righteousness and a systematic evasion of all questions raised even while pretending to answer them. And, to the end, there is Eloise vainly crying out for some word other than "ikon."

Assuming, however, that this book is going to be published for the same reasons that the modern materialistic secularistic world publishes other non-books, namely to cash in on a hot name in Catholic spirituality, what can be done? Nothing at all in terms of an integrated text-with-pix package. The reason is that the text never gets close . . . to specific pictures or statues. It is always and everywhere up on cloud nine. . . . Devote more pictures . . . in order to make this seminary essay look like a book. . . . But the selection should actually be an independent work, ignoring Merton's absurd text. . . .

You can count on my secret collaboration in the selection of the pictures and the writing of the captions, or their editing. But . . . the text is beyond any real salvation. Again, I do hope you'll reconsider getting further involved in this because I think it is almost certainly doomed to ridicule if it gets noticed at all by the non-Catholic press.[14]

Giroux almost certainly saw this biting evaluation of Merton's art book and it probably turned him against the project, considering especially its prediction that *Art and Worship* would be drubbed by the critics. Judging from Merton's correspondence with all parties involved in the project (Giroux, Ed Rice, Mrs. Spaeth, and Merton's agent), the memo was most likely written in mid-1964 when all references to *Art and Worship* suddenly disappear until Giroux mailed the manuscript back to Gethsemani in February 1967. As late as February 1964, *Art and Worship* was still under contract. And in March of the same year Merton announced to Giroux the "good news" that the revised manuscript had been passed by the censors.

Whether Merton himself read this attack on his decade-old art book is a matter of pure conjecture. If he did, the report might have only confirmed his own misgivings over the kind of "adolescent-Catholic ravings at the modern world" that muddled the argument of *Art and Worship* and also caused Merton considerable embarrassment, about this time, when thinking, for example, about his best-selling autobiography of 1948. More than a year before Mrs. Spaeth's friend leveled Merton, he was gently backing away from the project and telling his agent that he was no longer "keen" on it. "Bob [Giroux] was always insisting," Merton wrote, "on a bit about modern sacred art and I had no way of handling that. Besides, a lot of water has gone under the bridge since the book was written, and I would rather just drop it altogether if I could."[15]

Even if Merton never read the report, the current of his changing attitudes toward art and modernity was moving swiftly of its own accord. It was stirred most powerfully by Merton's old Columbia University friend, the abstract expressionist Ad Reinhardt, a paragon of modern art and one of the contemporary artists who had inherited from the Romantics a tradition that Merton claimed made modern art "a dead thing."

$$-7-$$

An excellent illustration of how radically Merton's views on art changed over the years was his decision, in the spring of 1968, to reprint Ad Reinhardt's Abstract Expressionist manifesto, "Art-As-Art," as the lead piece in the inaugural number of *Monks Pond*, edited and "published" by Merton from the desk of his hermitage. What Reinhardt had to say about the ultimate ends of modern art would have appalled Merton in 1954 when he first pieced together the argument of *Art and Worship*. If Merton had a copy of Reinhardt's manifesto then he may well have used it in service of his antimodernism, as a good example of how art in the modern age had been desecrated by its abandonment of ultimate spiritual and liturgical causes. "No one in his right mind goes to an art-museum to worship anything but art," Reinhardt wrote.

> *The one subject* of a hundred years of modern art is that awareness of art of itself, of art preoccupied with its own process and means, with its own identity and distinction, art concerned with its own unique statement, art conscious of its own evolution and history and destiny, towards its own freedom, its own dignity, its own essence, its own reason, its own morality and its own conscience. Art needs no justification in our day with "realism" or "naturalism," "regionalism" or "nationalism," "individualism" or "socialism" or "mysticism," or with any other ideas. . .
>
> Artists who claim that their art-work comes from . . . earth or heaven,

as "mirrors of the soul" or "reflections of conditions" . . . are subjectively and objectively, rascals or rustics.[16]

In choosing Reinhardt's manifesto as the centerpiece of the first edition of *Monks Pond*, Merton was announcing implicitly the editorial aesthetic which would govern his selection of material for the experimental magazine. And how different that aesthetic was from the infinitely more conservative one that underpinned his own manifesto ten years earlier! Merton had written, even as late as 1962 in a typescript revision, that "modern art . . . remains frustrated in its search for valid symbols, because it is out of touch with the Logos Who gives meaning as well as existence to the world of images and to the world of things." Reinhardt insisted that "art comes only from art only, not from anything else"; he claimed that anyone who used art to further anything but art itself "is out of his mind." Merton had also, in 1962, decried modern art for one of its "ruinous ambiguities": that modern art had transferred its attention from the ancient spiritual norms to "'art' as such." Reinhardt's "Art-As-Art" could easily have carried another title: "Art-As-Such."

Reinhardt was certainly no atheist. He could not be conveniently lumped into Merton's comprehensive index of modern artists who had taken "a fatal step into [the] puerile fiction" of considering his art as "an ikon of himself." In fact, Reinhardt shared Merton's interest in Christian mysticism, especially the tradition of "the negative way" (Merton's own) channeled, for example, through St. John of the Cross's Dark Night of the Soul. Reinhardt once spoke of how important it was for the artist "to enter into the darkness and to admit the coincidence of opposites to seek the truth where impossibility meets us."[17] And the religious implications of darkness were often cited by contemporary art critics when discussing Reinhardt's bold abstract experiments in all-black colossal canvases. In his "Notes on Contributors," Merton listed Reinhardt as "the 'black monk' of abstract art," "a rigorous contemplative . . . just beginning to be recognized as prophetic by a new generation" of artists.

Although Reinhardt once tried to talk Merton out of becoming a Trappist monk, they differed little in their spiritual sensitivities. Their differences, which often prompted lively, critical exchanges in their letters, hinged rather on a controversy over the ends and means of *art* itself. As a practicing and active artist, Reinhardt was naturally more concerned with the "process and means" of art, of art's "awareness of itself" and the artist's ability to identify with his tools and media of expression. As a practicing religious, Merton was naturally more concerned with the artist's "ends," with the Logos, as he said, which gives meaning to the artist's images.

It is worth digressing slightly to consider that the differences between Merton and Reinhardt, mediated by their shared religious sensibilities, became a kind of twentieth-century replay of the famous Iconoclastic Controversy that raged over the religious art of eighth-century Byzantium. Briefly, art historians date the beginning of the controversy at 726 when an imperial edict was issued prohibiting religious images. The art world was immediately split into two hostile groups: the iconoclasts (or image-destroyers) felt that any representation of Christ was a graven image conducive to idolatry; the iconophiles, led by the monks, insisted that religious art captured the relationship between the human and the divine in the person of Christ. The iconoclasts restricted religious art to abstract images and symbols. The iconophiles insisted on straight representation. In the pages of *Art and Worship* Merton had already wrestled with the aesthetic implications of the Iconoclastic Controversy. Sounding at first like an iconophile, he wrote that "since the Word of God . . . has been made Flesh, He has restored to human nature its full dignity as Image of God. . . . And so sacred art is able, in its representations of the Savior and of His saints, to portray to us something of the beauty and glory of God Himself revealed in them." In a later revision Merton blue-penciled that comment, turned a full one hundred and eighty degrees, and adopted an iconoclastic position. "Sacred art does not attempt to represent the divine and invisible mysteries, still less God Himself, 'Whom no man shall see and live' [Exodus]. . . . The sacredness of sacred art does not depend . . . on its capacity to 'represent' its subject. . . . The more art strives to create an illusion of sensible reality, the more it tends to depart from the . . . Spiritual dimension of reality which is proper to it."

Ad Reinhardt was eventually responsible for Merton's new iconoclasm, which brought with it an entirely renovated attitude about art and modernism. Clearly, as an abstract expressionist Reinhardt was a natural iconoclast; his tenets of abstractionism stressed "no shapes, no composings, no representings, no visions, no relations, no attributes, no qualities." Clearly too, the young Merton, like the eighth-century monks, was a staunch iconophile because he stressed the liturgical function of sacred art and sought to revive the purity and vitality of religious art in the service of Christian worship. When Merton wrote Reinhardt in 1959 and sketched in the argument of *Art and Worship*, Reinhardt's reply was predictably terse and critical. Merton's reply, in turn, showed that he tried to take his friend's criticisms to heart. "Now you come along," Merton said, "and ask me to fall into the iconoclast tradition. Which is admittedly something like my own (supposedly my own) Cistercian background. St. Bernard threw out all the statues. They were a distraction, he said. I used to believe it. I think it is an affectation, from the religious viewpoint, to hold that statues are a distraction. Who is there to be distracted?"[18]

The letters Merton and Reinhardt exchanged for the next three years continued to be marked by disagreements between Ad's "Art-As-Art" iconoclastic principles and Merton's determined efforts to defend the "Art-As-Worship" stance he had originally taken in his art book. Finally, however, Reinhardt launched a bitter attack against his old friend in 1962, an attack that jolted Merton into an acceptance of Reinhardt's distinctly modern views on art and, as a consequence, turned Merton against the "antimodern ravings" of his own art book.

Reinhardt was incensed by a jacket blurb Merton had written for a volume of paintings by the abstract expressionist and Catholic convert William Congdon, entitled *In My Disc of Gold: Itinerary to Christ of William Congdon*. Mrs. Spaeth thought Congdon had real possibilities for inclusion in *Art and Worship*, for he was one of the few contemporary artists who worked traditional themes with modern materials. After a brief correspondence, Merton agreed to write a preface to Congdon's "Itinerary to Christ," a pictorial record of his conversion. Merton wrote:

There is in the recent painting of William Congdon an . . . extraordinary breakthrough of genuine spiritual light in the art of an abstract expressionist. . . .
It is the inner truth of abstract expressionism that has led William Congdon to his religious conversion. . . .
Here we see a rare instance in which the latent spiritual *logos* of abstract art has been completely set free . . . from its compulsive, dionysian and potentially orgiastic self-frustrations and raised to the level of spirituality, innocence, and *theoria*. . . .
The religious spectator . . . , untutored in modern art but loyal to his

religion, may wish to rejoice that abstract art has once again entered into the service of the Church.[19]

When he received the prepublication publicity package from Congdon's publisher and read Merton's comments, Reinhardt fired off a letter which he later described as "chewing you up and down for that Billy-Congdon-business."

> Sometimes we see jolly old friends only at sad funerals, dear relatives and classmates only at tragedies, communicate only at crises. When everything is all right, everything is all right. The other day I received in my mail, a mailing piece and a blurb [sic] I couldn't believe my eyes when I saw . . . [sic]
> Why shouldn't you be human after all and to err is human, we all know, but why should I be forgiving? And you forgiven?
> . . . Imagine you after all these years. . . . [sic] Have you given up hope? . . . . Reality-schmearality, as long as you're sound of body? Are you throwing in the towel at long last? Can't you tell your impasto from a holy ground? . . . Just pack up your scribbles in your old kitch [sic] bag and smile, smile, smile, hey? . . . [I'll] send help, hold on, old man.[20]

Reinhardt was not so much annoyed at Merton's ranking of Congdon as a top-flight abstract expressionist, although, it is true, Reinhardt had no taste for Congdon's work; he thought of him as a "Palette-Knifer" and Reinhardt's "reality-schmearality" was pejorative reference to the way Congdon trowelled broad swaths of color on his canvases. What bothered Reinhardt was the reductionist mentality in Merton's praise of Congdon, in particular Merton's comment that Congdon's work proved "the protest of the abstract expressionist . . . *remains a deeply spiritual protest.*" He was even more angered by Merton's claim that Congdon's abstractions showed "the latent spiritual *logos* of abstract art . . . completely set free . . . free from its compulsive, dionysian and potentially orgiastic self-frustration and raised to the level of spirituality, innocence and *theoria.*" In so many words, Reinhardt was telling Merton that he did not know what he was talking about and had no business with nor claim on evaluating the principles and aims of modern abstract art. Everything Merton said about Congdon's work violated the principles of abstract expressionism which Reinhardt had just outlined in his original 1962 draft of the "Art-As-Art" manifesto. Merton had a copy of the manifesto; he knew too that Reinhardt was generally accepted as the central spokesman for modern abstract art. Why hadn't Merton considered Reinhardt's insistence that abstract art as "Art-as-art is nothing but art"? That "art is not what is not art"? *"The one object* of fifty years of abstract art," Reinhardt wrote, "is to present art-as-art and as nothing else, to make it into the one thing it is only, separating and defining it more and more, making it purer and emptier, more absolute and more exclusive,—non-objective, non-representational, non-figurative, non-imagist, non-expressionist."[21] Reinhardt would not forgive Merton for his errors: for the simple fact, above all, that the *logos* of abstract art was situated in the work of art itself, not derived, as Merton claimed, from "spirituality, innocence, . . . [or] *theoria."*

Merton was stung by Reinhardt's letter. "Once, twice, often, repeatedly, I have reached out for your letter and for the typewriter," he wrote.

Choked with sobs, or rather more often carried away by the futilities of life, I have desisted. Dear relatives and classmates at tragedies. Ah yes, how true. As life goes on, as we descend more and more into the hebetude of middle age, as the brain coagulates, as the members lose their spring, as the spirit fades, as the mind dims, we come together face to face with one another and with our lamentable errors.

Our lamentable errors. My lamentable errors. . . .

I have embraced a bucket of schmalz. I have accepted the mish mash of kitsch. I have been made public with a mitre of marshmellows [sic] upon my dumkopf. This is the price of folly and the wages of middle aged perversity.

I thought my friends would never know. . . . I shall weave rugs out of cornsilk, equivalent in substance to my artistic judgements which I eternally regret.

My artistic judgement has contracted the measles.

My love of kunst has become mumped.

My appreciation of the sacreds hath a great whoreson pox and is reproved by all with good tastings and holy lauds. . . .

You are pro-iconoclast and you are right. . . . You are non-objectivist and you are right. Down with object. Down with damn subject. Down with matter and form. . . .

I am in the wash. I am under the mangle. I am publicly identified with all the idols. I am the byword of the critics and galleries. I am eaten alive by the art racket. I am threatened with publication of a great book of horrors which I have despised and do recant. . . . Help, help, rescue your old fellow sachem.[22]

Although masked somewhat by a gush of camp rhetoric, Merton's embarrassment over the Congdon affair was felt deeply in his letter to Reinhardt. Perhaps more than anything else, Merton's exchanges with Reinhardt helped to break the chain of logic that reduced *Art and Worship* to little more than a "masterpiece of theological tautology." The links between art, sacredness, and antimodernism were shattered by Merton's willingness to announce to his friend, "Down with object. Down with damn subject. Down with matter and form." For Merton, art no longer had to be a subject serving only the object of Christian faith in a profane century.

It would be tempting to conclude that Merton's new Reinhardtian iconoclasm and the effect of the scathing memo written by Mrs. Spaeth's friend came together in an irreversible catharsis and finally resolved the dilemmas Merton experienced during the ten years he worked on his study of sacred art. But he still had hopes for his art book. Although by the mid-sixties he was no longer as persistent and impatient as he had once been, he nonetheless sounded out opportunities to publish more sections of *Art and Worship;* in late 1963, for example—a year after he recanted his "book of horrors" to Reinhardt—Merton asked his agent if she would object to his placing bits of the manuscript in small magazines. In fairness to Merton, however, he was not indulging in his old game of contradictions. He had matured to the point where he could contain contradictions within the framework of a broader point of view. He believed that art should serve Christian faith. He believed art ought to liberate itself from subservience to doctrines and formulas.

One measure of Merton's ability to transcend contradictory points of view with respect to art was his relationship with another artist-friend, the classicist Victor Hammer. At the same time Merton was coming around to the iconoclasm of the black monk of abstract modern art he was praising, in another catalogue announcement, the traditional style of Hammer's religious paintings and applauding their freedom from "a certain Dionysian romanticism abroad at the present time. . . ."[23] Hammer's classical realism in art—accompanied by a traditional conservatism that led him to describe himself as an "anachronism [who does not] 'belong' to my time, my century"[24]—suited Merton's own conservatism and fueled his persistent anti-modern inclinations. In the art of his friend Victor Hammer, Merton found justification for the tenets underpinning his study of sacred art. Hammer's insistence, for example, that the art public "(and not a Philistine public) . . . will not be satisfied by the elimination of recognizable, ordinarily human, subject matter" in art confirmed Merton's belief, expressed especially in the early drafts of *Art and Worship,* that sacred art must maintain fidelity to the sensible details of the sacred subjects it depicts. Clearly too, Merton shared Hammer's commitment to the ultimate "ends" of art: "the plain subject matter on which the artist can feed," Hammer wrote, " . . . must be spiritual, never material alone." These two factors led Hammer, as they had moved Merton, into a critique of the avant-garde and a distaste for all movements in modern art. Sounding very much like the Merton of *Art and Worship,* Hammer boldly admitted "I cannot spiritually cooperate with or acknowledge the validity of visual chaos, . . . the chaos of the modern movement in art."

Although he shared Hammer's conservative temperament, still it must have been difficult for Merton to weather Hammer's attacks on "daubers and abstractionists," especially Reinhardt. When Ad came to visit Merton at Gethsemani , for example, Hammer, who lived nearby in Lexington, was sorry he missed him. "I would have liked to talk to Reinhardt," Hammer wrote in a letter to Merton, "as I am still unable to see anything in abstract art. . . . If we were insects with the hard crust outside, abstract art would be appropriate. . . . To me abstract art is pure perversion. Reinhardt may be sincere, but as an abstractionist he is a sinner against the holy Ghost."[25] But just as he had successfully navigated the inevitable confrontations with Reinhardt, Merton diplomatically maneuvered away from any potential conflicts with Victor Hammer. Even after Merton, choked with sobs, fully surrendered himself to Reinhardt's abstractionists principles in 1962 (admitting that his "appreciation of the sacreds hath a whoreson pox"!), he could still accommodate Hammer by admitting that "one has to be able to say that abstract expression is *not* art." He added,

> I think that clarifies most of what needs to be said about it, both for and against. That is precisely what is "for" it: that it is not art, though it seems to be. I know this statement is scandalous, and I think the ambi-

guities are bad ones in the long run (it should not pretend to be art, which in fact it does). I do not think that throwing paint on canvas and saying "This is not art" merits twenty thousand dollars. It is too obvious. However, even the obvious has its place.[26]

Merton's catering to the opposing views of Reinhardt and Hammer was more than a matter of maintaining cordial interpersonal relationships with two close friends. Merton had wrestled with the conflicting views of his friends throughout the years of his own private struggle with *Art and Worship,* never entirely willing to surrender himself to either. The tension between "Art-As-Art" and "Art-As-Worship" was not a mere intellectual problem, however, that could be solved intellectually, nor was it a matter, really, of aesthetics. It was a tension rooted deeper in the opposing branches of Merton's evolving personality—between his inclinations as an artist himself and his spiritual commitments as a man of deep Christian faith trying to come to terms with a post-Christian century. Unable, in spite of a tenacious ten year struggle, to resolve that tension satisfactorily, Merton eventually grew large enough to contain it. As far as his study of sacred art was concerned, Merton's exceptionally broad depth of field rendered his art book unpublishable, but it gave him the rare ability to embrace, accept, and understand two artist/friends of immeasurably different temperaments. More important, by rising above the sacred/profane dialectic, Merton began to accommodate himself to his own age while simultaneously strengthening his faith and commitment to the traditions of his church and monastic order. He became eventually, in the words of Amiya Chakravarty, unwilling to accept "a fixed medieval line between the sacred and profane," a line that had hobbled the logic of his art book and stunted his inherent humanist inclinations. "In this," Chakravarty continues, in his preface to *The Asian Journal,* "he was a modern Christian thinker and believer who had to redefine, or leave undefined, the subtle balance of the religious life."

Back in 1954, Merton had warned the scholastics at Gethsemani that certain trends in modern art were witness to "a disturbing symptom of the ills of our time": "the total insensitiveness to the *sacred,* and to the *life* and *character* of an art to measure up to the holiness of God's house and of divine worship."[27] Ten years later, in August of 1964, he spoke on "The Importance of Art" in the novitiate again, with a different message: "In spite of the fact that the majority of people," like Merton himself ten years earlier, have derided modern nonrepresentational art, have attacked it, and have taken for granted that it was all a fraud, all complete nonsense, have been frightened, shocked, scandalized by it, this art has gone its own way and has established itself as one of the most important expressions of man's intellectual and spiritual life, in the world today.

Through an understanding of [this] art, we can enter into communion with the world of our time on a deep and significant level and can therefore come to a knowledge of its needs and its problems. We can be more in communion with our own time. *We have to be men of our time.*[28]

Although Hammer would not admit it and Reinhardt was perhaps too eager to broadcast it, both, at least in Merton's mind, were just such men of their time. Like Merton, his two friends communed with their age and understood it through the *protest* of their art. Reinhardt's and Hammer's protests, to be sure, were so different that they were virtually leveled against each other. Reinhardt rebelled against artistic conventions that compromised the freedom of abstract art and its total consciousness only of itself. Hammer rebelled against the incompetence of daubers who abandoned the discipline and dignity of traditional techniques. But both, through their identity and commitment as artists, were, like Merton, marginal men critical of their culture and their age but in communion with it. Like Merton, they were artists practicing the art of the radical critique.

PART II

A Radical Humanist and the Radical Critique

It is possible to doubt whether I have become a
monk (a doubt I have to live with), but it is not
possible to doubt that I am a writer, that I was born
one and will most probably die as one.
Disconcerting, disedifying as it is, this seems to be
my lot and my vocation.

5

A Modern Man in Reverse
Looking Forward

The new iconoclastic spirit that grew partly out of Thomas Merton's struggles with *Art and Worship* contributed to the content and style of the radical social critique which would later dominate his writing during the 1960s, win for him an entire new generation of readers, and reveal a temperament suited to the climate of a tumultuous new decade. By the late 1950s, Merton began to envision for himself a new role. He developed a new voice. He assumed new obligations arising from a sense of new responsibilities. "Basically," as he said to a correspondent during the 1960s, "I think it should be the job of the monk to do this kind of iconoclastic criticism . . . [and] to be effectively iconoclastic in the modern world."[1]

Not surprisingly, then, new books began to appear. No longer entirely satisfied with his public image as a Catholic convert and author of pious inspirational works, Merton began to rework his image into that of a candid and informed social critic. No longer content to address the problems of his day from the perspective of an otherworldly devotional writer, Merton began to speak more globally on a wider range of complex contemporary issues. He began to admit freely that the conventional Catholic answers, which he had committed himself to with such totality and abandon as a young monk, were becoming increasingly irrelevant to the malaise of intellectual, social, moral, and political problems facing the contemporary person. Merton grew to accept fully and openly a new reading of history, one which positioned the modern era squarely in a post-Christian age—which would have been anathema to his antisecular disposition years earlier. He evolved, in short, from a medieval ascetic who trumpeted disdain for his own century into a postmodern intellectual who could celebrate, among other things, the dignified humanism of Boris Pasternak and the agnostic credo of absurdity championed by Albert Camus.

Most important, the interior divisions that triggered and sustained the crisis of Merton's middle years began to heal by the end of the 1950s. Merton came to accept his instincts as a writer. He no longer viewed his literary inclinations as a serious impediment to progress in his spiritual life. This profound renewal of his sense of purpose and calling as a writer encouraged Merton to redefine the earlier standards of his monastic commitment and to compromise the rigidity of his old self-image as contemplative, mystic, would-be saint. Merton's self-image during the missing years was essentially biblical—a Jonas snatched away from the life of an ordinary mortal being into the jaws of the contemplative life, a life of withdrawal and negation. Like Jonas, "the waters had closed over his head, and he was submerged. . . . He was lost. The world would hear of him no more." But the new self-image Merton began to cultivate in the sixties was unmistakably existential—that of a bystander whose failure to address the crises, confusions, errors, crimes and suffering of his contemporaries became a tacit admission of guilt for and complicity in that suffering. This was a fully modern self-image, borrowed no doubt from Merton's enthusiastic embrace of Camus: that of a stranger whose frail protestations of innocence and pleas of noninvolvement only implicated him further in crimes he never committed. "A witness of a crime," Merton wrote in his turgid "Letter to an Innocent Bystander," "who just stands by and makes a mental note of the fact he is an innocent bystander, tends by that very fact to become an accomplice" (*Raids*, 55). If, in other words, the monk of the missing years took the offensive, accusing the writer (who remained stubbornly attached to the "world") of stunting his spiritual progress, the writer after 1957 gained, so to speak, the upper hand and criticized the monk for his pious enthusiasms and for the oversimplifications of his world-denying slogans and cliches. From the shadow of a somewhat arrogant young contemplative who seemed to have all the right answers, Merton emerged in the sixties as a far less self-conscious humanist who could share with his contemporaries, whether Catholic or Protestant, agnostic or atheist, the uncertainties of living in turbulent and confusing times—a man, in fact, who became harshly critical of all obligatory answers to the most pressing questions facing the new decade.

As early as 1955, Merton began to revise his earlier feelings concerning the fundamental incompatibility between the artistic and contemplative vocations, a revision that played no little role in the evolution of his new persona. He learned to see that the monk's ability to respond to reality, to perceive "the value and beauty in ordinary things" and "to come alive to the splendor that is all around us" were not, as he had earlier suspected, impediments to contemplation, but rather they were "the most important—and the most neglected—elements . . . of the interior life" (*TMR*, 386). He later maintained that the first step in the interior life called for a sharpening of the monk's sensory powers, essentially a refurbishing of his native poetic instincts. The monk, Merton came to believe, must rearm his ability to see, taste, and feel. Earlier Merton had made the fatal mistake, as he himself admitted, of viewing art as an entertainment and a diversion, a mistake that led inexorably to a poetics of negation which meant that the poet/ascetic must renounce art along with television, cigarettes, and gin. But he retooled his aesthetics and came to view the creation of a work of art as a sublime act, one of the highest and most perfect fulfillments of monastic life. Art, in short, became an *affirmation*. Perhaps he was describing himself during the crisis of the missing years when he wrote, in 1955, that "the soul that picks and pries at itself in the isolation of its own dull self-analysis arrives at a self-consciousness that is a torment and a disfigurement of our whole personality. But the spirit that finds itself above itself in the intensity . . . of its reaction to a work of art is 'self-conscious' in a way that is productive as well as sublime" (387).

The most significant signal of Merton's change in attitude toward art came in 1958 when he published a revision of his article on poetry and the contemplative life. "Poetry and Contemplation: A Reappraisal" first appeared in *Commonweal* in October 1958; it was also published as an appendix to Merton's *Selected Poems* (1959), and it reappeared, at Merton's suggestion, in *A Thomas Merton Reader*, edited by Thomas McDonnell in 1962. In this latter volume Merton even added an author's note, all in an effort to redeem the dogmatic stance he had taken a few years earlier.

Merton states that in the first version of the essay, he had applied "a rather crude 'solution'" to the problem of art and spirituality, a solution "wisely rejected" by many of his readers "because of its . . . puritanical implications." Since then, "I have found the confident pronouncements made in my earlier writing lay more and more heavily on my conscience as a writer and as a priest." The real problem with that earlier essay was its "altogether misleading insistence on the terms 'contemplation' and 'contemplative life' as something apart from the rest of man's existence." Merton is his own best critic on this account; in his apology he makes it clear that to consider "aesthetic reflection" as somehow interfering with contemplation is an altogether "naive presupposition." Moreover, "In actual fact, neither religious nor artistic contemplation should be regarded as 'things' which happen or 'objects' which one can 'have.' They belong to the much more mysterious realm of what one 'is'—or rather 'who' one is" (*LE*, 339). As a contemplative, Merton awoke to the realization that his quest for a "great wordless wilderness" was, like the poet's search for the words to name the unnameable, nothing more than a quest for an "object" or a "thing." Once Merton realized this, his search for a spiritual identity evolved into the "more mysterious" and challenging quest for an existential identity, still dependent, to be sure, on monastic ideals, but not tyrannized by those ideals. The new ground that emerged, then, from the crisis of Merton's middle years was not an exclusively spiritual or literary ground: it was an existential ground that encompassed spirituality and art. The monk needed the poet to help explore this new territory because, as Merton makes clear in his revision, "aesthetic intuition [leads to] a heightening and intensification of . . . personal identity."

Looking back on the logic he defended in 1947, Merton was now able to realize that "the implied conflict between 'contemplation' as rest and poetic creation as activity" was a dangerous and misleading polarization. He felt that the monk's will to mortify his senses, as a means of achieving a stillness wherein he could contemplate divine things, was, in a qualitative sense, no better than the poet's will to saturate his senses with the splendor and dynamism of created things as a stepping stone to affirming creation. "In actual fact, true con-

templation is inseparable from life and from the dynamism of life—
which includes work, creation, production, fruitfulness, and above
all *love*. Contemplation is not to be thought of as a separate depart-
ment of life, cut off from all man's other interests and superseding
them. It is the very fullness of a fully integrated life. It is the crown of
life and all life's activities" (*LE*, 339).

Merton made one thing abundantly clear in his apologetic reappraisal: he would no longer tolerate artificial, institutional divisions as
he sought a unity between his inclinations as artist and his vocation
as monk. He reflected more intimately on that quest when, a few
years later, a correspondent asked him to comment further on "Poetry
and Contemplation: A Reappraisal." "Should one be a poet and a
monk at the same time?" Merton asked. In 1947, Merton deftly answered that question by insisting that the monk's ruthless sacrifice of
art was the only possible course he could take. In 1964, he admitted
that comparing "an abstract essence of 'monk'" with "an equally abstract essence of 'poet' and [seeing] if they can be accommodated with
one another . . . answers nothing. Obviously," he wrote,

> there is some sort of conflict between the kind of inner life that one
> associates with poetry and the inner life of a monk. At least there ap-
> pears to be. The level of poetry and the level of interior prayer are quite
> different in many respects. . . . But in the long run, all life consists of
> growth toward unity and maturity and every man whether he be a monk
> or a street sweeper has to find in the end that his life gains meaning only
> when, by the right and responsible use of his freedom, in response to
> grace, everything is brought into a unified direction in accordance with
> his vocation and situation in life.
>
> In order to be honest with myself, with God and with other men, I
> find it is necessary to take the facts of my own life as they are, and admit
> to begin with that nothing in my life is ideal, and nothing fits the ac-
> cepted formulas. I am the first one to declare that I am not what I ought
> to be. At the same time I tend to question the declarations of those who
> might say I ought to be something other than I am. As I grow older I find
> it more and more necessary to respect the mystery of one's personal life,
> everyone's. We do not have clear answers to fit everybody's case, and we
> do not have ways of judging and solving all cases. . . .
>
> It seems to me that the particular configuration of my own life, with all
> its shortcomings, demands some sort of synthesis of poetry and prayer. I
> fully realize that I might perhaps aspire to a technically "higher" kind of
> life if I would try to refuse to be a poet. But I have reason to think that if I

made this refusal it would in fact be an act of pride and disobedience. Others will assume, on the other hand, that it is pride for me to continue to be a poet, especially when I am not a very good one. . . . I owe to the Lord my feeble efforts to synthesize, in my own life, the disparate elements that have been given to me. Hence I am to some extent monk, to some extent poet, and so on, and trying to reduce all this to unity. . . . [I]t would be wrong to say I was satisfied. On the contrary, I am more dissatisfied with the results than anyone else, but they are what they are, and they have to be accepted by me for the moment. . . .

[A]s time goes on, I have become more and more distrustful of the abstract and artificial divisions that men have devised.[2]

— 2 —

The dramatic changes which overtook Thomas Merton at the threshold of a new decade can be further illustrated, and their essences more generally defined, by contrasting two essays which span roughly the same period as Merton's decade-long struggle with *Art and Worship.* The first, "A Modern Man in Reverse" by Aelred Graham (a fellow Benedictine), was published in the *Atlantic* in 1953, when Merton was drafting the notes for his art book with its aggressive criticisms of the endemic godlessness of modern life and when Merton was resolving, in *The Sign of Jonas,* to surrender his identity as a writer. The second essay, by Merton himself, was written a dozen years later in 1965 when, armed with Bob Dylan records and Faulkner novels, Merton took up residence in his hermitage, pleased with a new role he described to a friend as a "laicized and deinstitutionalized . . . anti-ascetic humanist." In that essay he addressed the question, "Is the World a Problem?" and his answer then was the very antithesis of the rejoinder delivered by a "God-intoxicated man" Aelred Graham had scolded in 1953. Graham quoted Merton: "'Monks neither drink wine (in America) nor do they swim,' wrote the subject of our essay in 1949."[3] And Merton in 1965: "I drink beer whenever I can lay my hands on any. I love beer and, by that very fact, the world" (*CWA,* 70).

Of course, the basis of Aelred Graham's criticism of the young "modern man in reverse" and the essentials of Merton's change a decade later went considerably beyond his choice of beverages. What prompted Graham's critical assessment was Merton's "intense, one-sided, humorless, propagandist, morally indignant" propensity, clearly evident in *The Seven Storey Mountain*, to hypostatize the idea of "the world"—the fallacy of "embodying in the concrete what belongs to the sphere of [the] abstract." Merton's enthusiastic and uncritical reduction of worldliness to all that was sinfully wicked and morally corrupt seduced him, Graham argued, into a twofold fallacy. First, there was no alternative but for Christians to "affirm their Christianity by [a] full and unequivocal rejection of the world." The world was not, in effect, an object of Christian choice; one just didn't choose sin. Second, such inscrutable dogmatism blinded Merton to the crucial differences between an abstruse ideology of world-contempt and the reality of human "worldliness" manifested in concrete human situations. This failure to comprehend a basic distinction—between an attitude which "exists nowhere but in the . . . heart of man" and an abstract vision of evil and moral vacuity embodied in the Christless avenues of the secular city—rendered Thomas Merton, in Graham's view, "diffuse and uneven," simplistic, and incapable of "intellectual patience and [the] capacity to handle ideas"—in short, unworthy of the distinction lavished upon him in the wake of his best-selling autobiography.

What disturbed Graham was not so much the "inhuman hardness" of Thomas Merton or the lack of intellectual sophistication and nuance apparent in his simplistic dialectics. Graham was more frightened by the potential consequences the tyranny of choices offered Merton's receptive readers. "At a time when men are perplexed with fear and disillusionment," Graham wrote, when "their call is not to take flight from society but to revivify it with Christian values from within : . . . and incarnate an element of divine truth and goodness in each human situation," Merton offered only the choice of disengagement and renunciation, the exclusive and elitist alternative of contemplative prayer. "Let it be said at once," Graham warned, that "he is concerned . . . with what the Catholic Church holds to be the highest form of union with God to which man can attain on earth. This is the experience of God Himself granted to the Christian saints and mystics. What distinguishes Merton . . . is that he believes it to be an urgent necessity for all; he is in fact a propagandist of mysticism for the masses." Such a message of ascetic world-renunciation, Graham feared, could go to the head like wine and absolve people from the responsibility for concrete moral action in a world threatened by moral crisis. "One element of popular success in Merton's writing may be its power to bring vicarious satisfaction to those who remain in normal society yet share his indignation at its evils, a pleasing sense of being on the side of the angels. Denunciation of the unregenerate 'they' is only a step removed from 'I am holier than thou.'" Graham willed, then, to leave Father Louis, melancholy and unhappy, to the higher pleasures of mystical contemplation, doubtful "whether his well-intentioned simplifications can serve any lasting purpose."

Years later Merton noted in his private diary that Aelred Graham had visited Gethsemani; grateful now that they were good friends, he was pleased that "a lot of water has gone under the bridge since the *Atlantic* article years ago, in which he severely criticized me and in which no doubt he was not too far wrong."[4] During the intervening years Merton had developed a more sophisticated and less monolithic notion of the world and, more important, a far more responsible understanding of his relationship to that world than the simplistic stereotype of world renunciation which Graham had found both facile and frightening. The "mere automatic 'rejection of the world' and 'contempt for the world,'" Merton wrote in 1965, were only evasions of human choice, charades of irresponsibility which had earlier only diverted him from "the work I am capable of doing . . . to make the world . . . more human." Perhaps prompted by his recent "good talk" with Aelred Graham, Merton drafted "Is the World a Problem?" where he addressed directly the crux of Graham's earlier criticisms. "When 'the world' is hypostatized," Merton now admitted, "it becomes [a] dangerous and destructive fiction." "As long as I imagine that the world is something to be 'escaped' in a monastery—that wearing a special costume and following a quaint observance takes me 'out of this world,' I am dedicating my life to an illusion." Merton acknowledged and assumed blame for the "stereotype of the world-denying contemplative" he had foisted upon the public years earlier in his bellicose autobiography—the heroic image of "the man who spurned New York, spat on Chicago, and tromped on Louisville, heading for the woods with Thoreau in one pocket, John of the Cross in another, and holding the Bible open at the Apocalypse" (*CWA*, 159).

The apologetic undercurrents of this new essay amounted to nothing less than a critique of the contemplative ideal of *contemptus mundi* and a personal rejection, on Merton's part, of a life dedicated entirely to professional asceticism. "As regards the so-called contemplative life," Merton put it simply in a letter to a fellow priest, "please don't think that I am for a whole lot of introversion and introspection. True, in the past I have been much more inclined to that kind of 'contemplation' which looks into the ground of one's being, the Rhenish tradition, St. John of the Cross, etc. . . . but one learns over a period of years to go beyond the limits of a narrow and subjective absorption in one's own 'interiority' (ugh)" (*SofD*, 325).

It was precisely that immersion in interiority and the ideal of world-rejection that inspired it which had enraptured Merton during the missing years. Merton cultivated an attitude of *contemptus mundi* then, I believe, in an effort to palliate the bitter and painful disappointments, uncertainties, and failures of his own experiences in secular life. He saw no alternative but to embrace the authority of monastic dogma rooted in the middle ages, with its fixed view of the world's structure, its radical subordination of personal freedom and human choice to the predictable, changeless exigencies of a routinized daily life, and its promise of eternal salvation. This allusion to Merton's personal history did not go unnoticed by his severest critic in 1953. "It has been impossible," Aelred Graham insisted, "to display in isolation the more significant items in [Merton's] personal history and at the same time keep out a note of irony. Merton emerged from his youthful troubles, nourished by an apocalyptic imagination, to become a God-intoxicated man. Having conceived for himself a sublime ideal, he has heroically given it effect."

That he emerged in the 1960s as a critic of the "sublime ideal" which had prompted Graham to question Thomas Merton as a "preacher of pseudo-perfectionism" is certainly one measure of the extraordinary changes evident in Merton's later writing. In "Is the World a Problem?", for example, Merton himself now argued that such a "hierarchic ideal," with its fixed sacred hegemonies, was "sterile" and "unreal." It had ceased to be, he argued, "really fruitful and productive." Emerging from his personal struggles during the 1950s, Merton now celebrated a triumph over "the old immobilism" of a medieval world view which had so charmed him as a younger man. "The world," he now insisted, "can once again become an object of choice." In fact, "not only can it be chosen, but . . . it must be chosen." Echoing a vital concern for the ongoing, living events of his own age which would dominate his thinking during the sixties, Merton could find no freedom whatsoever in turning his back, for example, on the horrors of Auschwitz or the nightmare of Vietnam. For the Merton of a new decade, to choose the world, therefore, was to choose humanity in an anguished time "fraught with frightful difficulties." He could no longer deny history. "To choose the world . . . is first of all an acceptance of a task and vocation in the world, in history and in time. In my time, which is the present. To choose the world is to choose to do the work I am capable of doing, in collaboration with my brother, to make the world better, more free, more just, more livable, more human" (*CWA*, 164–65).

This revolution in personal perspective and world view led Merton to a new vision of his purpose and vocation as a writer and paved the way for the development and refinement of the humanistic themes which would characterize his later writing. No longer tolerant of his earlier calling as a "propagandist of mysticism for the masses," Merton arrived in the sixties with an entirely new complex of responsibilities and inspired by a new mandate: "to restore communication with our brother," as he said in a letter to Dorothy Day, *on his own terms,* and "to see our oneness of nature with him, and respect his personal rights, his integrity, his worthiness of love" (*Ground*, 141).

The burden of proof in the balance of this chapter will be to identify the sources in Merton's life during the pivotal years of the late 1950s which inspired this new mandate. As the vivid contrast between Aelred Graham's critical portrait of Merton in 1953 and his own revisionist essay of 1965 has shown, the key to that development rests in Merton's realization that the world was inescapable. He accepted, in the course of his struggles and personal development, that flight from the world into prayer and loneliness—"the damnable abstractness of 'the spiritual life,'" as he expressed it in *Conjectures of a Guilty Bystander* (1966)—was too self-limiting and inconsistent with his true bent of nature. Merton learned, in short, the wisdom of uncertainty in terribly uncertain times. In a world racked by racism, stockpiled with weapons of mass destruction, governed by the paranoia of the Cold War mentality, in a world increasingly diseased with alienation and fear, the official voice of Trappist silence would no longer suffice. So, beginning tentatively with *Disputed Questions* in 1960 and maturing in later books like *Seeds of Destruction, Conjectures of a Guilty Bystander,* and *Raids on the Unspeakable,* Merton cultivated a new voice. He described that voice best in "Is the World a Problem?"

This is not the petulant and uncanonizable modern Jerome who never got over the fact that he could give up beer. . . . This is simply the voice of a self-questioning human person who, like all his brothers, struggles to cope with turbulent, mysterious, demanding, exciting, frustrating, confused existence in which almost nothing is really predictable, in which most definitions, explanations and justifications become incredible even before they are uttered, in which people suffer together and are sometimes utterly beautiful, at other times impossibly pathetic. In which there is much that is frightening, in which almost everything public is patently phony, and in which there is at the same time an immense ground of personal authenticity that is right there and so obvious that no one can talk about it and most cannot even believe that it is there. (*CWA*, 160)

— 3 —

We can identify two principal factors which help explain Thomas Merton's growth from a petulant ascetic to a radical humanist. Such factors, from a biographical perspective, are not separate or mutually exclusive, nor do they evolve linearly. They commingle and mesh, often through continued conflict and struggle, during the last decade of Merton's life, like broad existential movements seeking a unity in Merton's intricate and evolving personal narrative. First, to put it bluntly, Thomas Merton failed as a mystic. Second, he underwent, as he entered his final decade, what can be called a process of secularization. The combination of his failure as a mystic and his successful reconciliations with a modern, post-Christian world freed him to develop, pursue, and refine the humanistic themes characteristic of his writing during a decade when Merton reached full maturity as a writer. Such issues, bound as they are to stir controversy, need some serious qualification before we turn to examine them more fully in the following chapters.

It is doubtful, for example, that Merton ever fully accepted his failure to achieve that level of infused contemplation which he was willing, as a young monk, to sacrifice everything (including his career as a writer and his habit as a Trappist cenobite) to attain. It is doubtful, too, that he completely surrendered his desire to be a saint, although as a more mature monk the goal of sainthood had become far more difficult to reach than it had been for the pious athlete of *The Seven*

Storey Mountain who confidently announced, "All that is necessary to be a saint is to want to be one." Over the years such naive enthusiasms were dampened by complexities of personal struggle and Merton's trials of self-doubt. After nearly two decades of growth through personal crisis, progress in the spiritual life would become far more problematic than it had seemed when Merton entered the monastery and described himself, with guileless confidence, as "a weak, proud, self-centered little guy, interested in writing, who wants to belong to God."[5] Merton gradually grew to understand that the ascetic ideal was not, as he had insisted in _Mountain,_ open to everybody, something which required no extraordinary spiritual equipment to attain. He came to accept the real wisdom of Aelred Graham's reminder that sainthood was not simply a matter of choosing what was at any man's disposal, that mysticism was not for the masses but for a divinely elected elite.

In a more subtle sense, then, Merton cultivated ambivalence about his self-image as a mystic. Such ambivalences certainly complicated his public image and were responsible, in large part, for the preposterous stories about him that circulated even in his own lifetime. Was he a mystic, as some wanted to believe, or a Christian anarchist, one of the leaders of a conspiracy to overthrow the CIA? Some accounts had Merton leaving Gethsemani, an alcoholic, and living in New York City with a woman. Other stories pictured Merton working miracles, like healing a crippled deer with his tears. Although Merton issued disclaimers to quiet such rumors, he was nonetheless partially responsible for those legendary inflations, due primarily to the ambivalences which enshrouded his apparent mystical quest.

For example, in his farewell conference with the novices of Gethsemani, just before taking up full time residence in his new hermitage, Merton explained his purpose in entering the hermit life as nothing less than an effort to "completely forget my own will and completely surrender to the Will of God." The solitary life, he told the novices, was "a life free from care," where "you don't have a great many contacts with the world, you're not terribly occupied with a lot of people and a lot of works and projects."[6] Thus it may have seemed that Merton's journey to the hermitage was the final assault in his mystical quest.

Yet in one of the first of thousands of letters he wrote from the cinderblock cabin built for him on a picturesque knoll, he described himself to Rosemary Ruether as an "active sinner as yet far from converted."[7] He later referred to "my 'secularized' existence as a hermit," "leading a more 'worldly' life [and] subtly infecting the monastery with worldly ideas."[8] His contacts with the world increased. A growing number of visitors were more frequently escorted to the hermitage from Gethsemani's gatehouse. His mailbag bloated. "I am thriving in the hermitage," he wrote Erich Fromm, "it is the ideal milieu for me. . . . Really I feel much more human and natural on my own than when tied up in the routines of an institution."[9] In his farewell address to the novices, Merton compared his hermit life to the spiritual enterprise of the monks at Mt. Athos. In another letter to Rosemary Ruether he explained that "being a hermit [means to] me being nothing but man, or nothing but a mere man reduced to this simple condition as man, that is to say as non-monk."[10]

Merton's descriptions of his daily life and routines at the hermitage often reflect similar ambivalences. "The outline of my daily life in the hermitage," he explained in 1966 to Abdul Aziz, a life-long student of Sufi mysticism, consisted of hours of meditation and prayer, interspersed with solitary celebrations of the canonical hours, and interrupted only by brief periods of manual labor and spiritual reading (*Ground*, 63). When asked a year earlier by a South American editor to describe a "typical day" at the hermitage, Merton affected considerably less piety as he projected the image of a hip, cool, anti-institutional counterculture hermit/hero in what was to become the essay, "Day of a Stranger." Picturing himself as a modern-day Thoreau, Merton speaks of rituals in stark contrast to those of the monastic Offices, rituals such as arriving at the outhouse every morning and, wary of "the king snake who likes to curl up on one of the beams inside [,] . . . asking the formal ritual question that is asked at this time every morning: 'Are you in there, you bastard?' " If, in his letters to a Sufi scholar, Merton could detail his methods of meditation and prayer as hermit/monk, he could simultaneously adopt a different persona as rebel forest ranger who claimed that "the spiritual life is guilt" and wisecracked, "If you see a meditation going by, shoot it" (*DofS*, 41).

So the question of Merton's success or failure as a mystic is a complicated one, obfuscated by ambivalences he himself sowed. Such ambivalences suggest nonetheless that he had broadened his expectations and modified his priorities considerably from the single-minded dedication to the mystical life to which he had subjugated his self-identity during the missing years. Even a slight measure of genuine doubt that he could achieve a full mystical union freed Merton from the tensions of his middle years. Such doubts rendered the matter of his literary instincts blocking his spiritual progress increasingly moot. Doubt gave him the freedom to write, the freedom, as he said in one of the new poems to appear in 1957 after a silence of eight years, to break out of "the trap set by my own / Lie to myself" (*CP*, 231). The fact that fully three-quarters of the bulk of the prodigious *Collected Poems of Thomas Merton* was written after 1957 surely indicates that he had outgrown his earlier need to surrender poetry solely for the sake of a fuller spiritual life.

The issue of Merton's "secularization" needs some initial qualification too. He remained, to be sure, a critic of the ideology of *secularism* and its world view, which pictured the modern person as the sole architect of his own destiny. Merton was frightened by such a world view because he saw in it the basis of a cultural omnipotence and narcissism which would only justify tragic abuses of power. That fear led him to distrust and criticize, in his later writing, for example, any spirit of strident nationalism, whether expressed through the economic individualism of the West or the revolutionary determinism of totalitarian societies, which only aggravated, he felt, the crisis of human alienation in the modern world. Any ideology of arbitrary self-determination, cast in the popular new image of Secular Man, was, Merton continued to believe, a seductive collective fiction in which he saw no real concern for persons and genuine human values. To Merton, secularism remained indistinguishable from an involvement in the fraudulent mythology of technological culture. His rejection of secularism as an ideology "focuses on the sham," he explains in *Conjectures of a Guilty Bystander*, "the unreality, the alienation, the forced systematization of life and not on the human reality that is alienated and suppressed" (*CGB*, 284).

Critical, then, of the pop-secular mindset, Merton eventually accepted the historical process of secularization as inevitable and irreversible, a process which liberated post-Christian culture from the strictures of a premodern world view with its radical separation of the sacred from the profane. In many respects, Merton experienced within himself the same process of self-examination and reassessment that the Church underwent in the early sixties in an effort to better accommodate herself to the new demands of modern life. He broke free from an archaic metaphysic that depicted the human person as naturally corrupt and secular society at odds with a sacred cosmos and divine plan. Merton outgrew the view of human nature as naturally unregenerate, a view that had forced him, years earlier, to confuse worldliness with a grandiose and abstract idea of the world and to identify the secular city as the seat of evil. Merton, along with a new generation of radical religious thinkers with whom he largely sympathized, surrendered the traditional stereotype of God, the supernatural and the sacred in opposition to the world, the dualism of the natural and the profane, as no longer valid for the modern individual. Eventually willing to accept the historical validity of a post-Christian ethos, Merton came to embrace secularization as a necessary choosing of the world, a choice that demanded social witness, a concern for social justice for the alienated masses, and even an appropriate application of technology to serve the needs of human persons in their alienation and despair. Critical, then, of secularism, Merton nonetheless evolved a new attitude which reconciled him to modern life in all its fullness, its ambiguity, and its potential destructiveness and absurdity, and freed him to refine, as we shall see, the radical post-Christian humanism which pervades his later writing.

Finally, not everything Merton wrote after he renewed his relationship to modern life and accepted a measure of failure in his monastic quest was entirely devoted to the content and style of a new post-Christian humanism. He continued to publish books of a basically inspirational nature, books which dealt solely with matters of the spiritual life and differed little from the focus of his earlier writings. *Spiritual Meditation and Direction*, for example, along with *Life and Holiness* and *Seasons of Celebration*, all written after 1960, were essentially works of spiritual instruction anchored in reflections of the interior life and largely unconcerned with contemporary social issues. But beginning with *Disputed Questions* in 1960, a cluster of new books appeared which suggest that Merton had become considerably less interested in devotional writing. He made a point of insisting, in the preface to *Disputed Questions*, for example, that the title itself was intended "to preserve the reader from the delusion that the book is 'inspirational.'" He continued, "It is not supposed to make anyone break out with a sudden attack of spiritual happiness." If the purpose of inspirational writing was to polish "the bright side of things" at the expense of ignoring the darker manifold crises of modern life, then

Merton boldly laid "claim to the honor of never having written [an inspirational book]." He became increasingly skeptical of the kind of devotional writing that might only pander to false hope—"the leprosy," as he described it in a letter to Daniel Berrigan, "of that particular kind of . . . hope, that special expectation . . . young monks [and] priests have."[11] Merton's renewed sense of involvement in and contact with the world and its human problems brought with it a "real repugnance," he said to another correspondent, "for writing things that tell everyone specifically how to do something spiritual now."[12] He frankly admitted to Ernesto Cardenal, "I think it is really a waste of time for me to write more books on 'the spiritual life.' . . . I have done enough already."[13]

In 1950, when Merton agonized over his desire, as he said in *Jonas*, to be "free of words," he had in mind the "human expressions that bind men to one another." Ensnared in ambivalences over his self-image as a writer, however, Merton could not abdicate all language. If he must write, he must choose a language superior to mere human expression, namely, "the Word of God. This I proclaim and I live to proclaim it." A comment he made to Dorothy Day eleven years later suggests that Merton had thoroughly reconsidered his obligations as a writer and was now ready to choose the kind of language that binds people together in their common predicaments over the lofty proclamations of Christian inspiration. "As for writing," he wrote, "I don't feel that I can in conscience, at a time like this, go on writing just about things like meditation, though that has its point. I cannot just bury my head in a lot of rather tiny and secondary monastic studies either. I think I have to face the big issues, the life-and-death issues: and this is what everyone is afraid of."[14]

In the balance, then, Merton's literary interests turned, after 1960, to books, essays and poems of a distinctly noninspirational character in which he engaged the intellectual, moral, political, and social issues facing the modern person. This new strain of writing was more concerned with the darker side of contemporary human affairs, with the human shadow cast by racism, war, the technologies of mass destruction, abuses of power and authority. After *Disputed Questions*, Merton wrote no fewer than nine books in which he responded to social issues with a profoundly personalistic humanism and continued to refine the art of the radical social critique. Ironically, Merton might have given himself over entirely to this kind of hard-hitting criticism if his superiors, whose fears Merton alluded to in his letter to

Dorothy Day, had not ordered him to stop writing about political issues in 1962. The writing ban itself was strangely symbolic of the revolution in Merton's self-identity and the difficulties, compromises, and ambiguities that continued to accompany that change. Ironically, Merton, fully reconciled to modern life and inspired by a renewal of his purpose as a writer, was held in check by his old self-image as the official voice of Trappist silence. After all, monks had no business discussing such things as fallout shelters or analyzing modern warfare. "What is the competency," complained one censor who denied a Nihil Obstat to Merton's seminal *Peace in the Post Christian Era*, "of cloistered Cistercians in [these] fields? If Cistercians are separated from the world, then why are they discussing [such] fields?"[15] During the missing years, Merton deplored the shadow of the writer who followed him into the cloister. During the sixties, those institutional proscriptions and stipulations he had so enthusiastically embraced returned to stymie and frustrate a writer now anxious to enter a worldly terrain from which he had officially withdrawn. Writing to Daniel Berrigan about the ban, Merton candidly admitted that it reflected a

> monastic party line [that] . . . ends up by being unadulterated s---crap. In the name of lifeless and graven letters on parchment we are told that our life consists in the peaceful and pious meditation on Scripture and a quiet withdrawal from the world. I have gone through the whole gamut in this business. In the beginning I was all pro-contemplation because I was against . . . trivial and meaningless activism. . . . [But] now I have been told . . . that I am destroying the image of the contemplative vocation, when I write about peace. . . . In a word, it is all right for the monk to break his ass putting out packages of cheese . . . for the old monastery, but as to doing anything that is *really* fruitful . . . , that is another matter altogether.[16]

The levels of intolerance evident in Merton's caustic remarks to Berrigan are a far cry from the sentiments expressed by a young convert who, two decades earlier, had been over-awed with the prospect of the initials "O.C.S.O." affixed to his name.

The issues discussed above help explain the gamut of changes Thomas Merton underwent as he entered a new decade: from a staunch and uncritical position in favor of contemplation, as an advocate of withdrawal from the trivial events of the world, to a new activist status he later identified as that of a Christian anarchist dedicated to an authentic and productive dialogue with the events of his day. Once again: Merton failed as a mystic. He simultaneously underwent a process of secularization which emancipated him from an archaic world view and from twelve years of "monastic life with no further object than . . . meditation and contemplation, silence, withdrawal, renunciation and so on." Looking back on those years he "began to see that [that life] was insignificant and indeed deceptive. It was unreal."[17] So he emerged from that life with new objectives, equipped with a new reading of history and a new sense of his place in it. And out of that new perspective he wrote new books of a decidedly different stamp than anything he had written before.

But this process of transformation and change, as the qualifications discussed above indicate, risks oversimplifying a far more complicated story of Merton's growth, a story marked by subtle ambiguities and ambivalences, denials and familiar self-contradictions. If he failed as a mystic, he never surrendered his dedication to the promise and fullness of the mystical life. If he rebelled against his old self-image as a professional ascetic and cultivated a new persona as a secularized hermit/humanist/activist, he did so very much on his own special terms, terms which encompassed severe criticism of secular values. And if his needs as a writer during the sixties were best met through new works of humanist social criticism, Merton nevertheless acquiesced obediently to a gag order enjoining him to cease publishing on issues of social justice.

— 4 —

Before moving on to explore the evolution of Merton's radical humanism in greater detail in the next chapters, it will be useful to consider a couple of Merton's earlier pivotal books. *The Strange Islands* (1957)— the first volume of poems to appear since Merton's poetic farewell in 1949—and *Disputed Questions* (1960) were both written during an interim period of gradual change. As such, they reflect elements of Merton's old self-image as an ascetic elitist while simultaneously planting seeds of a still-nascent new identity, that of a more expansive and curious mind less smugly content with narrow interests, less certain of itself, less committed to the exclusive agenda of the contemplative life, and less beholden to an archaic world view.

"The Tower of Babel," for example—a morality play Merton included in *The Strange Islands*—was a stinging and contemptuous condemnation of materialism and worldliness. Its zealousness suggested that Merton still harbored umbrage toward secular life and that he still clung to an abstract split between the purity of the contemplative enterprise and the programmatic vulgarity of worldly life, a split which had frightened Aelred Graham and stirred, quite frankly, the misanthropic undercurrents of much of Merton's early writing. The dialectic which led Merton to identify life in the world with the contemptible activities of an Antichrist in the play derived from an epigraph Merton cited from St. Augustine's *The City of God:* "Two kinds of love have created two Cities: the earthly city is created by the love of self to the point of contempt for God: the heavenly city is created by the love of God to the point of self-contempt." There was no room then for any middle ground, no freedom as yet from a theological formulation which obligated Merton to condemn the human community as godless and institute the monastic ideal of self-contempt as the only alternative to profane life in the Secular City.

Although published in 1957, "Babel" was written three years before a far more significant day in 1957 when Merton recorded in his journal, later published as *Conjectures of a Guilty Bystander*, an incident which would begin to free him from a theology of world-denial. That incident occurred during one of Merton's rare trips to Louisville during the fifties; it struck him as an epiphany, as a kind of existential conversion episode as intense, perhaps, as his religious conversion in Rome years earlier.

> In Louisville, at the corner of Fourth and Walnut, in the center of the shopping district, I was suddenly overwhelmed with the realization that I loved all those people, that they were mine and I theirs, that we could not be alien to one another even though we were total strangers. It was like waking from a dream of separateness, of spurious self-isolation in a special world, the world of renunciation and supposed holiness. The whole illusion of a separate holy existence is a dream. Not that I question the reality of my vocation, or of my monastic life: but the conception of "separation from the world" that we have in the monastery too easily presents itself as a complete illusion: the illusion that by making vows

we become a different species of being, pseudoangels, "spiritual men,"
men of interior life, what have you (*CGB*, 140–41).

"Tower of Babel," of course, was written from the perspective of a
man who still believed in the efficacy of separateness. But even as the
play was being published, Merton might well have felt already alien
to its theme.

Not all of the poems in *The Strange Islands*, however, are as ada-
mantly contemptuous of worldly life as "Babel." Some of the poems
suggest that Merton had already begun to grow weary of a self-isolation which had suddenly struck him in the streets of Louisville as
spurious and illusory. A couple of years before his epiphanic realization of a deep and loving kinship with total strangers, he had warned
that "the soul that picks and pries at itself in the isolation of its own
dull self-analysis arrives at a self-consciousness that is a torment and
a disfigurement of . . . personality." So some of the poems of 1957
began to question, with a new note of uncertainty, whether the contemplative alternative of a separate holy existence was as fruitful and
efficacious as perhaps Merton wished it could be. For example, in
"Whether There Is Enjoyment in Bitterness" Merton voices considerable self-doubt, angry and disillusioned with the agony his convictions inflicted upon him, embittered by the possibility that "life and
death / Are killing one another in my flesh," and questioning whether
his asceticism had indeed disfigured his personality.

> . . . let me
> Be a sad person. Am I not
> Permitted (like other men)
> To be sick of myself?
>
> Am I not allowed to be hollow,
> Or fall in the hole
> Or break my bones (within me)
> In the trap set by my own
> Lie to myself?
>
> (*CP*, 231).

Elsewhere Merton confesses to being "a man without patience . . .
thinking to blame only men / And defend Him Who does not need to
be defended." Other new poems dealt with self-deception, as in
"Sincerity," where Merton warns that "one who thinks himself
sincere . . . / Can deceive you with a good conscience." And in an-

other poem Merton is considerably less chary over the consequences of solitude than he had ever been before; he apprised "A Severe Nun" of the price she must pay for choosing "A path too steep for others to follow": a "long agony" with "no visible companions." Merton's ability to integrate a degree of self-doubt into the new poems opened to him the capacity to accept human frailty and failure; "One who doubts his own truth / May mistrust another less." That easing of mistrust, forged from trials of self-doubt, must have helped prepare his heart for the love he would soon feel for those strangers he encountered in the streets of Louisville.

Merton was also more trusting of his senses in some of the new poems, more willing to enjoy the simple sensory pleasures and beauty of ordinary things. Poems like "Stranger" and the often-anthologized "Elegy for the Monastery Barn" are etched in finer perceptual detail than most of Merton's earlier poems which were rendered so heavy and gray by a poetics of mortification. Moreover, other poems, like "How to Enter a Big City" and "Exploits of the Machine Age," are less bellicose and accusatory than Merton's earlier, more baldly polemical anti-city tirades. The city becomes more of an existential symbol of human discontent—of "optimism without love / And pessimism without understanding"—and less of a geo-religious locus of godlessness through which Merton, in his previous poems, had channeled his hostility to worldliness. It was not the unholiness of city dwellers that bothered Merton now; it is their human angst, their failure to be "at peace with their own images." Merton still believed that the way to achieve such serenity was through the discipline of solitude, but in a poem like "In Silence," it is no longer a brand of solitude patterned exclusively after the Cistercian model, a solitude of disengagement and self-estrangement; it becomes a solitude through which one discovers, on the contrary, the very fullness of self and recovers a personal authenticity that survives after false self-images are stripped away. A silence, in other words, that "speaks your name." "Be what you are," Merton admonishes, "be / The unthinkable one / You do not know."

These aspects of the new poems in *The Strange Islands*—the tone of uncertainty and self-doubt, the perceptual detail, the existential treatment of solitude—reveal Merton turning back to the world in more human terms, questioning, if only tentatively, whether a monastic disengagement could be valid if it meant a total separation from humankind. What Merton said of T. S. Eliot's poetry may well apply to the new cluster of poems appearing in 1957: "everything that was big, vast, universal, is brought down to the pointed, the moral, the human. The heavens are indifferent, but here are real wounds in a real moral order" (*SJ*, 94).

The poem that best illustrates a shift from the detached, monolithic themes of Merton's earlier poetry to the existential, concrete human concerns evident in some of the new poems was not published in *The Strange Islands*. Although Merton wanted to include "The Sting of Conscience," his agent, after an unusually heated exchange of several letters with Merton, urged him to drop the poem. Merton admitted that the poem was "neurotic," but he still felt it was a good poem unlike anything he had written before, and he only reluctantly acquiesced to his agent's advice. Inspired by Graham Greene's stinging indictment of smug inaction amid social injustice in his novel *The Quiet American*, Merton's "The Sting of Conscience (Letter to Graham Greene)" brought that indictment squarely to bear on his own conscience as a professional world-denyer who was fast preparing to awake from a dream of "spurious self-isolation in a special world."

> You have written, Greene, in your last book
> The reasons why I so hate milk.
> You have diagnosed the war in my own gut
> Against the innocence, yes, against the dead mother
> Who became, some twenty years ago,
> My famous refuge.
>
> This one place that claims to know peace,
> This is the very den
> Where most damage is planned and done.
> Oh, there are quiet ones among us
> And I live with the quietest of all.
> Here we are, victims, making all the trouble
> Loving the pity and the ignorance
> With which the light stands firm
> On our most righteous candlestick.
>
> And now your book has come
> To plague the hapless conscience of the just
> While war boils in my own hard-praying heart.
> Not out of charity,
> Rather out of idleness do we refuse to hate.

O, if I were less desperately meek
And could win back some malice, once again
And tell the people what I mean
I would perhaps hate them less
For having so loved me.

I know: the decision is fatally made.
I shall never return. I cannot reach again
Those dear bad shores, to which prolific life
Is not altogether alien.
I cannot see again
The world of lively, prodigal sin!

Yet look, Greene! See Christ there,
Not in this innocent building,
But there, there, walking up and down,
Walking in the smoke and not in our fresh air,
But there, there, right in the middle
Of the God-hating sinners!

But here I stand, with my glass in my hand
And drink the pasteurized beatitudes
And fight the damned Ohio in my blood!

*

Tell me, at last, Greene, if you can
Tell me what can come of this?
Will I yet be redeemed, and will I
Break silence after all with such a cry
As I have always been afraid of?
Will I so scandalize these innocents
As to be thrown clean out of the wide-eyed dairies
And land in heaven with a millstone round my neck?[18]

As Patrick O'Connell, who discovered the poem buried in the Curtis Brown archives at the Friedsan Library of St. Bonaventure University, points out in his essay "Sunken Islands," "The Sting of Conscience" anticipates Merton's vigorous turn toward the world during the following decade. Written out of a mood of intense confession, the poem shows too that Merton's humanistic epiphany on a Louisville street corner was triggered by nothing less than a crisis of personal conscience. The "refuge" he had sought after his conversion, the peace he had found in his monastic retreat, and the pious public image he had since fostered all turn against him in the poem as a "war in my own gut." The poem foreshadows as well the major motif of Merton's later social criticism: that inaction in the face of "real wounds in a real moral order" is tantamount to culpability for man's inhumanity to man. It is especially telling that Merton focuses such blame on his monastic refuge as he diagnoses the cause of a conflict that "boils in my own hard-praying heart." He leaves little doubt that one who has taken up residence in the "innocent building" of monastic life has chosen "ignorance," "idleness," and "pasteurized beatitudes" over "prolific life . . . [in] the world of lively, prodigal sin!" The consequences of that choice might be linked to the recurrent images of fatality in the poem, as if Merton was drowning in the very springs from which, twenty years earlier, he had sought nourishment and renewal: the dead mother Church, the monk victimized by a plague of righteous immobilism, and, perhaps most interesting, Merton's not-so-subtle insinuation that his choice to abandon the world was one "fatally made." Yet in the final stanza Merton begins to speculate on avenues of redemption: to be reborn to the world may demand that he break his silence and overcome the fears that for so many years had attended his self-image as writer. Should the writer be given full rein, the prospect of scandalizing the "innocents . . . of the wide-eyed dairies"—an obvious allusion to religious cloistered in monasteries—seems particularly prescient in light of the writing ban looming ahead. The self-doubt and uncertainty that plagues Merton's conscience in the poem intimates a crisis of vocation that stands in stark contrast to the righteous triumphalism of Merton's previous poetry and reveals him on the brink of a significant, if painful, transition.

Of course, not all of the new poems were shaken down to the human plane that Merton admired in Eliot's poetry and that Merton's agent had found as the source of some indiscretion in "The Sting of Conscience." "The Tower of Babel" was still firmly anchored in universal archetypes, monolithic and biblical. The heavens were not indifferent in the play. And the order of the drama was not a human moral order, but that of the biblical Apocalypse. Besides, the poetics that still govern most of the new poems derived, as in Merton's earlier poetry, from liturgical models which only later he would abandon for the radical poetics of the antipoem, first seen in the laconic, deadpan style of "Original Child Bomb" (1962). We must keep in mind too that Merton had not yet formally revised his earlier stand in "Poetry and the Contemplative Life" that poetry and contemplation were essentially incompatible. It wasn't until the following year that Merton issued his reappraisal and admitted that the "implied conflict between 'contemplation' as rest and poetic creation as activity" was an illusion no longer worth consideration. A couple of the 1957 poems—notably "Spring Storm"—still resonate with that conflict, their poet suspicious of words. Although Merton might have been moving in a new direction in 1957, the movement was, as yet, still tentative and provisional—a tentativeness, incidentally (and not surprisingly) that may help explain why *The Strange Islands* was uniformly panned by the critics.

— 5 —

That same tentativeness is evident in an uneven collection of essays Merton published in 1960. As noted above, Merton insisted in the preface to *Disputed Questions* that, unlike his earlier writing, the new volume was distinctly noninspirational and more concerned with engaging important contemporary issues. "I am simply thinking out loud," he announced, "about certain events and ideas which seem to me to be significant . . . for the spiritual and intellectual life of modern man." Merton followed through on that claim in his sensitive monograph on "The Pasternak Affair," which he selected to lead off the new essays. His discussion of the controversy surrounding Pasternak's refusal of the Nobel Prize in 1958 was a searching tribute to the resilient humanity of the Russian poet whose quiet, personal protest of an antagonistic political regime moved Merton deeply. For the first time, he discovered in Pasternak's life and writing a theme which would engage him throughout the sixties and prove critical to the evolution of his mature humanism: "the relation of the *person*," as Merton said in the preface, "to the *social organization*." He saw in Pasternak the triumph of individual human integrity over the enormous power of the collectivity, the power, Merton continued, of a "mass society . . . constructed out of disconnected individuals—out of empty and alienated human beings who have lost their center and extinguished their own inner light in order to depend in abject passivity upon the mass in which they cohere without affectivity or intelligent purpose" (*DQ*, x).

This topic of human alienation as an inevitable by-product of mass social movements was worked out concretely and in poignant detail in Merton's tribute to Pasternak, which I will discuss in greater detail below. Merton might have looked, then, perhaps for the first time, like an informed modern man moving forward, grappling with some of the important issues of the time. But the balance of essays in the new volume seemed only to betray Merton's claim in the preface that he was turning to events and ideas relevant to the intellectual and spiritual life of the modern person. He admitted as much himself when he scanned his table of contents; aside from the Pasternak monograph and a short essay on "Christianity and Totalitarianism," there was little else there to justify his new interest in contemporary affairs. "[O]ne might ask," he questioned in the preface, "what on earth do Mount Athos, the reformer of the Camaldolese hermits, the early Carmelite Friars, and most of all Saint John Climacus, have to do with the contemporary world?" Such subjects, which occupy fully three-quarters of *Disputed Questions*, might have made Merton look more like Aelred Graham's "Modern Man in Reverse," an essayist concerned principally, as he had always been before, with the world-denying protest of legendary figures in the history of monasticism, not, as he said of Pasternak, with the existential "protest of life itself, of humanity itself, of love" against the potentially dehumanizing effects of contemporary mass movements such as Pasternak had faced in post-Stalinist Russia. This imbalance of subjects forced Merton to issue an awkward disclaimer and admit that the social relevance of such subjects "may turn out to be apparent to me only." "Let us settle for the fact that [those] subjects may have some interest in themselves and may, perhaps, obliquely reflect some light upon contemporary spiritual life which can be seen if one looks closely."

Notwithstanding his disclaimer, the social relevance of Merton's treatise on the monks of Mt. Athos or his scholastic inquiry into the ascetic principles of St. John of the Ladder may have remained ob- lique indeed to many readers. No prefatory disclaimer could effec- tively unify a collection of essays whose subjects ranged from the humanism of a modern Russian novelist to "The Primitive Carmelite Ideal."

But it was not simply poor editing that unbalanced *Disputed Ques- tions*. Its unevenness was indicative of the interim transitions and gradual changes that Merton himself was undergoing in the late 1950s. Still intent on pursuing the call of his own inner experience as a contemplative, his interest turned naturally to the heroic figures in Christian mysticism. Yet, as some of the new poems in *The Strange Islands* suggest, Merton was growing more doubtful of the relevance of a life of isolation and withdrawal. Such doubts moved him, if only tentatively at first, to reevaluate his relationship to his own age and to reconsider his personal perspectives in response to its problems and needs. One of the first things he saw, with the help of a modern voice like that of Pasternak's, was "that in the last twenty years," as he said in the far-reaching preface to *Disputed Questions,* he was startled to have discovered that "the world [had] moved a long way towards conformism and passivity." This new interest in the survival of authentic human freedom in a age increasingly dominated by collectivist ideologies was expressed through the Pasternak monograph, while Merton's old interest in religious salvation in a world delirious with godlessness and self-love found expression through his essays on the monolithic asceticism of figures like St. John of the Cross. Both interests contributed to the imbalance of *Disputed Questions.*

That imbalance, I believe, reflects the deeper ambivalences that still puzzled Merton as he confronted his self-image as a contemplative. Even after he awoke, in 1957, from the dream of separateness in the streets of Louisville, he still pursued schemes, as he had in 1955, to leave Gethsemani and embark on a life of complete isolation, this time in Mexico—an isolation that he had already dismissed as spurious and illusory. Even as Merton drafted his preface to *Disputed Questions*—where he acknowledged his growing discontent "with the idea that a contemplative monk is one who takes flight from the . . . world and turns his back on it completely"—he was busy petitioning Rome again for permission to live as a hermit. And it only deepens the almost manic ambivalences to note that in the summer of 1959 Merton was writing Dorothy Day to explain yet another plan to live as a "hermit/missionary" among the Hopis (*Ground,* 136).

The pattern of ambivalences in Merton's plans to leave Gethsemani in 1959 was evident in his similar efforts in 1955, which culminated in the aborted scheme to set up a hermitage in the Fire Tower and Merton's acceptance of the Novice Mastership. In 1955, he felt that his literary drives seriously impeded his spiritual progress; he resolved then that the hermit life would revitalize him spiritually and free him from the writer's shadow. In 1959, perhaps he felt equally threatened by the new humanistic feelings welling up within him and calling him back into contact with a world he had vowed to renounce. On both occasions, Merton's desire to further his spiritual aims was driven by his need to deny expression to the natural tendencies of his personality: in 1955, his innate inclinations as a writer; a few years later, his gregariousness and the warmth he suddenly felt for human companionship.

On both occasions too Merton seemed more motivated by criticisms of Cistercian life than by a genuine dedication to an eremitical ideal. "Gethsemani is *terrible*," he wrote to Ernesto Cardenal shortly after drafting the request for a *transitus* in September of 1959. "Tremendous commerce—everybody going mad with cheese business. I want to leave very badly." "My mind is completely made up," he continued, in a letter aggressively underscoring his dissatisfactions, "to totally cut off all ties that attach me here. It is *essential* not just for my own peace but for the glory of God. I *must* advance in the way He has chosen for me."[19] Cardenal, a former novice of Merton's who had left Gethsemani because of bad health, became Merton's confidant during this time; he assumed the same role that Dom Jean Leclercq had in 1955 when Merton tendered his first request to leave Gethsemani. And Merton's letters to Cardenal, like those he had fired off to Dom Jean, were punctuated by criticisms of "the inertia of conventional religious life" and the "state of almost passive irresponsibility here." "[T]hat is one of the qualities and one of the vices of this monastery: everything is geared to keep one passive and, in a certain sense, infantile. . . . Unfortunately, . . . the peculiar circumstances of this monastery prevent real spiritual growth. Underneath the superficial and somewhat false good humor, with its facade of juvenile insouciance, lies the deep fear and anxiety that comes from a lack of real interior life."[20]

Merton's strident criticism of a conventional religious life may only have masked deeper misgivings over his own failure to advance spiritually. Criticism vented off the more painful suspicion that maybe he had failed as a monk; it diverted him from a deeper realization too that the hermit life might not mitigate that sense of personal failure. As in 1955, when the question of Merton's living as a hermit came closer to being resolved, in 1959 he grew less enthusiastic as his superiors' response to the dispensation closed in on him. Even after preliminary permission had been granted, Merton wrote to Cardenal and mentioned that his health was bad and that "complications in my usual infirmities" may prevent his leaving. "I think it is . . . a providential event," he said. "Often sickness has the function of slowing a man down when he is about to turn a corner." Ironically, back in 1955 the sudden availability of the Novice Mastership was another such providential event that, like his ill-health in 1959, turned him back from a life of total detachment and withdrawal. When Merton was finally denied permission to leave, in January of 1960, he greeted the decision with a complacency strangely disproportionate to the intensity of his earlier criticisms and their implied conviction. He shared the news with Cardenal and admitted that "my life is one of deepening contradictions and frequent darkness."

It is not surprising, then, that the books Merton wrote during the late fifties were uneven and tentative. *The Strange Islands* and *Disputed Questions* were literary by-products of a period of personal limbo for Merton, written, as he said to Cardenal, during a time of deepening inner contradictions. He was a man still bent, as he had been in 1955, on disappearing into the bushes, yet a man capable now of questioning the logic of withdrawal as a complete fiction.

As the balance of his letters to Cardenal show, however, Merton quickly rebounded from a crisis of self-contradictions and emerged with a new unity of purpose. After being denied permission to leave Gethsemani, Merton's letters quickly shifted to matters of immediate topical interest, focused primarily on peace and issues of social justice. "I am deeply concerned about peace," he announced to Cardenal with sudden conviction, "and am united in working with other Christians for protest against nuclear war."[21] If the letters of the late fifties revolved around Merton's schemes to acquire a life of greater self-isolation and interior solitude, the letters of the new decade centered around a far different sense of personal responsibility and purpose, a duty Merton later described to Cardenal as "our *first* duty . . . to human truth in its existential reality."[22] Merton still remained critical of the conventional religious life, but the target of his criticisms also shifted radically. Earlier, he had condemned the passivity of conventional monastic life as a serious threat to interior spiritual growth. Soon, however, he became critical of an entirely different expression of passivity he detected among both monks and the Catholic laity, one which encouraged indifference to social and political problems such as the threat of nuclear war. "I observe with a kind of numb silence," he complained to Cardenal, "the inaction, the passivity, the apparent indifference and incomprehension with which most Catholics . . . watch the development of pressure that builds up to nuclear war. It is as if they had all become lotus eaters, as if they were under a spell."[23] He committed himself to resist, "with all my force," that "same coma" by vowing to stay clear of "that comatose fog" of inaction.

His letters to Cardenal indicate, then, that the profound changes Merton underwent pivoted roughly around 1960, when his personal convictions shifted in a radical new direction, although it is impossible to trace the essence of such a profound transformation to any single cathartic flashpoint. A variety of incidents throughout the latter half of the 1950s gradually supplied impetus to Merton's personal evolution. Such episodes certainly include the events of 1955 and 1959, when Merton could not help but see that his desire for total detachment and solitude was seriously compromised and weakened by self-deceptions; an incident in Collegeville, Minnesota, when Merton received a brutal but bracing chewing-out from the psychiatrist Gregory Zilboorg for deceiving and manipulating his superiors;[24] the epiphany of love and human companionship that struck him on a street corner in Louisville in 1957; some of the poems he wrote in 1956 which freed him to express self-doubt and personal uncertainty; and the prolonged embarrassment he suffered throughout those years over the failure of his art book with its rancorous and indefensible antimodern prejudices.

Finally, of no little significance was the influence of Boris Pasternak, an influence Merton chronicled in his moving tribute in *Disputed Questions*. That influence, briefly, derived from Merton's sensitive reading of Pasternak's poetry and his novel, *Dr. Zhivago*. Merton was drawn as well to the international uproar surrounding the events of 1958, when Pasternak, pressured by Soviet authorities who feared that his less-than-sympathetic treatment of the Bolshevik revolution in *Dr. Zhivago* would lead to a campaign of anti-communist propaganda in the West, refused the Nobel Prize for Literature. Through the personal sacrifices suffered by Pasternak himself—and through Merton's exposure to the sacrifices and ultimate human triumph of the protagonist of Pasternak's great novel—Merton saw "an embodiment," as he says in his tribute, "of that personal warmth and generosity which we seek more and more vainly among the alienated mass-men of our too organized world." Pasternak emerged for Merton as "a genuine human being stranded in a mad world." His personal witness was a "sign" to Merton that the human person, dedicated to fundamental human values, could survive the increasingly dehumanizing tendencies of mass social organization. Inspired by a new humanism, and stunned by what he considered a serious threat to its basic precepts, on 29 October 1958 Merton even wrote the president of the Soviet Writers' Union, Aleksei Surkov, a passionate plea in support of Pasternak. He did not write as a monk, he explained. Rather, he wrote as a man "passionately opposed to every form of violent aggression, and no matter for what 'good' ends. I am a man dedicated entirely to peace and to justice, and to the rights of man whether as a citizen, a worker, or, in this case, a *writer*" (*TMR*, 272).

The Pasternak affair planted in Merton, then, the seeds of a social conscience that began to strike him as more legitimate than a quietistic philosophy of world-denial. More specifically, Merton discovered in Pasternak a new role for the artist as revolutionary; he encountered as well a new motive for criticism: a criticism purified by love, not contaminated by personal bitterness. Pasternak helped clarify for Merton the function of art as a protest, energized by love, against the dehumanizing proclivities of collective social movements, a protest further fortified by Merton's enthusiastic reading, a few years later, of Albert Camus. And Pasternak revealed to Merton a more relevant spirituality, one fully responsive to modern life that made no distinctions, as Merton later said, between "building the kingdom of God . . . [and] *building a better world here and now."*

On the role of the artist as revolutionary, Merton wrote:

> All great writing is in some sense revolutionary. Life itself is revolutionary, because it constantly strives to surpass itself. . . . The thing that attracted people to Pasternak was not a social or political theory, . . . not a collectivist panacea for all the evils in the world: it was the man himself, the truth that was in him, his simplicity, his direct contact with life, and the fact that he was full of the only revolutionary force that is capable of providing anything new: he is full of love. . . . [Pasternak's] protest is . . . the protest of life itself, of humanity itself, of love, speaking not with theories and programs but simply affirming itself and asking to be judged on its own merits (*DQ*, 10–11).

On the larger function of art as a critique of socio-political forces which dehumanize and alienate:

Pasternak's ability to rise above dichotomies [is] his greatest strength. This transcendence is the power and essence of *Dr. Zhivago*. One of the more important judgments made by this book is a condemnation of the chaotic meaninglessness of all twentieth-century political life. . . . [For Pasternak] the whole political chaos of our world is a kind of enormous spiritual cancer, running wild with a strange, admirable and disastrous life of its own and feeding on the spiritual substance of man. The deep interest in *Dr. Zhivago* is precisely its diagnosis of man's spiritual situation as a struggle for freedom *in spite of* and *against* the virulence of this enormous political disease. . . . [Pasternak's] view of life . . . is that the individual is more important than the collectivity. His spirit, his freedom, his ability to love, raise him above the state. The state exists for man, not man for the state (46–52).

And Merton found in the spirituality of Pasternak a bracing freedom from the "churchly and hierarchal [spirituality] of the Apocalypse." Merton especially admired in Pasternak "the ingenuousness of a spirituality that has never yet become quite conscious of itself and has therefore never needed to be purified." He wrote,

And so, though Pasternak is deeply and purely Christian, his simplicity, untainted by ritualistic routine, unstrained by formal or hieratic rigidities of any sort, has a kind of *pre-Christian* character. . . . It is a Christianity that is not perfectly at home with dogmatic formulas, but gropes after revealed truth in its own clumsy way (14–15).

This is the very key to Pasternak's "religious philosophy"[:] He is a complete existentialist (in the most favorable and religious sense of the word) (21).

To me . . . one of the most persuasive and moving aspects of Pasternak's religious mood is its slightly off-beat spontaneity. It is precisely because he says practically nothing that he has not discovered on his own, that he convinces me of the authenticity of his religious experience. When one is immersed in a wide and free-flowing stream of articulate tradition, he can easily say more than he knows and more than he means, and get away with it (29).

This last comment of Merton's may have been an autobiographical assertion masking as literary commentary. After all, the spirituality articulated in contemporaneous works like "Tower of Babel" was a spirituality firmly anchored in an articulate tradition, very much at home with "formal and hieratic rigidities" and "dogmatic formulas." But the new spirituality he celebrated in Pasternak—spontaneous, authentic, world-affirming, slightly off-beat—would help liberate Merton from that tradition and prepare the way for a new purpose in a new decade: "to get down," as Merton said so simply of Pasternak, "to the business of living productively on this earth, in unity and peace."

6

Failed Mysticism—
The Crisis of a "Finally Integrated Man"

"Let us walk along here, says my shadow, and compose a number of sentences, each one of which begins: 'You think you are a monk, but . . .'"

Any portrait of Thomas Merton during the sixties would lack depth and credibility if it did not include the shadow of his self-doubt. One of Merton's remarkable personal attributes during his final decade was, in fact, his courage to face up to uncertainty, especially with respect to his long-cherished self-image as mystic. Never before had he been quite so willing to listen to his misgivings when assessing the aspirations of his spiritual life. Facing the shadow of self-doubt was painful for Merton; uncertainty forced him to ride out, as he said in a 1964 entry in his private journal, "the usual anguish and struggle [of] . . . spiritual crisis." But uncertainty also broadened him and made him increasingly "aware of the need," as he noted in his fiftieth year, "for constant self-revision and growth, leaving behind the renunciations of yesterday." As we shall see below, Thomas Merton was, psychologically speaking, *completed* by his shadow. Self-doubt nourished the fullness of his humanity.

The most visible result of this process of growth and self-revision through uncertainty was the extraordinary breadth of vision encompassed by Merton's journal of the sixties, *Conjectures of a Guilty Bystander*. Merton welcomed the voice of his shadow into the dialogue of self-reflection in *Conjectures*. His willingness to admit, for example, that "the very idea of 'spirituality' tends to be unhealthy in so far as it is divisive and itself makes total response impossible" actually freed him for a more total response in the journal. Unlike the journals of the two previous decades, *Conjectures* encompassed a broader range of issues and events, its author open to and tolerant of a range of divergent attitudes. "These entries," Merton claimed in the preface, "are not of the intimate and introspective kind that go to make up a spiritual journal."

Merton made a point of insisting, then, that his new journal was in no sense a sequel to *The Sign of Jonas*. While *Jonas* consisted largely of a stream of laconic meditations on an inner world, the entries in *Conjectures* come across more like transcriptions of the real world of the sixties, extrospective, searching, and distinctly colored by Merton's emerging humanism. His characteristic exuberance and totality of response energizes the new journal as Merton hurls himself into a complex matrix of social, cultural, political, and technological institutions which comprise the very fabric of modern life. The result is a rich and spontaneous dialogue that anticipates many of the issues that would surface during the turbulent decade ahead: racism, technological millennialism, superpower antagonisms, the presence of poverty amid affluence, the crude materialism of contemporary American life, ideological fanaticism, passive submission to power politics, political opportunism, the impoverishment of moral reason and the concomitant degradation of language and Christian social inaction. The journal also includes a series of frequently disjointed but probing reflections on the collapse of once vital American myths, such as the Adamic myth of individualism, into dysfunctional collective evasions. Compared to such works as *Disputed Questions*, *Conjectures of a Guilty Bystander* proves unmistakably that the transition Merton was undergoing in the mid-to-late fifties was now complete and that he stood ready, without compromise, for a direct confrontation with questions relevant to twentieth-century life.

Although it differs radically from his previous public journals with respect to content, theme, and narrative form, *Conjectures* does conform to a similar dynamic pattern present in both *The Seven Storey Mountain* and *The Sign of Jonas*. That pattern reveals the key, I believe, to Merton's personal evolution during the course of the three decades covered by his three major journals. Like *Mountain* and *Jonas*, *Conjectures* is driven at its deepest levels by a psychological scenario consisting of interlocking transitions from *denial*, through *self-doubt*, to final *reconciliation*. In *Mountain*, for example, that scenario is worked out first through Merton's renunciation of the cruelty of his personal history, his rejection of a worldly life which had unmercifully robbed him of his childhood; that denial gives way to the uncertainty and confusion he encountered as he desperately sought escape from the grip of an unfeeling world until he achieves a final liberation when he comes home to Gethsemani and celebrates the sweet savor of his new liberty. Similarly, in *Jonas*, Merton's trenchant denials of his self-image as a writer are accompanied by self-doubts which seize him as he judges the spiritual immaturity of a monk seemingly paralyzed by that writer's ubiquitous shadow—until, again, those conflicting self-images arrive at a final synthesis in the "Fire Watch" epilogue. And in *Conjectures* that scenario recurs again: a renunciation of his two-decade commitment to withdraw from worldly life ignites new uncertainties that challenge Merton as he seeks then to redefine his place in that world; out of that process of redefinition Merton discovers a profound renewal of personal calling as a post-Christian humanist now bent on engaging, as he says in *Conjectures*, in "concerns appropriate to an age of transition and crisis, of war and racial conflict, of technology and expansion" (vi).

Conjectures shows, too, that Merton had made such a complete break from the posture of bellicose self-assurance that characterized his autobiography of the forties that he no longer even felt the story of *The Seven Storey Mountain* was his. Years earlier, Merton had begun to evince some embarrassment over *Mountain*. In *Jonas*, for example, the protagonist of his previous autobiography had already come to seem "completely alien" to him. By the early sixties, the divorce was complete. "The story," Merton admitted in a 1963 preface to the first Japanese edition of *Mountain*, "no longer belongs to me. . . . The author no longer has an exclusive claim upon his story."

Merton's comments in the Japanese preface are worth quoting in more detail, for they capture the essence of two decades of growth that culminate in the new temperament resonating throughout *Conjectures*. "When I wrote [*Mountain*]," Merton reflected, "the fact uppermost in my mind was that I had seceded from the world of my time in all clarity and with total freedom. The break and secession were, to me, matters of the greatest importance. Hence the somewhat negative tone of so many parts of this book. Since that time, I have learned, I believe, to look back into that world with greater compassion, seeing those in it not as alien to myself, not as peculiar and deluded strangers, but as identified with myself."[1]

It was that motive of greater human compassion that inspired the expansive vision of *Conjectures* and no doubt contributed as well to the success of the journal with the broader-based reading public Merton was now addressing. Merton was so inspired by the popularity of *Conjectures* that he immediately proposed two new books to his agent, *The Church in the Godless World* and *Worldly Essays*, whose titles alone suggest that he wanted to push even further into new territory, "leaving behind," as he had in *Conjectures*, "the renunciations of yesterday."

Merton could never have moved into that new territory, however, had he not resigned himself first to his growing antipathy to the monastic commitment, an antipathy tempered by two decades of personal sacrifice and struggle. Pestered by uncertainties and gradually more willing to accept doubt that he could make it to sainthood, he could begin to see, as he said in a letter to Daniel Berrigan, that "it is not God's will that a religious or a priest should spend his life more or less in frustration and defeat." In accepting himself as a less-than-perfect monk, Merton could realize, as he continued to confess in this letter to Berrigan which bore the caveat "conscience matter," "that I am about at the end of some kind of line. . . . It is burning out, in a lot of sweat and pain if you like, but it is burning out for real. . . . As a priest I am a burnt out case, repeat, burnt out case."

Perhaps it is best to let Merton speak for himself on this admittedly sensitive issue of his private uncertainty. To that end, what follows is a comprehensive post-1960 portrait of Thomas Merton, trained on the shadow of his uncertainties and constructed out of fragments from his most intimate writing of the period, including quotations from his published journals, and excerpts from his letters, poems, and private notebooks. The editorial infrastructure of the portrait derives from a method Merton himself described in *Conjectures* and employed later on in other journal narratives such as *The Day of a Stranger* and *Woods*,

Shore, Desert, as well as in his experiments with the long poem (*Cables to the Ace,* for example, and *The Geography of Lograire*): namely, "a series of sketches and meditations . . . fitted together in a spontaneous, informal . . . scheme in such a way that they react upon one another" (v).

Let us walk along here, says my shadow, and compose a number of sentences, each one of which begins: "You think you are a monk, but . . ."

Perhaps I am stronger than I think.

Perhaps I am even afraid of my strength, and turn it against myself, thus making myself weak. Making myself secure. Making myself guilty.

Perhaps I am most afraid of the strength of God in me. Perhaps I would rather be guilty and weak in myself, than strong in Him whom I cannot understand (*CGB*, 131).

We have the words, the slogans, the notions. We cultivate the pageantry of the monastic life. We go in for singing, ritual, and all the externals. And the ceremonies are very useful in dazzling the newcomer, and keeping him happy for a while. But there seems to be a growing realization that for a great many in the community this is all a surface of piety which overlies a fake mysticism and a complete vacuity of soul. Hence the growing restlessness, the rebellions, the strange departures of priests, the hopelessness which only the very stubborn can resist, with the aid of their self-fabricated methods of reassurance.[2]

I do not have the impression of being especially happy, and I am in definite reaction against my surroundings: for a "happy monk" I must admit that I certainly protest a great deal against the monastic Order, and the Order itself thinks I protest a great deal too much . . .

I am willing to admit that in the sight of God I do not protest enough, and that the protests I generally make are always beside the target. I have the impression that when I am indignant in print, I am always indignant about something vague and abstract, and not about something more concrete which I really hate and which I cannot recognize.[3]

The Lord said [to the Russian mystic Staretz Sylvan]: "Keep thy soul in hell and despair not." At first it sounds a bit dreadful, or perhaps at best eccentric. Yet to me it is in a strange way comforting. Men still share deeply and silently the anguish of Christ abandoned by His Father (to be abandoned by God is to be "in hell") and they "despair not." How much better and saner it is to face despair and not give in than to work away at keeping up appearances and patching up our conviction that a bogus spirituality is real! That we are not really facing dread! That we are all triumphantly advancing "getting somewhere" (where?), accomplishing great things for Christ, and changing the face of the world!

We can still choose between the way of Job and the way of Job's friends, and we have to have the sense (I say sense, not courage) to choose the way of Job: it takes far more than courage to start out on a way that obviously leads to the far end of nothing, and to walk over the abyss of our own absurdity in order to be found and saved by God, who has called us to walk that way. . . .

I have praised the saints and I have told at what cost they strove to surpass lesser men. What madness have I not preached in sermons! (*CGB*, 147–49).

Many of the problems and suffering of the spiritual life today are either fictitious or they should not have to be put up with. But because of our mentality we block the "total response" that is needed for a fully healthy and fruitful spirituality. In fact the very idea of "spirituality" tends to be unhealthy in so far as it is divisive and itself makes total response impossible. The "spiritual" life thus becomes something to be lived "interiorly" and in "the spirit" (or worse still in the "mind"—indeed in the "imagination"). The body is left out of it, because the body is "bad" or at best "unspiritual". . . .

So we create problems that should never arise, simply because we "believe" with our mind, but heart and body do not follow. Or else the heart and the emotions drive on in some direction of their own, with the mind in total confusion. The damnable abstractness of the "spiritual life" in this sense is ruining people. . . . All is reduced to "intentions" and "interior acts," and one is instructed to "purify one's intention" and bear the Cross mentally, while physically and psychologically one is more and more deeply involved in an overworked, unbalanced, irrational, even inhuman existence (253–54).

. . . a monk is a person who sets himself to meet demands that cannot be met, and exists only as an ideal. True. Nevertheless, he who is called to be a monk is precisely the one who, when he finally realizes that he is engaged in the pure folly of meeting an impossible demand, instead of renouncing the whole thing proceeds to devote himself even more completely to the task. Aware that, precisely because he cannot meet it, it will be met for him. And at this point he goes beyond philosophy.

Here he admits finally that the problem of being a monk cannot be resolved merely by fidelity to a religious ideal (266).

I am for the most part very gay and hearty in spite of solid despairs, but I have discovered that despairs make jolly and all consolations and no despairs is for the dull monk to enjoy, but I do not say this out of vain hopes. Let all the glad abandon vain hopes and laugh until silly. There is little else to do. But plenty to laugh at.[4]

What matters is the struggle to make the right adjustment in my own life and this upsets me because there is no pattern for me to follow and I don't have either the courage or the insight to follow the Holy Spirit in all freedom. Hence, my fear and my guilt, my indecisiveness, my hesitations, my back-tracking, my attempts to cover myself when wrong, etc. Actually, it is a matter of deciding what limited and concrete view to take so as to fulfill my actual duty to God and to my community and thus be the monk I am supposed to be. I need only seek truth as I am personally called to do in my own situation. If I were more a man of love and spirit, more a man of God, I would have no problem. So my job is to advance with the difficulty of one who lacks love and yet seeks it, in the realization that I am not supposed to solve my problems for myself. Nor am I supposed to be a man of God in the sense of "having no problem." One of the sources of futile struggle in the spiritual life is the assumption that one has to become a person without problems which is, of course, impossible.[5]

I am aware of the need for constant self-revision and growth, leaving behind the renunciations of yesterday and yet in continuity with all my yesterdays. For to cling to the past is to lose one's continuity with the past since this means clinging to what is no longer there.

My ideas are always changing, always moving around one center, and I am always seeing that center from somewhere else.

Hence, I will always be accused of inconsistency. But I will no longer be there to hear the accusation.[6]

I suppose that I am now going through another small spiritual crisis. It is nothing new, only the usual anguish and struggle. Perhaps a little intensified by the fact that I am now in my 50th year. And yet I think this might be a decisive struggle because now fewer and fewer evasions are possible.[7]

It is of course not God's will that a religious or a priest should spend his life more or less in frustration and defeat. . . . But . . . I know that in fact, this is what a lot of people have to face. . . . I realize that I am about at the end of some kind of line. What line? What is the trolley I am probably getting off? The trolley is called a special kind of hope. The streetcar of expectation, of . . . desire of betterment, of things becoming much more intelligible, of things being set in a new kind of order, and so on. Point one, things are not going to get better. Point two, things are going to get worse. I will not dwell on point two. Point three, I don't need to be on the trolley car anyway, I don't belong riding in a trolley. You can call the trolley a form of religious leprosy if you like. It is burning out. In a lot of sweat and pain if you like, but it is burning out for real. . . . As a priest I am a burnt out case, repeat, burnt out case. So burnt out that the question of standing and so forth becomes irrelevant. I just continue to stand there where I was hit by the bullet. . . . I have been shot dead.[8]

This is not a hermitage—it is a house. . . . What I wear is pants. What I do is live. How I pray is breathe. . . . If you see a meditation going by, shoot it. Who said "Love"? Love is in the movies. The spiritual life is something that people worry about when they are so busy with something else they think they ought to be spiritual. Spiritual life is guilt (*DofS*, 41).

[A] man would perhaps do anything to evade [union with God], once he realizes it means the *end* of his own ego-self-realization. . . . Am I ready? Of course not. Yet the course of my life is set in this direction.[9]

> . . . today they have hit me hard in the city
> They have beat me with their official chain
> They have hit the easy places of my head with the heel
>   of a clerical shoe
> And now I am flying dead over the town sending you
> The rush signals of emergency love and dread
> As I speed homeward full of cancer by the neutral
> Highways out of Town.[10]

> Every beautiful day
> Is invention and evidence
> Of that one morning
> When the fields of May forever
> Sing their slow hymn
> This is the morning when God
> Takes you out of my side
> To be my companion
> Glory and worship
>
> O my divided rib
> It is good to be willing
> To be taken apart
> To come together[11]

I always tend to assume that everyone knows I have had a monumental struggle with monasticism as it now is and still disagree violently with most of the party line policies. . . . I have the usual agonia with my vocation . . . but now I am in a position where I am practically laicized and deinstitutionalized, and living like all the other old bats who live alone in the hills. . . . I feel like a human person again. My hermit life is expressly a *lay* life.[12]

. . . about the crisis bit. . . . I am in one of those situations when so much is surfacing that I can't even read and I have to talk to someone. . . . Problem: unrecognized assumption of my own that I have to get out of here. Below that: recognition that life here is to some extent (not entirely) a lie and that I can no longer just say the community lies and I don't. With that: sense of being totally unable to do anything about it that is not a feeble gesture. But also a genuine realization that this *is* my vocation, but that I have not yet found the way of being really true to it. Rock bottom: I don't know what is down there. I just don't know.[13]

In our monasticism, we have been content to find our way to a kind of peace, a simple undisturbed thoughtful life. And this is certainly good, but is it good enough?

I, for one, realize that now I need more. Not simply to be quiet, somewhat productive, to pray, to read, to cultivate leisure—*otium sanctum!* There is a need of effort, deepening, change and transformation. Not that I must undertake a special project of self-transformation or that I must "work on myself." In that regard, it would be better to forget it. Just to go for walks, live in peace, let change come quietly and invisibly on the inside.

But I do have a past to break with, an accumulation of inertia, waste, wrong, foolishness, rot, junk, a great need of clarification of mindfulness, or rather of no mind—a return to genuine practice, right effort, need to push on to the great doubt (*Woods*, 48).

How can one laugh and shudder at the same time? The book [Kierkegaard's *Attack upon Christianity*] is so uncontrovertibly *true*. And to find myself a priest. And to find my own life so utterly false and trivial—in light of the New Testament. And to look around me everywhere and find people desperately—or complacently—going through certain motions to prove that they are Christians. (And far more people not giving a damn and not even paying attention, so that "proving one is a Christian" comes to mean begging for *just a little attention* from the world— some grudging admission that a Christian can be an honest man.)

At least this: I have enough self respect left to refuse to be abbot, and to refuse to go around to meetings and lectures and functions. And I have felt a little compunction about continuing to proclaim a "message" just because that is what people expect of me. It is not easy to talk of

prayer in a world where a President claims he prays for light in his decisions and then decides on genocidal attacks upon a small nation. And
where a Catholic Bishop praises this as a "work of love."

Paralyzing incomprehension—what does one do when he realizes he
is part of an organization whose members systematically try to "make a
fool out of God"? I suppose I begin by recognizing that I have done it as
much as the best of them.[14]

The purpose of this portrait is not to put Thomas Merton's foibles on parade. These excerpts may reveal a side of Merton rarely
glimpsed by the public. But it is a side, to my way of seeing, which
vividly, indeed beautifully illustrates the evolution of Merton's humanness. Such a portrait may only offend those who, as Monica
Furlong says, "have idealized [Merton's life] into unrecognizably
saintly proportions"—to those who "label him 'saint' and use him as
a dummy to be dressed up in garments that say more about our own
illusions of holiness than anything Merton himself affected or believed."[15] These passages attest to Merton's extraordinary capacity for
honest self-scrutiny in the face of personal uncertainties, never for a
moment indulging in self-pity or misreading self-doubt as utter personal failure. Our portrait reveals a man capable of confronting his
fears, misgivings, hesitations and indecisiveness with remarkable
frankness and candor—a man increasingly incapable, as a result, of
self-deception and evasion, even when experiencing, as in his fiftieth
year, the personal anguish and struggle of spiritual crisis. The very
fact that Merton could admit doubt and uncertainty when assessing
his spiritual aspirations only strengthened his faith and underscored
the integrity of his dedication to a vocation he knew existed "only as
an ideal." What Merton praised in Pasternak is equally true of Merton
himself as he faced his "monumental struggle with monasticism": "It
is precisely because he says practically nothing that he has not discovered on his own, that he convinces me of the authenticity of his religious experience" (*DQ*, 29).

With such considerations in mind, there are three elements of this
portrait that shed light on the evolution of Merton's mature humanism and especially the stages he passed through as he began to project a new vision in his major writings of the sixties. First, some of the
early entries echo the by-now-familiar opprobrium that marked Merton's attitudes toward the conventional monastic life. But the entries
are arranged chronologically. Merton's terse criticism of the ceremoni-

ousness of the conventional monastery routine surfaces only in the early passages—in a letter to Cardenal late in 1959 and a couple of fragments from *Conjectures*, written in 1960. This was a pivotal period for Merton, as we may recall from the last chapter, when he had just been denied permission to leave Gethsemani and strike out on a more solitary, less conventional life in Mexico. His bitterness at the time may only have been an expression of the great disappointment he felt over his superiors' decision, for he still clung to a belief that the solitary life would fulfill him spiritually. But Merton's protests against "the pageantry of the monastic life" abate considerably when, a few years later, he was finally given permission to live the solitary life and he actually took up residence in his own hermitage. "This is not a hermitage," however, "it is a house," Merton wrote in May 1965. His new hermit life, which five years earlier had held the only promise of advancing him beyond "the surface of piety" ingrained in ritual routines, had become, not, as he said to Cardenal, an opportunity to perfect "the simplicity of the monastic ideal," but rather, in effect, "an expressly lay life." Perhaps Merton had come to realize that his earlier chagrin and indignation over the apparent "vacuity of soul" inherent in conventional community life had only shielded him, as he hints in a May 1960 letter to Czeslaw Milosz, from "something more concrete which I really hate and which I cannot recognize"—specifically, I would suggest, his own failure to advance spiritually and his unrealistic hope that the solitary life would bring him closer to a union with God. Once able to accept that such hope sprung from a demand he could not personally meet and that his vision of the solitary life "exists only as an ideal," Merton toned down his protests, and, while he may still have disagreed with the monastic party line, he entered more fully into a life frankly uninhibited by conventions and institutional proscriptions: a life open to a more "total response," less hemmed in by "the words, the slogans, the notions" of an institutional religiosity and its problems and sufferings which Merton eventually dismissed as fictitious, irrational, "even inhuman." "Alone in the hills," he admitted simply to Rosemary Ruether in 1967, "I feel like a human person again." If the essence of Merton's complaints to Cardenal in 1959 was that the machinations of ritual life were distractions to meditation, he had certainly shifted his perspective by 1965 when he intoned from his hermitage, "If you see a meditation going by, shoot it."

Second, this portrait is punctuated, especially in the early entries, by wrenching internal conflicts. Paraphrasing Merton, the central conflict is between "the monk I am supposed to be" and "the man that in fact I am." Such a conflict arises from Merton's fidelity to a monastic ideal, on the one hand, and, on the other, his growing existential recognition of, once again, the mere appearances, the "fake mysticism" and the "bogus spirituality" that render his ideals illusory. This is the conflict experienced by a man struggling to meet demands that cannot possibly be met, a man who realizes that he is not capable of surrendering his own "ego-self-realization" yet charts the course of his life in that direction. The conflict, as Merton further maintains in a letter to Rosemary Ruether, is between his "genuine realization that [the monastic life] *is* my vocation" and the utter honesty of his admission that he is not true to that life; "Below that," he concedes: "recognition that life here is to some extent (not entirely) a lie and that I can no longer just say the community lies and I don't." . . . "So my job is to advance with the difficulty of one who lacks love and yet seeks it."

But, third, underlying those conflicts, and ultimately overpowering them, there emerges, in the later entries of the portrait, a catharsis of transformation, growth, and change. Merton was not paralyzed by his internal conflicts. His courage in confronting them led him gradually to accept that "what matters," as he reflects in a 1964 entry in his private journal, "is the struggle to make the right adjustment in my life." Such adjustments were inevitable as Merton grew less tolerant of his own self-contradictions and realized that "fewer and fewer evasions are possible." "I am sick of the contradiction," he confessed with a simple clarity after moving into the hermitage, "[of] wanting a hidden life that is not hidden, but famous."[16] It is significant, then, that the internal conflicts evident in our portrait eventually inspire the language of change and prepare the way for an awareness on Merton's part "of the need," he writes in his private notebook, "for constant self-revision and growth." In his letter to Berrigan, Merton further emphasized that need for self-revision by announcing "that I am about at the end of some kind of line," anxious to depart from a "trolley" of frustration and defeat, of idealistic expectations and false hopes, which were slowly burning out of him in "a lot of sweat and pain." Such anxiety gives way to Merton's peaceful affirmation that change will indeed "come quietly and invisibly on the inside." "I, for one, realize," he says in May 1968, "that I now need more" than the unruffled contentment of the monastic life. "There is a need of effort, deepening, change and transformation"—a need to break with the "waste, wrong, foolishness" of his past, a need to bridge action and intention and "push on to the great doubt." He struck a similar note a few years later when he left on his ill-fated Asian journey with "a great sense of destiny, of being at last on my . . . way after years of waiting and wondering and fooling around" (*AJ*, 4).

Our portrait of Merton's shadow of self-doubt reinforces, then, the dynamic stages of Merton's evolution that unify three decades of intense personal scrutiny: the interlocking cycles, that is to say, of denial, doubt, and reconciliation. His denials of the efficacy of monastic life force Merton into a painful but bracing confrontation with the potential fraudulence of his commitments. That confrontation nourishes in turn the ground of new commitments from which spring a more global sense of purpose as well as a more vital concept of self-identity that serves to reconnect Merton to the community of humankind. Such stages, more broadly speaking, reflect those movements of the life cycle that Erik Erikson has shown to be crucial to the "epigenesis" of personal identity. I will return to Erikson later, but for now his comments about the role of crisis in the evolution of self-identity seem particularly relevant to Merton, especially as Erikson "present[s] human growth," in his study of *Identity: Youth and Crisis*, "from the point of view of the conflicts, inner and outer, which the vital personality weathers, re-emerging from each crisis with an increased sense of inner unity, with an increase in good judgment, and an increase in the capacity 'to do well' according to his own standards and to the standards of those who are significant to him."[17]

In Merton's case, at no point in his life would his nascent "vital personality" weather a crisis of greater proportions than when, in the mid-sixties, he experienced a crisis of intimacy: the crisis of a monk drawn to the joys of affective human love. Out of that crisis of inner division, out of that conflict of "love and dread" Merton writes about in one of his love poems to a Louisville nurse, comes, not destruction and defeat, but "invention." For a man whose "head" felt the full brunt of "the heel of a clerical shoe," his heart discovers that "It is good to be willing / To be taken apart / To come together."

— 2 —

The post-1960 portrait of Merton's shadow suggests, then, that his protests against the conventions of cenobitic life were projections of his own failure to advance spiritually; his dedication to unrealizable monastic ideals sparked painful internal conflicts; and those conflicts, in turn, eventually inspired the need for self-transformation and change. These factors combine to reveal a broader pattern of growth through personal crisis in which Merton's self-doubt and uncertainties compelled him to break with his past and seek a new direction in his life course.

Two notable influences during the sixties—one intellectual, the other experiential—further intensified and clarified for Merton that growth through personal crisis was as viable as it was inevitable. And each confirmed for Merton that the central conflict at the heart of his own crisis of personal growth was—as our portrait indeed indicates—between his ideal self-image as "the monk I am supposed to be" and, at its other extreme, the "laicized and deinstitutionalized . . . human person" who struggled to emerge from the shell of a burnt-out priest. Merton framed that conflict most succinctly himself in a 1966 entry in his private journal; reflecting on his intense and "frightful longing" for a woman he loved, he squarely confronted the acute contrast, he wrote, between "what I think I should be . . . [and] what I am."[18]

Let's consider the intellectual influence first. Merton was deeply impressed by a book written by the Persian psychoanalyst Reza Arasteh entitled *Final Integration in the Adult Personality*. When Merton read the book early in 1968, he wrote Arasteh to share with him "how much I enjoyed your book and profited by it."[19] People close to Merton at the time corroborate his claim that he had benefitted from the book. They recall that Arasteh cropped up frequently in Merton's conversations and that his responses were unreservedly enthusiastic. *Final Integration in the Adult Personality* was not Merton's first venture into psychology. He had already developed a considerable interest in psychotherapy by this time—an interest, incidentally, somewhat unusual among monks, most of whom remain, by tradition, suspicious of modern psychology. During the previous years Merton had filled a couple of working notebooks with quotations from borrowed books, including the work of Freud, Karen Horney, and Carl Jung. Moreover, Merton's interest in abstract calligraphy grew out of his experiments, conducted in the novitiate among the novices, with Rorschach blots. He continued, as well, to carry on a sophisticated and informed correspondence, begun in the fifties, with Erich Fromm, and, by 1966, Merton was even undergoing his own analysis with a Louisville psychiatrist. In spite of such active interest, Merton hesitated to publish anything in the area of psychotherapy. Perhaps he was still stung by Gregory Zilboorg's brutal criticism of the never-published "Neurotic Personality in the Monastic Life," an essay Merton had written in the mid-fifties. But Merton was so moved by *Final Integration in the Adult Personality* that he overcame his hesitations, wrote a long essay on the book, and published it under the title "Final Integration: Toward a 'Monastic Therapy.'"

Merton was especially struck by Arasteh's thesis that anxieties suffered by adults are not necessarily symptoms of neurosis; anxiety can in fact be a sign of health, Arasteh argued, a vital and necessary, albeit distressing call to full adult maturity. "This is one of the main points made by Dr. Arasteh's book," Merton emphasized in his essay: *"the importance of existential anxiety seen not as a symptom of something wrong but as a summons to growth and painful development."* Merton stressed repeatedly the "important distinction between mere neurotic anxiety which comes from a *commitment to defeat* and existential anxiety which is the healthy pain caused by the blocking of vital energies that still remain available for radical change" (*CWA*, 223). Unlike the crippling debilitation suffered by "the petulant, self-defeating neurotic," Arasteh's existential anxiety, to borrow Abraham Maslow's phrase, is a self-actualizing psychic energy, an invitation to self-fulfillment and self-completion. The adult who approaches final integration and perseveres in "the human task of maturation and self-discovery," Merton further argued, experiences nothing less than "rebirth . . . as a new being"—"this anxiety is a sign of health and generates the necessary strength for psychic rebirth into a new transcultural identity."

It won't push the logic of comparison to extremes to argue that Merton's descriptions of this "new transcultural identity"—this "new being"—seem entirely fitting descriptions of Merton himself. The qualities Merton celebrates in the person who achieves "final integration" read like a profile of the man who eventually emerges from our forgoing portrait of Merton's own inner struggles. Like Arasteh's "finally integrated adult," Merton courageously resists defeat, weathers the storms of existential anxiety, and arrives at a higher plateau of personal development—precisely that process, according to Arasteh, that unleashes "vital energies," in Merton's words, "for radical change." Furthermore, in his essay Merton stresses above all that final integration means health and wholeness. "The man who is 'fully born' . . . apprehends his life fully and wholly from an inner ground that is at once . . . universal . . . and yet entirely his own. He is in a certain sense 'cosmic' and 'universal man'. . . . He . . . is identified with everybody. . . . He is able to experience their joys and sufferings as his own" (225). Such language would not be inappropriate on the dust jacket of *Conjectures of a Guilty Bystander* or perhaps in an uncritical review of a piece like *Day of a Stranger* or in an examination of Merton's leading role in the Ecumenical movement of the sixties. Merton's comments about the "universality" of Arasteh's finally integrated adult by no means contradict the kind of treatment accorded to Merton himself in recent scholarship: Anthony Padovano's study of Merton, for example, as an Everyman whose life transcends to cosmic proportions as a "Symbol of a Century" comes immediately to mind. Monica Furlong further supports this popular view of Merton's psychological "wholeness" and his extraordinary ability to relate to others when she notes that his psychiatrist marvelled over Merton's mental acuity and pronounced him "as one of the least neurotic personalities he had known, with an exceptional capacity to relate to others."[20] And Merton himself may have anticipated Arasteh's distinction between neurosis and existential anxiety when he countered his Abbot's claim and wrote to another superior: "I have consulted the psychiatrist in Louisville who tells me that I am not neurotic and that my problem here in the monastery is quite a natural reaction."[21]

Consider further some of Merton's descriptions of the "new being" who experiences final integration:

> This new being is entirely personal, original, creative, unique, and it transcends the limits imposed by . . . convention and prejudice. . . .
>
> The man who has attained final integration is no longer limited by the culture in which he has grown up. "He has embraced *all of life*" [writes Dr. Arasteh.] "He has experienced qualities of every type of life": ordinary human existence, intellectual life, artistic creation, human love, religious life. He passes beyond all these limiting forms, . . . "finally giving birth to a fully comprehensive Self." He accepts not only his own community, his own society, his own friends, his own culture, but all

mankind. He does not remain bound to one limited set of values in such a way that he opposes them aggressively or defensibly to others. He is fully "catholic" in the best sense of the word. He has a unified vision. . . . With this view of life he is able to bring perspective, liberty and spontaneity into the lives of others. The finally integrated man is a peacemaker. (225–26)

Written in 1968, the essay on Arasteh may have been both a book review and a retrospective celebration of Merton's own radical transformation through personal crisis. Those existential traits of character Merton identified in Arasteh's "finally integrated man" have much in common with the Merton of the late sixties, so much, in fact, that one is tempted to interpret the essay as largely autobiographical, as if Merton had discovered through Arasteh's typology a new reading of his personal history. One is quickly reminded, for example, of the global breadth of interests—intellectual, religious, artistic, political, even domestic—that expand the boundaries of *Conjectures* and, unlike the journals of the previous decades, the absence of an aggressive defense, on Merton's part, of any limited set of values to which he remains bound and must therefore justify. The very "catholicity" of *Conjectures* constitutes it as the journal of a finally integrated man. Furthermore, Merton certainly developed the capacity to transcend his own culture. And he continued unstintingly to refine that capacity by studying non-Western cultures, writing new books—such as *Mystics and Zen Masters, Zen and the Birds of Appetite,* and essays on the Cargo Cults and Native American culture later collected in *Ishi Means Man*—and laying plans to visit Asia. In short, "He has," in Arasteh's words, "experienced qualities of every type of life." Merton celebrates, for example, the harmonies of "ordinary human existence" in *Day of a Stranger* where he exults that "What I wear is pants" and extols the virtues of domestic rituals, like washing out the coffee pot, sweeping the floor, and making his bed. Merton expanded the boundaries of his "intellectual life" as well through his excursions into Faulkner, Camus, Rilke, Roland Barthes and others. Moreover, Merton's growing interest in abstract calligraphy, his enthusiastic embrace of photography, and his new experiments in poetry and innovative prose forms exemplify, indeed almost caricature, that quality of "artistic creation" that Arasteh highlighted in his portrait of the finally integrated adult. Other hallmarks of character mirror further linkages between the post-1960 Merton and Arasteh's self-actualized adult whose experience of final integration gives birth to a "fully comprehensive Self" capable of accepting all mankind: simply put, a peacemaker. We need only mention Merton's solidarity with Black Americans in *Seeds of Destruction*, his concern for the plight of the Vietnamese in "Nhat Hanh Is My Brother," and the important contributions Merton made to both the theory and practice of non-violence in such later works as *Gandhi on Non-Violence, Peace in the Post Christian Era*, and *Faith and Violence*.

With its emphasis on global self-realization in near-mystical proportions, Arasteh's paean to self-actualized adulthood may strike us today as too overstated, rooted, as it were, in the transient enthusiasms of the human potential movement flourishing in the late sixties. We may detect in Merton's effervescent endorsement of Arasteh's theory, then, a kind of seduction, especially in light of Merton's efforts to redress his earlier self-image as "a modern man in reverse" and reposition himself on the leading edge of the sixties vanguard. I don't wish to brush aside that critique. But, viewed in the context of Merton's personal evolution, Arasteh's book nonetheless arrived at a propitious moment. Merton was drawn to Arasteh's theory of final integration in the adult personality because it confirmed, authenticated, and legitimized his own experience of growth through personal crisis. It helped him to see that the pain of his own self-doubt and uncertainties in his struggles with "the monastic party line," modernity, solitude, and his drives as a writer did not issue from neurotic frustrations (as his Abbot and Gregory Zilboorg had implied), but signaled instead a rebirth into a more authentic identity. Arasteh's theory also reinforced Merton's need to break with his past, for final integration demanded, above all, that one surrender attachments to an ideal role, which, in Merton's case as we have seen, had always been "the monk I am supposed to be." The "finally integrated man"—"entirely personal, original, . . . unique"—"transcends," Merton stresses in his essay, "the limits imposed by . . . convention." "He passes beyond limiting forms. . . . He does not remain bound to one limited set of values."

Merton frankly admitted in the essay on Arasteh that the conventions of monastic life—"the monastic role defined by the *ideal* to which we hold"—constituted just such "limiting forms" and, as such, threatened to stunt the process of final integration for monks dedicated exclusively to conventional proscriptions. He concluded that the kind of maturity defined by Arasteh "is exactly what the monastic life *should* produce." But he conceded that the "institutional straitjacketing" prevalent in Catholic monasticism impedes maturity and thus leads to "a serious impoverishment of the personalities of the monks." Merton utilized Arasteh's vocabulary to remind his fellow monks "that people are called to the monastic life, so that they may grow and be transformed, 'reborn' to a new and more complete identity, and to a more profoundly fruitful existence in peace, in wisdom, in creativity, in love. When rigidity and limitation become ends in themselves," he cautioned, "they no longer favor growth, they stifle it" (221–22).

Here again, autobiographical undercurrents surfaced in Merton's essay as he launched into a familiar critique of monasticism. Perhaps the insights of psychiatry provided him with a springboard to discuss publicly something he had already wrestled with privately: namely, his failure to fulfill his monastic aspirations and his determination, arising from that failure, to transcend the limits imposed by an idealized monk persona. Although he framed his discussion in the third person, his comments—especially as he turned to the matter of "vocational crisis"—accurately trace the course of his own painful development and reintegration, while his conclusions sound almost like an abstract of our post-1960 portrait of Merton's shadow. "To put it quite simply," he wrote,

> many people come to the monastery with a strong, if inchoate, sense that they are called to *make something* out of their lives. But after a few years of struggle they find out that this "thing" they are supposed to do is not clarified, and though they may have become acquainted with formulas which explain the monastic life and justify it, they still do not feel that they are able to do anything about them. In addition, they begin to question the relevance of such formulas for modern man. The most difficult kind of vocational crisis is that in which a monk with genuine monastic aspirations comes to feel that such aspirations cannot be fulfilled in a monastery. Which means that they probably cannot be fulfilled anywhere. . . .
>
> All of us who have had to work through vocation problems with professed monks can, on reflection, easily distinguish obvious neurotics from men whose monastic crisis has taken the form of existential anxiety: this is a crisis of authentic growth which cannot be resolved in the situation in which they find themselves and the situation cannot be changed. (224)

Above all else, his interpretation and application of Arasteh's theory of final integration to problems of the monastic life clarified for Merton the rock-bottom conflict at the heart of his own monastic crisis— "the monastic role defined by the *ideal* to which we hold is one thing: and the role as defined by the *actual situation* of our community and of ourselves in it, quite another" (220).

In "Final Integration: Toward a 'Monastic Therapy,'" Merton addressed his growth through personal crisis from a somewhat detached intellectual perspective. When he fell in love with a young woman, he wrestled with its experiential equivalent.

The conflict between an ideal role and an actual human situation could not have been felt more deeply, with greater emotional impact or potential consequence, than when Merton, in April 1966, found himself "so much loved and loving so much , when according to all standards it is all wrong, absurd, insane."[22] Existential anxiety as a summons to painful development was indeed more than an intellectual proposition or psychological theory to a 54-year-old monk, vowed to celibacy, who had once chanted the name of a 19-year-old woman "as magic to break the grip of awful loneliness on my heart."[23]

For better or worse, Merton's brief but intense affair with a young nurse he met in a Louisville hospital is a matter of public record since the publication of John Howard Griffin's *Follow the Ecstasy* and Michael Mott's authorized biography of Merton. Our purpose here is not to rehash the details of the romance itself. We can, however, borrow some of Griffin's generous quotations from Merton's private journal and trace, through them, the existential ramifications of that theory of personal growth Merton himself both defined and endorsed in his essay on Arasteh. "The process of disintegration and reintegration," Merton noted in "Final Integration," "involves a terrible interior . . . crisis and an anguish which cannot be analyzed or intellectualized." It must in fact be lived, Merton implied; "after all, the rebirth which precedes final integration involves a crisis which is extremely severe" (*CWA*, 227).

The crisis of uncertainty Merton lived through during this five-month episode was more severe than any he had ever faced before. His violent confrontation with the vow of celibacy—far more intense, one can easily imagine, than his earlier brushes with the vows of silence and stability—stirred terrible misgivings within him. In the only poem published during his lifetime in which Merton broached the relationship directly, he wrote, not about the joys of affective human love, but about the doubts descending upon him as he confronted "the questions in my blood" raised by a "man's enormous want." "Whose life is this?" he asked in desperation. "I wonder who the hell I am." Such doubts and misgivings were further exacerbated by sensual undercurrents which eddied within Merton for the first time in thirty years. Restrained by three decades of ascetic discipline, irrepressible feelings of "enormous want" surfaced. Suddenly Merton found himself, as suggested by the title of the poem alluded to above, "With the World in My Bloodstream" (*CP*, 615), wrestling with an anguish of ambivalences and trying to extricate himself from a "maze" of new "questions" and "meanings." "I have no more sweet home," he confessed. Drawn to what he called "the spring's plasm" and "the accurate little spark" of carnal love, Merton sought to recover his monastic bearings, his "lost Zen breathing," and return to the fold of "the technical community of men" where he had vowed "the wild gift . . . of unmarried fancy." Unable, however, to reconcile an ambivalence of sensuality and asceticism, Merton was left hanging in the precarious balance, as he put it in the essay on Arasteh, "of a terrible interior crisis . . . which is extremely severe." By "loving and [being] loved so much," Merton encountered, at the outset of the affair, "the gambles and the blue rhythms / Of individual despair."

Merton made every effort to convince himself in his journal "that our love must be spiritual and chaste, but the longing for her," he admitted, "is frightful—and of course so is the conflict that goes with it." As if the torment of such internal conflicts was not enough, there was also the potential for public scandal to be reckoned with. Merton wrote about just such a possibility in a fragment he later included in *Cables to the Ace.*

> I seek you in the hospital where you work.
> Will you be a patch of white moving rapidly across
> the end of the next hall? I begin again in every
> shadow, surrounded by the sound of scandal and the
> buzzer calling all doctors to the presence of alarm (*CP*, 445).

Just a few months before he met the woman, Merton began to reflect seriously in his journal on the potential human "tragedy" of chastity. He gently approached, for the first time in many years, "the *refusal* of woman which is a fault in my chastity," and he evaluated that refusal as a profound and "irreparable loss . . . I have not fully accepted." Having just moved into the hermitage full-time, he was experiencing the felt burden of loneliness to a degree he had never experienced before. Perhaps the day-to-day reality of solitude instilled in Merton (as his Abbot later concluded after he learned of the affair) the need for human companionship. In any event, judging from the most recent entries in his journal, Merton was perhaps then primed for the avalanche of emotion which awaited him when he checked into the hospital for a cervical spine operation and noted in his journal, soon after meeting the nurse who attended him during his convalescence, that "we did not know, of course, that we were now in love."[24]

During the next few months, "swept in love and lost in it," Merton could hear little more than "metaphysical howls" and "silent cries [that came] slowly tearing and rending their way up out of the very ground of my being." After being discharged from the hospital, Merton continued to tap some of his friends who visited Gethsemani to drive him back into Louisville for lunches with the woman and picnics in Cherokee Park. Merton's psychiatrist, who had become a close friend and confidant, continued to caution Merton with appeals to better sense and vivid reminders of the potential tragic consequences of his infatuation. But Merton's love was apparently so strong that it even left him bewildered and incredulous. He lamented, "I just don't know what to do with my life."[25]

The bouts of desperation Merton experienced during this time render many of his later comments in "Final Integration" more credible (and less hyperbolic) than they might be had Merton been merely speculating about Arasteh's thesis. His feeling of love, tearing at him from "the very ground of my being," reached a pitch of intense existential anxiety as the interior divisions he suffered grew to crisis proportions. The "howls" and "silent cries" that surfaced in his journal record attest to his later conclusion that "the process of disintegration and reintegration . . . involves a terrible interior . . . crisis and an anguish . . . which is extremely severe." Moreover, the exact nature of the interior division that threatened Merton's own disintegration at the time centered on that ideal/actual dichotomy he defined in "Final Integration"—a dichotomy struck from the conflict, he wrote, between "the monastic role as defined by the *ideal* to which we hold . . .

and the role defined by the *actual situation* of . . . ourselves." A priest in courtship knew that dichotomy firsthand.

Even while "floundering around in the dark" and witnessing himself doing "some very foolish and dangerous things" during the summer of 1966, there were moments nonetheless of great clarity, wisdom, and insight for Merton. Trying desperately to understand his "wrong, absurd, insane" feelings of love, he honestly confronted the "dissonance" of his situation and accepted the very real difference, he admitted in his journal, between "my ideal (monk) self . . . and my actual self"—the conflict, in other words, between "What I think I should be" and "What I am." Painful as it may have been, such self-scrutiny prepared Merton for the kind of reintegration that summoned an individual, as Reza Arasteh theorized, to become the "person one is truly meant to be." "I must manfully face . . . and find my center," Merton wrote, "not in an ideal self which just *is* . . . but in an actual self which does all it can to be honest and to love truly, though it still might fail."[26]

The facts concerning how Merton settled this affair are not as important as the extent to which he felt reconciled and reintegrated after it was in fact settled. Once he determined never to see the woman again, the freedom of his life in the hermitage—seriously jeopardized by the affair—meant more to him than it had ever meant before. His commitments and responsibilities as a writer deepened too as he realized how much trust his readers had invested in him and how close he had come to violating that trust. "This [writing] is a gift," he reflected in a crucial moment, "that has been given me not for myself, but for everyone. I cannot let it be squandered and dissipated foolishly."[27] This heightened sense of altruism with respect to his identity as a writer prompted Merton to issue a couple of veiled public apologies and reconfirmations. For example, in "Antipoem I," Merton thinly disguises an autobiographical reference to "the gentle fool / [Who] . . . fell in love."

> Obstinate fool
> What a future we face
> If one and all
> Follow your theology
>
> You owe the human race
> An abject apology.
>   (*CP*, 672).

No matter how foolish it may have been, Merton emerged a fuller person after experiencing the affective nature of human love. And ultimately he gained more than he might have lost by eventually refusing himself the love of a woman. The entire experience strengthened his human capacities and opened him to a depth of human feeling he had never directly experienced before. Like Arasteh's "finally integrated man," Merton could now say of himself, "He has embraced *all of life*," from "ordinary human existence" and "religious life" to "human love." And "while retaining all that is best and most universal in them," he was able "to pass beyond all these limiting forms." Merton best captured that spirit of growth and reintegration in several journal entries written soon after his last meeting with the woman, when "[we] fell on each other in desperation and love, . . . knowing it would . . . never be like that again."[28] He writes,

> . . . there is such a great good in human love, and I need this good, or thought I did. Well, I did. But I needed to know that I was called to something else. And the fact that I risked my other and special calling now frightens me.
>
> I have always wanted to be completely open, both about my mistakes and about my efforts to make sense out of my life. [My love for _____] shows my limitations as well as a side of me that is—well, it needs to be known, too, for it is a part of me. My need for love, my inner division, the struggle in which solitude is at once a problem and a solution. . . .
>
> [Even months after last seeing her] everything was still charged with the power of our love. But I see it as folly and infidelity for me to try to keep it going even in my own heart now. And that is what I am doing . . . and still retaining a warm and deep affection for her.[29]

— 4 —

Before reading Arasteh, and just a few weeks prior to finding himself "so much loved and loving so much," Merton drafted a comment in *Conjectures* which anticipated, with uncanny prescience, not only the contours of his own private experience of growth through personal crisis but Arasteh's psychological theory which would later authenticate it. He reflected on "the psychology of crisis and change." He argued that a person needed to surrender a preoccupation with "holding himself together." To become "a more developed person," Merton insisted, required that one muster the courage to face "the fear of change . . . the fear of disruption, [the] disintegration of one's own inner unity and the unity of one's accustomed world."

> A personal crisis occurs when one becomes aware of apparently irreconcilable opposites in oneself. If the tension between them is strong enough, one can no longer "keep himself together." His personal unity is fractured. . . .
>
> A personal crisis is creative and salutary if one can accept the conflict and restore unity on a higher level, incorporating the opposed elements in a higher unity. One thus becomes a more complete, a more developed person, capable of wider understanding, empathy, and love for others (*CGB*, 189).

Later, during the summer of 1966, Merton certainly experienced the fracturing of his unity as an ideal monk; he witnessed the disintegration of his accustomed world. But by accepting the conflict—as his own private comments clearly suggest—he restored himself to a unity on a higher level and "became a more complete, a more developed person." Merton discovered, that is to say, a fuller meaning to his life—not, as had been his practice for nearly thirty years, through solitude, but through an intense, thorough-going interrelatedness with another person. The relationship revealed to Merton the poverty of a self isolated in its interiority. His love lead him to a great and wonderful human gift: the selfless humility of being in the presence of someone he loved, a humility that Merton gave free expression to in the eighteen love poems he wrote during and just after the affair. He is able to realize in "Certain Proverbs Arise Out of Dreams," for example, that "No harm ever comes to / The one who loses himself entirely in the love of another."

> Why has God created you to be the center of my
> being? You are utterly holy to me, you have become a
> focus of inaccessible light. Suns explode from the light
> you spread through my guts and torn with love for you
> my cry becomes a hemorrhage of wild and cool stars.
> I wake with knowledge of my whole meaning,
> which is you. Our luck is irreversible. We are the chosen
> winners of sleep, whose secret light is now clear to us
> after five or six adventures.[30]

As is always the case, Merton's need for companionship, love, and interrelatedness brought with it an overwhelming desire to transcend the limits of an isolated self. So the process of self-actualization he traced abstractly in his essay on "Final Integration" was experienced personally as Merton's triumph over interiority and the reintegration of a self defined, not through its monastic quest for ideal separation and detachment, but through its actual, lived connectedness to another human being.

We can see in Merton's brief and isolated experience with affective love, then, that broader dynamic cycle of denial, doubt, and reconciliation integral to his previous decades of personal evolution. Unable to escape his feelings of "man's enormous want" by renouncing them, Merton wrestled with the anxiety of such feelings until he resolved them, as he says, on a higher level of personal unity and awoke to a new "knowledge of my whole meaning." Two important changes accompanied this latest stage of Merton's personal development. He emerged more determined than ever before to embrace a modern secular world he had once rejected with disgust and contempt. And his heightened capacity for "wider understanding, empathy and love for others" further reinforced and refined the humanistic vision that is the legacy of Thomas Merton's final years.

7

The Secularization of Thomas Merton— Modernity Reconciled

The foregoing portrait of Thomas Merton's shadow of self-doubt focuses on inner struggles and conflicts he experienced when witnessing the erosion of his ideal monk image. It is time to shift perspectives and examine some of the external influences working on Merton and consider, in particular, the extent to which those influences contributed to the evolution of his mature humanism.

Not the least significant of those external forces sprang from a ferment of new ideas brewing in the theological arena. Merton's three decades of monastic experience were cut against a contemporary backdrop of vigorous debate in theological circles, a debate sparked by a new generation of Protestant theologians, by and large, who sought to revise and revitalize Christian teaching and practice in the context of a modern secularized world by accommodating centuries of tradition in Christian culture to the radically new demands and climate of modern life. Most interestingly, the entire movement spanned Merton's monastic years, from the depths of World War II and the writings, initially, of Dietrich Bonhoeffer to the late 1960s when the so-called New Theology movement was eclipsed by a growing fundamentalist retrenchment.

I must note from the outset that the movement itself amounted to little more than a blip on the radar screen of twentieth century theological thought. I believe it is a fascinating blip, something we might classify as a near-collision of radical dissent and mainstream theological thought during an era when traffic in dissent was considerably more congested than it is today. Nonetheless, few tenets of the radical theology have been historically assimilated during the past twenty years, except perhaps for some trace elements showing up in phenomena as divergent as Liberation Theology and the facile new-wave video evangelicalism. Also, Merton himself was not terribly preoccupied with the work of the New Theologians. He did engage them with care and thoughtfulness and with his characteristic energy and thoroughness, but his writings on the radical theology hardly dominate the Merton bibliography. It is important, however, to examine such responses as there are because Merton, especially during the early sixties, was wrestling privately with many of the same issues that the radical theologians subjected to intense and lively public debate. Like the New Theologians, Merton struggled to reconcile himself to modernity; he sought, as they, to accommodate his faith, rooted in centuries of Christian tradition, to what both he and the New Theologians recognized and accepted as a post-Christian era.

The essential questions of most concern to the movement can be summarized by drawing from the contributions of two central figures. Writing from a Nazi prison in 1944, Dietrich Bonhoeffer, returning to fundamental questions characteristic of the movement, asked,

What *is* Christianity, and indeed what *is* Christ, for us today? The time when men could be told everything by means of words, whether theological or simply pious, is over, and so is the time of inwardness and conscience, which is to say the time of religion as such. We are proceeding towards a time of no religion at all: men as they are now simply cannot be religious any more. . . . Our whole nineteen-hundred-year-old Christian preaching and theology rests upon the "religious premise" of man. What we call Christianity has always been a pattern—perhaps a true pattern—of religion. But if one day it becomes apparent that this *a priori* "premise" simply does not exist, but was an historical and temporary form of human self-expression . . . what does that mean for Christianity?[1]

Two decades later, John A. T. Robinson—in an immensely popular synthesis of the ideas of Bonhoeffer and other leaders of the movement, notably Rudolf Bultmann and Paul Tillich—also wrestled with the collision of tradition and modernity in Christian thought and wondered whether the concept of God as "a super-Being 'out there' is really only a sophisticated version of the Old Man in the Sky?" He asked,

> Suppose belief in God does not, indeed cannot, mean being persuaded of the "existence" of some entity, even a supreme entity, which might or might not be there, like life on Mars? Suppose the atheists are right . . . ? [But] suppose that all such atheism does is to destroy an idol, and that we can and must get on without a God "out there" at all? Have we seriously faced the possibility that to abandon such an idol may in the future be the only way of making Christianity meaningful?[2]

To appreciate the impact of this movement, variously labeled the New Theology, Death of God Theology, and Religionless Religion, and to prepare for an assessment of its affect on Merton, other issues must be taken briefly into consideration. First, the very word "secular," in its historical context and usage, had always been locked into a dialectical relationship with its opposite, the "sacred." The separation between the secular and sacred was so rigid and clear-cut that in the Medieval era, for example, the rhetorical interrelationship between the two remained essentially spatial. The sacred became the world of religious—of monks cloistered in monasteries, a space bounded neatly by the walls of the monastic enclosure; the secular encompassed the world outside the monastery. The cleavage between the two was further underscored by institutional sanctions and the church's establishment of a hierarchy of values: the secular realm, in effect, was subordinate to the sacred space of the monastery. Reacting against the historical context of the secular, the new generation of modern theologians sought to bridge the rigid separation between the sacred and the secular, to ease the tension of the old dialectics, and to liberate, in essence, the usage of the secular from its traditional rhetorical stigma rooted in the old spatial hierarchy. Dietrich Bonhoeffer could then argue, for example, that historical developments converging on the modern person's "coming of age" must not be viewed as anti-Christian, but only that the reactionary polemics of Christian apologists, refusing to surrender the old dialectics, had made it seem so. And Robinson could insist that secularization must not be combated, but must be accepted dispassionately as a neutral historical fact.

Consider, too, the ontological and psychological ramifications for men and women of faith living a Christian life in a fully secularized world. Secularization implies a fundamental, radical change in the modern person's sense of being and existence in the world. Historically, earthly life was viewed as subordinate and inferior to a higher metaphysical reality. For Christians coming of age in the context of a modern reality, this other, higher, truer, supraterrestrial reality is no longer present; it no longer imposes itself on the modern person's capacities to judge and decide and solve problems and, most important, to derive identity through autonomous self-reflection. And, psychologically, secularization implies a profound liberation. Men and women are free to live their lives independently and assume full responsibility for their actions and shape their own destinies. With secularization comes a heightened sense of autonomous responsibility for moral and ethical, intellectual, familial, social, educational and aesthetic spheres of human existence, as well as a new freedom from authority where the burden of human responsibility is cut free from the approval or disapproval of a "god" or any sacral reality.

Such ontological and psychological implications threatened, thirdly, to undermine the institutional footings of the church itself. Secularization tacitly assumed a new relationship between the church and its role in the lives of the laity, a relationship requiring the church to surrender its control in all spheres of human life. Most obviously, science and politics, for example, become fully autonomous entities no longer subject to the church's approval or disapproval. Largely in response to a perceived threat to its traditional authority, the church naturally reacted against the secularization movement. Christians were called upon to reject and fight secularization, and the resistance was frequently characterized in institutional pronouncements as tantamount to a struggle against the Devil himself. The battle lines stiffened during nearly three decades of virulent debate. The reactionary wing of leadership in the churches, sensing the very fabric of Christian society beginning to fray, waged a campaign to discredit the radical theologians. The new theologians, in turn, persisted in their efforts to accept secularization as historically inevitable, surrender the old dialectics, and search for new pathways of Christian faith through the institutional, ontological and psychological realities arising from secularization. By trying to renegotiate Christian teaching and Christian practice in light of the modern secular world's experience of reality, this cadre of theologians continued to press their work beyond the religious premise of man. Like Bonhoeffer, they held that "God as a working hypothesis in morals, politics or science, has been surmounted and abolished; and the same thing has happened in philosophy and religion. . . . For the sake of intellectual honesty, that working hypothesis should be dropped, or as far as possible eliminated."[3]

For the young Thomas Merton—the Merton of *The Seven Storey Mountain*, a contemporary of Bonhoeffer's—the notion of eliminating God as a working hypothesis would surely have been viewed as heretical and greeted with considerable contempt. During the forties, committed as he was to a life within the sacred space of the monastery, Merton might have been a perfect caricature of what John A. T. Robinson later called a "flat-earther," clinging, philosophically and theologically, to a pre-Copernican hierarchy of separation between both secular and monastic life and the relationship between God and the human person mediated by the institutional authority of the church. But given Merton's personal evolution over three decades, it would be unfair to judge his response to this ferment of new ideas from the perspective of *The Seven Storey Mountain* and its bellicose apologetics. Merton eventually came to share, especially during the sixties, in the spirit of the new theologians, although he could never entirely accept the full range of conclusions argued by the new generation. Later in his life, for example, Merton remarked, on more than one occasion, how put off he was by the "religiousness" of religion—a religion of tactics, external observances, formalistic rituals—a "religiousness" that he, like the new radicals, dismissed as negative, ambiguous, moralizing, and, frankly, dysfunctional. Even as he looked back, in his journal of the sixties, to reconsider his own conversion, he was compelled to borrow the language of Bonhoeffer and Robinson, recalling then that "God was not for me a working hypothesis . . . Nor was He a God enthroned somewhere in outer space" (*CGB*, 292).

How, then, did Merton respond to the new climate of religious thought? What was the precise course in the evolution of those responses? To what extent did he embrace the historical process of secularization coming to fruition in the context of a modern world that he had once vowed to reject? What difficulties did he encounter and how did he resolve those difficulties? More important still, what principal influences worked upon Merton to temper his reconciliations to modernity? I will tackle that latter question first before returning, in section 5, to a full assessment of Merton's response to the Radical New Theology.

— 2 —

There is no question, first and most generally, that Thomas Merton underwent a significant reorientation in philosophical and theological perspectives, as well as a radical change in his openness to and acceptance of modern thinkers and modern thought. As a young monk, for example, Merton was thoroughly committed to a distinctly premodern separation between the natural order of human experience and a supranatural divine cosmos, a view governed by a traditional hierarchy of values. "In the concrete order of things," Merton announced in *The Seven Storey Mountain*, "God gave man a nature that was ordered to a supernatural life. He created man with a soul that was made not to bring itself to perfection in its own order, but to be perfected by Him in an order infinitely beyond the reach of human powers. . . . We were never destined to lead purely natural lives," Merton concluded, "and therefore we were never destined in God's plan for a purely natural beatitude" (*SSM*, 169). Twenty years later—after having encountered, as we have seen, considerable difficulties with self-transcendence—Merton arrived at a substantially altered view of what post-Enlightenment philosophy had come to accept as "natural rights" by declaring "it is a compelling necessity for me to be free to embrace the necessity of my own nature" (*DofS*, 33). Tapping into a leitmotif of existential freedom and the importance of personal authenticity common to his later writing—and sounding very much like a new theologian suspicious of a tradition of supranaturalism—Merton spoke of the mature modern identity as "liberated from the enclosing womb of myth and prejudice." He further granted a degree of autonomy to the modern person at odds with his earlier view of a sovereign, higher cosmic order by insisting that the mature modern individual must learn "to think for himself, guided no longer by the dictates of . . . systems and processes designed to create artificial needs and then 'satisfy' them" (*Raids*, 17).

Merton's theological bearings during the forties, anchored in a theology of supranaturalism, may account, too, for the anti-intellectualism of *The Seven Storey Mountain* and the more supple discounting of the intellect in another early book, *The Ascent to Truth*, his only full-scale venture into theology. By linking, for example in *Mountain*, intellectual activity to baser human desires, Merton could justify his reactionary indictments of modern intellectual trends. He insisted then that modern people needed desperately to learn one truth above all others: "the intellect is . . . constantly being blinded and perverted by the ends and aims of passion, and the evidence it presents to us with such a show of impartiality and objectivity is fraught with interest and propaganda." Intellectual activity is a source of self-delusion, he believed, because "our intellects . . . present to us everything distorted and accommodated to the norms of our desire" (*SSM*, 205). That distortion obligated him to dismiss figures like Freud and D. H. Lawrence and even to attribute the instability of his youth to reading books on psychoanalysis. "I don't know if I ever got very close to a padded cell," Merton wrote when discussing the books of Freud, Jung, and Adler checked out of the Columbia library, "but if I ever had gone crazy, I think psychoanalysis would have been the one thing chiefly responsible for it" (124).

But as he underwent a gradual reorientation in theological perspectives, Merton came to recognize the importance of opening himself to modern thinkers. Once he accepted, as he later said in *Seeds of Destruction*, the great facts of our own era—that, in particular, "we have come to a certain kind of 'end' of the development of Western Christian society"—he could argue against a Christianity that ignores currents of modern intellectual thought as "a lunar landscape of meaningless gestures and observances" (*SofD*, 246–48). "We have to come to grips with the great facts of our time," he wrote to a correspondent, "and see where we are in the midst of this colossal revolution" of modernity.[4]

Those facts included a full spectrum of modern, post-Christian intellectuals, from Darwin and Nietzsche to Freud and Mao Tse-Tung. And nowhere did Merton argue more strongly in favor of attending to modern intellectual thought than, interestingly enough, in his essays on monastic renewal. Written during the sixties when monastic communities witnessed a growing disaffection among monks, these essays, posthumously collected as *Contemplation in a World of Action*, address the crisis of religious vocations. Merton attributed that crisis, in large part, to the penchant among modern Christians, Catholics in particular, to ignore modern intellectuals, and especially with a failure in the novitiate to recognize the importance of such figures. He cited a litany of modern intellectuals who had "completely revolutionized the thought of modern man": including, among others, Marx, Darwin, Kierkegaard, Nietzsche, Freud, Jung, Lenin, Sartre and the existentialists—"Christian and otherwise"—Heidegger, Buber, Teilhard de Chardin, Gabriel Marcel, Bultmann, Tillich. Merton mocked contemporary Christian apologists who condemned these thinkers for inciting rebellion in modern youth by appealing to anarchist instincts which threatened to undermine order, authority, and morality. "All the most influential thinkers of modern times," he concluded with no little ridicule, "are thus regarded as disciples of demons and prophets of evil . . . responsible for . . . restlessness, dissatisfaction, doubt, and rebellion. . . . They have 'poisoned the mind of man.'" But "let us ask: Are all these men simply madmen or villains . . . trying, out of malice, passion or envy, to undermine a beautiful and well-ordered universe?" Merton thought not. Because they are principally concerned with the problems of the human person in the wake of the Industrial Revolution, because of their efforts to understand and explain the "progressive dehumanization of man in the world of the machine," Merton argued that we must "attend to their diagnosis of modern man." In his appeal, he took pains to stress the importance of coming to terms with an intellectual inheritance—moving from Nietzsche and Kierkegaard through Marx and Freud to the new theologians—generally perceived as anathema to traditional Christian thinking. "All these thinkers," Merton emphasized, "even the Christians, tend to regard conventional forms of religion as being in league with the forces which have diminished and depersonalized man" (*CWA*, 76–77).

By embracing, indeed immersing himself in modern thought and its bewildering array of developments, trends, and countertrends, Merton struck a delicate and healthy balance. Remembering, perhaps, the intellectual indulgences of his own youthful enthusiasms, Merton cautioned against the tendency to adopt superficial admixtures of mental clichés based on the variety of popular ideas acting upon the modern person. He remained acutely sensitive to the inclination toward intellectual fashion. "Obviously we must change," he wrote to an innovative Christian educator, "but just as obviously all meaningful change implies continuity. There is all the difference in the world between real development, growth, and mere change of fashion. . . . All that is needed is a wide-openness to what is really new in the new and what really points to significant development (and not to plain immersion in totalism)."[5] Wary of intellectual faddism, Merton was equally vigilant, however, in his efforts to thwart the reactionary retrenchment of certain Christians who dismissed modern intellectuals out of hand. What enabled him to balance superficial fashion against the arrogance of Christian reactionaries was that he sought out, in his own study of modern intellectuals, any elements of a vestigial humanism intrinsic to trends of modern thought. He emphasized that humanistic element by insisting, in an essay on "Vocation and Modern Thought," that the most significant modern thinkers "have all in one way or another concerned themselves very deeply with the predicament of modern man: with his special needs, his peculiar hopes, his chances of attaining these hopes." By focusing on the humanistic ramifications of modern thought, Merton discovered a meaningful continuity between radical new currents in contemporary thinking and a traditional Christian humanism. Christianity, he came to believe, was in fact fully compatible with the new intellectuals' radical humanistic critique of modernity. Merton admonished, then, that "Christianity too must be profoundly concerned with twentieth-century man, with technological man, 'post-historic' man, indeed. . . 'post-Christian' man" (*CWA*, 53–54).

Nowhere were Merton's efforts to resituate himself within the context of modern thought and appeal most directly to a new breed of "post-historic, post-Christian man" more determined than in the journal of the sixties, *Conjectures of a Guilty Bystander*. His aim there was to reconcile himself to the intellectual, existential, and religious dimensions comprising modernity in its fullest sense. And he achieved that reconciliation, first, through an honest and forthright abnegation of his earlier attitude of *contemptus mundi* and, second, through a synthesis, as we have seen above, of a viable Christian humanism relevant to modern realities yet maintaining all that he felt was best and most needed in the cultural tradition of Western Christendom. He spoke, then, as "a progressive with a deep respect and love for tradition." "I am more and more convinced," he announced, "that my job is to clarify something of the tradition that lives in me, and in which I live. . . . Man's sanity and balance and peace depend, I think, on his keeping alive a continuous sense of what has been valid in his past" (*CGB*, 176). Two figures occupy positions of central influence as Merton sought that synthesis through the open dialogue of his new journal: the Swiss theologian Karl Barth and the German ethicist Dietrich Bonhoeffer.

Merton engaged Karl Barth, first, through his reading of a collection of Barth's sermons and *Dogmatics in Outline*, a heavily redacted version of the multi-volume *Church Dogmatics*. Although Merton was not as well read in Barth as he was in Bonhoeffer, and even though a more thorough reading of Barth may have forced some compromises in *Conjectures*, Merton nonetheless found in Barth a fusion of orthodoxy and iconoclasm appropriate to the journal's agenda. Merton was particularly attracted to Barth's theological emphasis on the importance of faith as the sole end of a Christian life. Barth demoted, then, the importance of the church as a human institution and coined the famous aphorism "religion is the enemy of faith," defining religion as man's attempt to enter communion with God on his own terms. Barth argued that Christians must therefore transcend human religion if they hope to reach the self-transcendence of genuine faith. One indication of just how appealing Barth's stress on faith was to Merton concerns his retelling of a dream Barth had. Merton interpreted that dream as dealing with Barth's own personal salvation through faith, and Merton was so taken by Barth's account of the dream that he originally proposed *Barth's Dream* as the title of the journal, only later opting for it as a subtitle for part 1.

In his dream, Barth, a prominent Protestant theologian, is appointed to examine the child prodigy Mozart in theology. Antagonistically critical of Protestantism as a cerebral religion, Mozart sits dumb and passive in the dream, fidgeting like a child as Barth grills him about the theological aspects of his Masses. Merton interprets Mozart as a central symbol of faith, cast in the dream-image of a child—a "divine child," as Barth himself says of his dream, "who speaks in Mozart's music to us." Mozart's passivity in the face of Barth's abstruse theological questions, Merton suggests, shows that faith—"the hidden sophianic Mozart," a child "in the higher meaning of that word"—sits impassive and disinterested before a more cerebral theology, the kind of sophisticated adult thinking that Barth himself may have indicted as a task which makes of religion a human institution. So Merton concludes that "Barth perhaps is striving to admit that he will be saved more by the Mozart in himself than by his theology." By then internalizing Barth's dilemma—namely, that sophisticated discourse about religion is rendered virtually meaningless when confronted by the wisdom of simple faith—as his own, Merton addresses Barth with the sympathy of a fellow-traveller. "Fear not, Karl Barth! Trust in the divine mercy. Though you have grown up to become a theologian, Christ remains a child in you. Your books (and mine) matter less than we might think! There is in us a Mozart who will be our salvation" (4). In a similar vein, Merton elsewhere quotes a fragment from *Dogmatics in Outline* which he endorses enthusiastically as "magnificent lines from Barth" and "one of the great intuitions of Protestantism": "Everyone who has to contend with unbelief [Barth writes] should be advised that he ought not to take his own unbelief too seriously. Only faith is to be taken seriously; and if we have faith as a grain of mustard seed, that suffices, for the devil has lost his game."[6] In its context, that comment occurs as Barth discusses the human pain experienced when intensities of belief fluctuate during periods of confusion and doubt. Barth admonishes his readers not to fear such fluctuations but to accept them as an invitation, for faith is the only "final thing" from which a person "may take comfort of the fact that he is being upheld." Perhaps Merton took special comfort from Barth's assurances that faith, if even as a grain of mustard seed, invariably checks the waning intensities of belief and commitment, for we must remember that Merton himself was emerging from a decade of self-doubt over his ideal monk image. Moreover, Barth's theological discounting of institutional religion certainly must have appealed to Merton's own growing iconoclastic temperament.

Merton wavered, however, in his sympathies to Barth's more conservative side, with his emphasis, in particular, on a strictly God-centered theology. Often labeled the theologian of the sovereignty of God, Barth's watchword was, as Luther's, "Let God be God," the God Who was in Christ. Barth leaned heavily, then, on the Incarnation and biblical revelation, while taking care to treat them as suprarational categories lest he compromise his de-emphasis of human religion. Merton spoke kindly, then, of Barth's treatment of Incarnation and revelation as wholly-other categories which transcend rational human understanding. "The Incarnation," Merton concludes in apparent agreement with Barth, "is not something that can be fitted into a system." He quotes Barth further: "Divine revelation cannot be discovered in the same way as the beauty of a work of art or the genius of man is discovered. . . . It is the opening of a door that can only be unlocked from the inside" (9). No doubt Barth's conservative orthodoxy, his "wholly-other" theism, appealed to Merton because of its compatibility with his own apophatic tradition which stressed the unknowability of God. Given the ecumenical spirit of Merton's new journal, he could then forge an alliance between Cistercian monasticism and the theology of a prominent Protestant.

Merton may have found Barth's theology of the sovereignty of God consistent with his monastic agenda. But Merton's new progressivism nevertheless prompted him to object to Barth's conservative orthodoxy as hastening, Merton feared, a fatal separation between Christianity and modern society. Throughout his dialogue Merton frequently took Barth to task over the issue of social witness. Merton suspected, for example, that too "few people can maintain themselves in a world like ours with the austere faith of a Barth, and not simply submit in complete unreason to the forces of destruction" (176). Elsewhere he faulted Barth for inclining toward what Bonhoeffer criticized as "thinking in two spheres." By relying theologically on a separation of nature and grace—and emphasizing grace over nature—Merton felt that Barth risked de-emphasizing the rights of nature and the dignity of the human person, something Merton objected to as "Barthian radicalism." By centering his theology around justification by grace through faith, Merton, from the vantage point of his new social activism and its emphasis on good works, questioned Barth's adequacy in the arena of social action. On this score, Merton clearly preferred Bonhoeffer.

Interestingly, Merton either missed or ignored Barth's humanist bent. Merton's objections seemed more in line with the popular criticisms of a post-Barthian generation of new theologians, rather than in a thorough reading of Barth himself. It was fashionable during the early sixties to discredit Barth's conservative orthodoxy; singling out his emphasis on the disunity of the natural and the divine and the unbridgeable gap between God and man, Barth was criticized for, in effect, bringing original sin back into theology at a time when liberal theological trends aimed for the secularization of Christianity. But Merton, like the more radical of the new theologians, did not adequately balance Barth's conservative theism with his apostolic side—his call, in particular, for modern Christians to recognize their complete involvement in the human situation of their fellow man. While Barth was not, as Dietrich Bonhoeffer was, personally victimized by *en masse* social and political assaults on civilized values, he was nonetheless deeply disturbed by the human catastrophe of World War I and experienced, as a result, a crisis of inspiration in his preaching that left him questioning conventional assumptions governing relations between the church and state. That crisis prompted him to write the sprawling *Epistle to the Romans*, perhaps his most famous work. In spite of his conservative orthodoxy, Barth stressed that the "humanity of God" needed renewed emphasis in the modern context, so much so that Bonhoeffer later credited the Swiss theologian as the chief inspiration for his own doctrine of "holy worldliness." But Merton simply did not engage Barth's more humanistic predilections. He chose instead to use Barth's neo-orthodoxy as a foil to implement a rising social awareness that marked Merton's turn into the new decade. Nor was Merton aware, apparently, of Barth's ecumenical spirit; nowhere in *Conjectures* does Merton acknowledge the generally accepted claim that Barth was among the most genuinely ecumenical theologians of our time. Additionally, Merton makes only a glancing reference to Barth's "crisis theology" which held that religion enters a person's life at crisis junctures, during times of death, grief, guilt, self-doubt, for example, when the very basis of a person's existence is imperiled. There are existential resonances in that "crisis theology" certainly germane to Merton's own conversion experience and his subsequent bouts with self-doubt. At any rate, confronted with a choice in *Conjectures of a Guilty Bystander* between the "wholly-Other" theism of Karl Barth and the "holy worldliness" of Dietrich Bonhoeffer, Merton unhesitatingly cast his lot with Bonhoeffer.

As in the case of Barth, Merton uses passages from two of Bonhoeffer's most influential books—*Ethics* and *Letters and Papers from Prison*— as springboards into his own commentary and reflections. In the former work, Bonhoeffer argues that an exemplary Christian ethical life requires steady concentration on God coupled to an intimate involvement in the affairs of the world. His principal concern was one close to Merton's own heart: How are the two reconciled? Bonhoeffer proposed a logic of reconciliation based on the Incarnation. Thus "Man becomes man," Bonhoeffer writes, "because God became man." "In Christ," Bonhoeffer says in *Ethics,* "we are offered the possibility of partaking in the reality of the world, but not in the one without the other. The reality of God discloses itself only by setting me entirely in the reality of the world." In another passage, further emphasizing his humanistic orientation toward an ethic of social concern, Bonhoeffer states: "Just as in Christ the reality of God entered into the reality of the world, so, too, is that which is Christian to be found only in that which is of the world, the 'supernatural' only in the natural, the holy in the profane, and the revelational only in the rational."[7] Bonhoeffer's religious humanism was firmly rooted in his belief that Christian practice remains viable only insofar as Christians maintain fidelity to their historical situation. Keying on a quote from *Ethics* in which Bonhoeffer insists, then, that Christians have no choice but to accept their place in history, Merton writes approvingly, "In one word: the only way in which I can make sense in the unparalleled confusion and absurdity of the breakdown of Western culture is to recognize myself as part of a society both sentenced and redeemed" (*CGB,* 59). This is a far cry from the ascetic orientation from which Merton had argued, years earlier, that sanity amid the moral corruption of Western culture was only restored through separation, disengagement, and withdrawal. And there may have been no other more singular influence in that reorientation process than Dietrich Bonhoeffer.

Merton's dialogue with Bonhoeffer in *Conjectures* was not limited to an affable exchange of ideas and impressions on the theological plane. Merton internalized Bonhoeffer's position uniting the human and the divine. In many passages Merton moves in the spirit of Bonhoeffer with a existential commitment well beyond mere rational approval.

A good case in point occurs when Merton writes of a night when he had pulled duty as watchman. As his rounds took him through the novitiate, he was suddenly struck by the differences between his impressions now and those he had recorded nearly a decade earlier in the "Nightwatch" epilogue to *The Sign of Jonas.* What he had felt then during the night's solitude was the presence of a suprarational spirit speaking to him through the icons displayed austerely along the novitiate walls. Now the novices' desks spoke to him. Merton was touched by the humanity of the empty seats where each novice kept his letters and books and where he thought his most personal thoughts. In the darkness of the room, Merton's flashlight illuminated, he says, "the loveliness of the humanity . . . of our friends, our children, our brothers, the people we love and who love us." Negotiating a Bonhoefferesque leap from his existential impressions into their theological ramifications, Merton questions rhetorically, "Now that God has become Incarnate, why do we go to such lengths, all the time, to 'disincarnate' Him again, to unweave the garment of flesh and reduce Him once again to spirit?" Sounding very much like Bonhoeffer, Merton leaves the novitiate convinced that "you can see the beauty of Christ in each individual person, in that which is most his, most human, most personal to him, in things," he notes in a veiled reference to his own past, "which an ascetic might advise you to get rid of" (193).

Elsewhere in his reading of *Ethics*, Merton endorsed Bonhoeffer's strenuous objections to what he called "the tradition of thinking in terms of two spheres": specifically, the traditional scholastic separation of nature and grace which had divided life into Christian and pagan, the sacred and the profane. "There are not two realities," Bonhoeffer contends, "but only one reality, and that is the reality of God, which has become manifest in Christ in the reality of the world." In his revolt against the old dialectics, Bonhoeffer called for a recovery of the concept of the natural. He argued that the traditional theological emphasis on the sovereignty of grace had disastrous historical consequences because the realm of nature and the body politic had been allowed to fall prey to the forces of social disorder. "Before the light of grace everything human and natural sank into the night of sin, and . . . no one dared to consider the relative differences within the human and natural, for fear that by their doing so grace as grace might be diminished."[8]

Merton shared Bonhoeffer's fear that separating the realm of nature from a sacral reality bodes only the greatest religious disaster for society because it could legitimize inaction amid social evil. As Merton was well aware, Bonhoeffer himself, persecuted and eventually executed by Nazi authorities, was appalled that the church stood by while violence and wrong were being committed; he viewed such inaction as nothing less than the church's shaming "the name [of Jesus Christ] before the world." Reading one of Bonhoeffer's prison letters in which he spoke despairingly of the church's failure to resist the idolization of

arrogant Nazi teenagers during the time of the Hitler Youth Movement, Merton sensed a parallel in the situation of the United States
South when, during the height of the civil rights movement, a wave of
glossolalia swept the white Protestant churches. Merton writes about
the irony of that charism, recalling Bonhoeffer's claim that a preference
for grace over nature diminishes ethical responsibility. The tongue-
speaking phenomenon, Merton suggests, "seems to have been an ultimate protest against the inacceptable realities and challenges of the
historical situation—a convenient resort to immediate inspiration
rather than the difficult and humiliating business of hearing and obey-
ing the Word of God in the need of one's fellow man" (CGB, 110).
Merton was keenly accepting, in a broader sense then, Bonhoeffer's
position on social witness based on the ethical principle that, as Merton
summarizes with an extravagance of overstatement, "the peculiar evil
of our time . . . is to be sought not in the sins of the good, but in
apparent virtues of the evil. A time of confirmed liars who tell the truth
in the interest of what they themselves are—liars. A hive of murderers
who love their children and are kind to their pets" (53–54).

Given the ecumenical spirit of his new journal, Merton remarked
further that Bonhoeffer's emphasis on the rights and dignity of nature
was essentially Catholic and fully compatible with the humanistic tradition of Catholicism. And he accompanied Bonhoeffer to the logical
extreme of such an emphasis by offering no objection to Bonhoeffer's
view, for example, that "the life of the body assumes its full significance only with the fulfilment [sic] of its inherent claim to joy," a claim
that encompassed a full spectrum of sensual pleasures, from eating
and drinking, through recreation and play, to human sexuality. "This
is genuine Christian humanism," Merton concludes, "and Catholic too. . . . This is 'Christian worldliness' with which I thoroughly
agree. It is also the voice of all that is best in the cultural tradition of
Western Christendom" (183).

Merton discovered in Bonhoeffer's ethic of social responsibility—
an ethic grounded in Christology while rigorously oriented toward
the modern person's concrete situation in the world of his or her own
time—an axiomatic humanism extraordinarily appealing to Merton's
own burgeoning social conscience. Perhaps he found, too, in Bonhoeffer's doctrine of Christian worldliness a potential resolution to
the dilemma of the monk as "guilty bystander," the monk whose
withdrawal from the arena of contemporary social injustices only

alienates him, as Bonhoeffer said, from participation "in the sufferings of God at the hands of a godless world." On one level, then, Merton's dialogue with Bonhoeffer was that of an ecumenical-minded Catholic entering into the Protestant experience. At another, deeper level, Bonhoeffer's thoroughgoing Christian humanism helped ease the "guilt" Merton had begun to associate with his identity as a monastic "bystander." Bonhoeffer opened, that is to say, Merton's "monastic world," as he writes in the preface to *Conjectures*, "to the life and experience of the greater, more troubled, and more vocal world beyond the cloister." For both the worldly Christian and the cloistered monk, "Bonhoeffer's famous worldliness," Merton later insists, "begins [then] with a very clear recognition of the modern world as guilty and fallen—but also, therefore, as having the greatest claim on Christian mercy, all the more so as Christians themselves are deeply implicated in the same guilt. Thus Bonhoeffer's worldliness is [an] . . . 'entering into the fellowship of guilt for the sake of other men'" (231).

— 4 —

If, by the early sixties, Merton discovered a viable new humanism through his dialogue with Barth and Bonhoeffer, he still needed to push beyond a theistic framework in order to consummate his encounter with a post-Christian ethos in its entirety. That final push began in the summer of 1964 when Merton first read Albert Camus' *The Plague* and quickly wrote to Henry Miller, explaining how deeply moved he was by the novel's sobering truths. Merton came to the work of Camus only reluctantly through the prodding of the Polish poet Czeslaw Milosz, and there are only two passing references to Camus in *Conjectures*. Once having read *The Plague*, however, Merton's trepidation—owing, no doubt, to Camus' explicit disavowal of Christianity—gave way to a critical fervor equalled only by Merton's initial reading of Pasternak's *Dr. Zhivago* a few years earlier. For the next two years Merton focused his considerable energies on a full reading of Camus and a methodical study of the ethical, philosophical, political, religious and aesthetic questions of most concern to the French Algerian novelist. By summer, 1966, Merton had no reservations in his estimation of Camus as the greatest writer of our time. He parlayed that admiration into seven carefully considered essays which occupied much of Merton's attention from March 1966 to Spring 1967. The impression Camus made on Merton during his final years was so strong that it would be hard to imagine the mature Thomas Merton without considering the full extent of Camus' influence. Merton himself sensed how far he had come in his own journey, and he used, on more than one occasion, his response to Camus to gauge the distance travelled during previous decades of personal growth. For example, Merton noted in a private Midsummer Diary that he had just read "The Myth of Sisyphus," Camus' searching commentary on absurdity and suicide. "I had tried it before," Merton wrote, "and was not ready for it because I was too afraid of the destructive forces in myself. Now I can read it, because I no longer fear them, as I no longer fear the ardent and loving forces in myself. If they all turn against me I don't care, but I think for some strange reason they are all for me."[9]

Camus' influence on Merton stems from the fundamental issue of Camus' denial of God. It seems as though Merton needed to grapple with Camus' explicit non-Christian leanings and find a way to reconcile his admiration of Camus as a quintessential modern writer with his outspoken critique of Christian hope and grace. Almost as if called to a challenge, Merton struggled to distill from Camus' existential humanism an ethic compatible with Christian morality. While ultimately accepting Camus' agnosticism, Merton aimed nonetheless to illuminate, as he says in one of the Camus essays, "Camus' witness to the plight of man in that world with which the Christian still seeks to communicate."[10] Given the broader challenge of Camus' rejection of Christianity, Merton was drawn, more specifically, to Camus' philosophical orientation; the perspectives Merton found there enabled him to engage existentialism—the philosophy of modernity—while conveniently skirting such radical extremes as, for example, Sartre's uncompromising atheism. Merton also encountered, as he had in Bonhoeffer's ethic of social concern, a compelling political dimension in Camus' writing, coupled with what Merton came to see as a perfectly legitimate critique of Christian institutions in the arena of political action. The moral and humanistic underpinnings of Camus' political activism contributed much to the vitality of Merton's own social witness during the sixties. And Merton was deeply moved as well by Camus' vision of the artist's role in the modern world, a vision that suited Merton's own evolving identity as artist. Just as he had been challenged by Pasternak's personal witness, Merton was similarly drawn to Camus' prototype of the modern writer as rebel, as *artiste engagé*.

Although Camus publicly denied any connection to existentialism (a denial that derived more from his break with Sartre than from Camus' philosophical temperament), there are, nevertheless, expressly existential shadings in his work. In his novels, existential leanings are apparent, for example, in Camus' preference for dealing with characters caught in the web of coercive, collective systems and his depiction of the individual as exiled, abandoned, alienated, forever a stranger in his world. Merton may have sensed more than a relevant sociology in Camus' dramatic renderings of alienated characters. Merton may have seen a fictional counterpart to the existential situation of the monk, for the monk, too, lives an alienated life on the fringes of society, disenfranchised, in many ways a stranger in his own time and subject, as Merton knew only too well, to the constraints of a collective system. Moreover, Camus' antiromanticism— which rejected sentiment in favor of the primacy of the absurd—was typically existential. Not surprisingly, Merton had no quarrel with Camus' celebration of the absurd. Perhaps Merton's effortless appropriation of Camus' antiromanticism—reflected, for example, in "Original Child Bomb" and the turgid "Letter to Pablo Antonio Cuadra Concerning Giants"—further distanced Merton from the pietistic sentimentality and mystical triumphalism of his earlier years. Among other existential elements surfacing in Camus, Merton was especially attracted to Camus' preoccupation with exaggerated states of mind and his use of radical circumstances—for example in *The Stranger* and *The Plague*—as unexceptional representations of the contemporary historical situation. And Merton's frequent reliance on a false self/true self dichotomy in his late social criticism owed much, finally, to Camus' insistence that the greatest danger to the survival of free societies was the modern person's growing estrangement from his true self through unquestioning conformism dulled by banal routine.

But where Camus departed from existentialism, Merton followed. That departure arose over the ultimate question of achieving meaning and clarity of purpose in modern life. Camus held that no purpose can be found in the person's quest for the meaning of his existence, even if that quest subscribes to loosely defined tenets of existentialism like personal authenticity, nonconformity, liberation from closed col-

lective systems, acceptance of aloneness, abandonment, or alienation. If there is a Camusian absolute, it is that the modern person is
deeply and inextricably involved in the drama of the absurd and entrapped in an irrational world. The individual, however, must still
strive to live meaningfully. That is where Camus trained his vision as
a writer. And that is where Merton followed Camus with such interest and enthusiasm. Merton faced a compelling challenge to the tradition of Christian hope through Camus' acceptance, as Merton says in
his commentary on *The Plague,* of "the radical *absurdity* of an existence
into which evil or irrationality can always break without warning." If
the individual is condemned to the absurd, as Camus insisted, that
means, Merton writes elsewhere, "that instead of trying to justify his
life in terms of abstract formulas, man must create meaning in his
existence [only] by living in a meaningful way." Merton began to see,
in essence then, the contours of a viable ethic of action emerging from
Camus' hostility to abstract principles, either secular or religious,
based on his fear that they seduce people into imagining themselves
in possession of absolute truth and deter them from the business of
living their lives in authentic and meaningful ways. And, moreover,
Merton could bring himself to accept, without the slightest inclination
toward apologetics, that the Camusian ethic was "basically atheistic
and characteristically modern" (*LE,* 182, 191, 232).

Living meaningfully in the face of the absurd became the central
moral and critical issue, more specifically, in Merton's lengthy commentary on Camus' *The Plague.* Merton sought to recover from
Camus' story of evil, irrationality, and chaos erupting into the most
banal of social milieus the roots of an authentic humanism in the
novel, a humanism that Merton could endorse notwithstanding
Camus' rejection of such Christian concepts as grace and redemption.
From the morbid fictional situation of a French colonial town ravaged
by bubonic fever, Merton could detect, that is to say, Camus' positive
concern for a suffering humanity and celebrate the novelist's "classic
humanism . . . rooted in man as an authentic value"—an authenticity
derived, not from Christian theistic principles, but solely from an experiential love and compassion affirmed only through concrete actions "in defiance of suffering and death." From a strictly political
perspective, Merton interpreted the pestilence visited upon the unexceptional and placid little town of Oran, Algeria as representing the
brutalizing incursions of political fanaticism into the war-torn Europe

of World War II. In his accompanying biographical sketch of Camus, Merton cited such things as the Nazi occupation of France, the death camps, and Stalinism as contemporary evidence. Critically, Merton viewed the Plague as in fact "an excellent typological device for discussion of Nazism and other absolutisms." The question that most fascinated Merton, however, concerned the problem of moral paralysis and ethical degeneration brought on by political totalitarianism. How does one fashion an authentic and meaningful moral life in the fictional context of *The Plague* and, by extension, its sociopolitical manifestations in contemporary history? How, as Camus said in his Nobel Prize acceptance speech, do men and women "fashion an art of living in times of catastrophe"? (Quoted in *LE*, 186.) Not only is the bubonic plague a physical epidemic, then, but it parallels, Merton writes, "the moral sickness of men under repression by a hateful regime—a typological reign of evil."

In his search for answers to such moral questions, Merton identified most fully with the reactions of two characters: Dr. Rieux, a physician and healer, and Tarrou, who organizes the Oranian sanitation squads, both of whom confront the Plague and dedicate their efforts to alleviating the suffering of their fellowman. Dr. Rieux and Tarrou recognize the absurd, they endure it, and, most important to Merton, they do so unselfconsciously, and therefore authentically, without self-satisfaction, complacency or pride in their endeavors. For Merton, Dr. Rieux and Tarrou become models of "the sanity of that realistic self-assessment which delivers men from fatal *hubris*." They are "willing to do their job, do it well, and even lay down their lives," Merton continues, "*without insisting that anything is proved by their action* . . . without declaring that they were *justified* in doing what they did."[11] Touched by Camus' embodiment of a Sisyphian stoicism and a genuine altruism in the characters of Dr. Rieux and Tarrou, Merton praised their "Camusian modesty and its distrust of formal virtuousness" as the essential ground of compassionate humanism.

Camus' hostility to abstract principles of virtue and his preference for an ethic of modest self-sacrifice were not without their unflattering consequences for Christianity. In *The Plague*, Camus trained his critique of the Christian response to human suffering on the Jesuit theologian Père Paneloux. Unlike, in particular, Dr. Rieux, whose self-effacing modesty and ability to recognize the absurd elements of the Plague mark him with a certain Camusian heroism, Paneloux refuses to accept the rock-bottom absurdity of the pestilence. He chooses instead to justify it through theological rationalizations. Merton argues that Paneloux retreats, then, to "a basic immutable truth"— namely, that a punishing God visits retribution on a sinful people—which he uses to explain the absurd. His rationalizations, in turn, brand him with a certain inhuman hardness and deflect him from the awful burden of human suffering inflicted by the pestilence. Paneloux's "*idea* of God," Merton concludes, "his *abstractions* about God come between him and other human beings," thus violating the authentic humanism of Dr. Rieux by opting instead for an abstruse virtuousness. "One looks in vain for any evidence of a really deep human and Christian compassion in this stern, logical mind." Merton rejects Paneloux (as he had the chaplain in *The Stranger*) for much the same reason, as we have seen, that Aelred Graham rejected Merton himself years earlier: by hypostatizing the idea of God, Paneloux is deterred from a truly meaningful involvement in the suffering of his fellow man. Merton writes: "the ignorance which Camus rejects ignores the absurd, and fancying itself to be wisdom, prefers its own rightness to the values that are worth defending" (195).

Merton found in Camus' *The Plague* a humanism that advanced Bonhoeffer's ethic of social concern. It was a humanism that permitted a critique of conventional institutional Christianity while simultaneously endorsing a resilient tradition of Christian compassion that could endure the incursion of the absurd and serve, as in the case of Dr. Rieux, Merton believed, as a guide to living a meaningful, authentic moral life. And, perhaps most important to Merton himself, Camus' "classic humanism" carried the imprimatur of a truly representative modern mind. Addressing Camus' protest against Christianity, Merton accepted it as "typical of the 'Post-Christian' mentality which bases its criticism of Christianity on the historic gap between a glorious Christian ideal and a somewhat less edifying reality." "If Camus is severe with Christians," Merton further argued, "it is because he thinks they have abdicated their mission of opposing the Plague and [like Père Paneloux] have instead devoted their talents to excusing and justifying it in terms of an ambiguous theology or . . . by compromise with political absolutism." But Merton could still see in that protest a synthesis of traditional Christian values and a moral framework that remained responsive to modern realities. So Merton could both accept and praise Camus as "a typical 'post-Christian' thinker in the sense that he combines an obscure sense of certain Christian values—the lucidity and solidarity of men in their struggle against evil—with an accusatory, satirical analysis of the Christian establishment and of the faithful." Merton returned repeatedly throughout his exhaustive analysis of Camus' "ethic of revolt" to his successful fusion, as Merton saw it, of iconoclasm and a vestigial Christian humanism. Merton speaks of Camus as representative of "that secular and nonreligious thought of the . . . 'post-Christian era' which seeks to defend values that are essentially those of Western and Christian tradition against the nihilism and violence that have arisen out of the breakdown of Western civilization." In his renunciation of "illusions" and "misleading ideals" and "deceptive and hypocritical social forms," Camus' "deepest affirmation is that of an almost traditional and classic humanism with a few significant modern doubts, austerities, and reservations . . . a humanism rooted in man as authentic value, in life which is to be affirmed in defiance of suffering and death, in love, compassion, and understanding" (186).

After his study of *The Plague,* Merton turned to Camus' *The Rebel,* a largely autobiographical character study of the individual who transforms an ethic of revolt from moral philosophy into social action. Merton encountered, in the figure of the rebel, an existential model that brought further changes in Merton's identity as artist and served as a major catalyst for his later social criticism. Inspired by Camus' rebel, the numerous tracts of radical social criticism that Merton wrote during the sixties aimed, without exception, to affirm the human person as an authentic value in an era of increasing nihilism and violence. Camus envisioned the modern writer as a rebel who faces the absurd unflinchingly and seeks a creative revolt against it. The rebel's protest is against tyranny, whether from the political left or right, and his every action stands in opposition to any ideology that threatens to subvert human dignity. But the rebel's protest is tempered by reason and restraint; he is wary, for example, of the extremism of modern revolutionaries whose utopian dreams defy moderation and threaten the same coercive tendencies they aim to overthrow. The rebel pits tolerance and restraint against the ever-present proclivities of extremism. He "distrusts the nihilism," Merton writes approvingly, "that negates all virtue in order to dedicate itself to revolutionary action in history, regardless of whether it is 'moral' or not." Like Pasternak, Bonhoeffer, and Camus himself, the rebel "is the man who protests

. . . in the name of man, individual and concrete man of flesh and blood, against the war-making arrogance of total power, against the abstractions on which power bases its claim."[12]

Significant for Merton was Camus' insistence that the rebel engage in open dialogue, that he speak and listen as well as act. "The Rebel . . . refuses," Merton says, "to be silent and insists on open dialogue . . . a lucid and common decision to oppose absurdity and death and affirm man against all abstractions [because] the logic of revolt demands dialogue, openness, speech." Such a demand for discourse certainly suited Merton's natural inclinations as a writer, while Camus' insistence on the efficacy of open dialogue may itself have lead Merton to establish more personal contacts with intellectuals, activists, and writers—Christian and non-Christian alike—outside Gethsemani. Such contacts increased dramatically, especially after 1964, when Merton first read Camus. Merton began receiving more visitors and he even organized formal dialogue sessions at the monastery. He seemed alert to Camus' call for the open exchange of ideas, probably because Camus, an avowed agnostic, articulated it best in a statement emphasizing the importance of dialogue between Christians and unbelievers. When addressing a group of religious leaders at a Dominican monastery in 1948, Camus quickly asserted that "I shall never start from the supposition that Christian truth is illusory, but merely from the fact that I could not accept it." "I share with you the same revulsion from evil. But I do not share your hope." Camus emphasized, however, that dialogue between believer and unbeliever is nonetheless invaluable, and he recommended "the kind of dialogue between people who remain what they are and speak their minds." In speaking his own mind, Camus did not hesitate to remind responsible Christians to voice their condemnation of human suffering and of their failure to do so. The previous years had seen a Europe wracked by totalitarian tyrannies in Spain, Germany and Italy, and even then dreadful repressions were occurring in Russia. The Christian response, Camus believed, had simply not measured up. Camus' intolerance of Christian inaction and silence, and his equally vehement condemnation of mere formalities of action (as, for example, in the form of the Encyclical), was the very same intolerance that had emboldened Merton from his earlier encounter with Bonhoeffer. And there is every indication in Merton's later writings that he had taken to heart Camus' similarly uncompromising appeal to Christian duty and adopted Camus' ideal vision of the Christian as would-be rebel. "What the world expects of Christians," Camus declared, "is that Christians should speak out loud and clear, and that they should voice their condemnation in such a way that never a doubt, never the slightest doubt, could arise in the heart of the simplest man. That they should get away from abstraction and confront the blood-stained face history has taken on today. The grouping we need is a grouping of men resolved to speak out clearly and pay up personally."[13]

Clearly, then, Camus' rebel provided Merton with a durable and practicable existential model. If that model was slightly at odds with the more conventional image of a monk, it still maintained allegiance to a legitimate sense of Christian duty. And even further, Camus' rebel appealed to Merton's identity as artist and writer. In fact, Camus' influence redoubled as Merton discovered in the rebel a fusion of viable self-images: a uniting of the Christian *and* the artist. Camus' conviction that modern literature, of necessity, must be a literature of revolt meant that the modern artist is, most properly, a rebel himself. Camus argued passionately that art is inherently revolutionary, a point that Merton had stressed repeatedly in his earlier Pasternak monograph. But Camus, like Merton, could not endorse that injunction as fully and unreservedly as some of the more indulgent modernist contemporaries. The rebel as artist must not, Camus believed, succumb to the mere fashion of rejecting everything, for that only sterilizes art and cuts it off from "the fecundity we associate with true art." Almost as if addressing directly Merton's own personal history as an artist and writer, Camus wrote that "art is neither a complete rejection nor a complete acceptance of what is. It is simultaneously rejection and acceptance, and this is why it must be a perpetually renewed wrenching apart. The artist constantly lives in such a state of ambiguity, incapable of negating the real and yet eternally bound to question it."[14] Camus' comments on the purpose of art were instrumental in shaping the aesthetics of the radical humanist critique which govern much of Merton's late writing. "The aim of art," Camus said, "the aim of life can only be to increase the sum of freedom and responsibility to be found in every man in the world. . . . There is not a single true work of art that has not in the end added to the inner freedom of each person who has known and loved it. . . . An artist may make a success or a failure of his work. He may make a success or a failure of his life. But if he can tell himself that, finally, as a result of his long effort, he has eased or decreased the various forms of bondage weighing upon men, then in a sense he is justified and, to some extent, he can forgive himself."[15]

Camus' comment that the modern artist is "incapable of separating himself from the world's misfortune [while] passionately longing for solitude and silence" captures beautifully the dilemma of Merton's monastic situation, especially during the so-called "hermitage years": a reaching out to engage loudly and clearly the crucial questions of the era and, simultaneously, a fervent inner need to withdraw and disengage. Sounding very much like the secluded monk who still insisted on maintaining a "quiet but articulate place" amid the cacophonous events of the sixties, Camus wrote: "the artist of today becomes unreal if he remains in his ivory tower or sterilized if he spends his time galloping around the political arena. Yet between the two lies the arduous way of true art. It seems to me that the writer must be fully aware of the dramas of his time and that he must take sides every time he can or knows how to do so. But he must also maintain or resume from time to time a certain distance in relation to our history. . . . The artist, if he must share the misfortune of his time, must also tear himself away in order to consider that misfortune and give it form."[16]

— 5 —

I noted in the first section of this chapter that Thomas Merton's response to the Radical New Theology, judging at least from his pivotal public journal of the sixties, was, although not without reservations, largely sympathetic and understanding. His preference for Bonhoeffer's "holy worldliness" over the relatively conservative orthodoxy of Karl Barth situates Merton rather more neatly in the fold of the moderns. And the ardor of his Camus essays further aligns Merton with the new radicals, many of whom utilized Camus' writings to forge a neo-Christian existentialism compatible with the New Theology. Merton might not have been as inclined to join the Death-of-God debate had it not been for Camus' insistence that open dialogue is essential in an era of increasingly oppressive and monolithic ideologies. Elsewhere, especially in the private journal *Vow of Conversation* where he engages the writings of Rudolf Bultmann, Merton was equally hospitable to a movement which, at first glance, may seem entirely anathema to his monastic agenda.

But Merton's overall reactions to the movement are complicated considerably by the context of his responses. As he shifted perspectives and personae—from self-reflective, introspective journal writing, for example, to a more formal and authoritative public discourse—Merton's sympathetic understanding gave way to a sustained, near-polemical critique, especially as he discussed the Death-of-God theologians (the most radical wing of the new radicals) in a collection of late essays to which we will presently turn. In examining the full range of Merton's reactions, we encounter, in a word, his return to a familiar posture of ambivalences. Merton could accommodate the radical theologians in the context of private self-reflection where his aim was to reconcile himself to modernity, and where he could more freely reckon with the personal experience of religious crisis central to the Radical Theology. And he could be less obliging in extrospective rhetorical situations when he adopted the persona of an influential Catholic writer who had amassed a considerable following and who recognized his responsibility to such a wide readership. Many of those readers had repeatedly turned to Merton to shore up a flagging belief. How could he, in good conscience, publicly endorse a movement that preached the efficacy of unbelief?

Such a pattern of ambivalences can be seen in other contexts as well. In his letters Merton routinely tailored his comments concerning the Death-of-God movement to his correspondents' sympathies. For example, Merton could share with Marco Pallis, who was deeply devoted to Tibetan monasticism, how utterly struck he was "by the limitless depth of despair . . . implicit in the pitiful 'hopes' of so many moderns, Christians, who are trying to come out with justifications for a completely secularized and optimistic eschatology of pseudo-science, in which the eventual triumph of religion is to discover that God is 'dead' and that there is no religion anyway."[17] In chameleon-like fashion, Merton responded quite differently in his letters to the theologian Rosemary Ruether, whose thinking was shaped by Bonhoeffer, Bultmann, and especially Gabriel Vahanian, who had first popularized the phrase "God-is-dead" in its contemporary theological context. Naturally, Rosemary Ruether remained unsympathetic to the monastic project, referring to it disparagingly on one occasion as "anti-matter theology" totally irrelevant to "the arena of real historical action." In an effort to tailor his responses to Ms. Ruether's theological bearings, Merton experimented throughout his letters with a variety of labels for himself: "Christian anarchist," "anti-ascetic humanist," "secularized hermit," "non-monk," "man as mere man," among others, some of which might have made fine lapel buttons for the jacket of a new theologian.

These ambivalences may only blunt Merton's public criticisms of the Death-of-God movement. Nonetheless, his sharpest critical pronouncements came in a carefully edited cluster of six essays which comprise part 4 of *Faith and Violence,* culminating in the polemical pitch of the final two essays: "The Death of God and the End of History" and "Godless Christianity." Merton most certainly had something in mind, incidentally, when he selected "Apologies to an Unbeliever" to precede those essays. In that piece he adopted an epistolary style and engaged unbelievers in an intimate dialogue not unlike that kind of dialogue prescribed by Camus' rebel—a free and open exchange of ideas "between people who remain what they are and speak their minds." Merton's aim, however, was not to justify his faith and belief to an audience of unbelievers. He was not out to win their confidence. He chose instead to apologize for the penchant among Christian faithful to proselytize their message. Announcing the Good News with evangelical zeal, Merton readily admitted, only alienated unbelievers and shut down dialogue between Christians and atheists, thus breaching a "compassionate respect for one another in their common predicament." Most important, Merton did not characterize himself as the kind of believer whose tenacity of faith alone might justify an upcoming attack on a new brand of Christian thinking that stressed the utility of unbelief and aimed to accommodate secular atheism. Rather, Merton viewed "my own peculiar task in my Church [as] . . . that of the solitary explorer who . . . is bound to search the existential depths of faith in its silences, its ambiguities" (*F&V,* 213). In the course of that search Merton freely acknowledged that he had encountered his own faith "mysteriously [taking] on the aspect of doubt." He was fully prepared to accept, then, that "the division between Believer and Unbeliever ceases to be so crystal clear," that both believer and unbeliever "are bound to seek in honest perplexity," and that, ultimately, "Everybody is an Unbeliever more or less." By taking such an egalitarian position in "Apologies to an Unbeliever," Merton may have been trying to cushion, from the outset, his disagreements with the Death-of-God theologians which would follow in the next essays. No acute reader would likely mistake such criticisms as issuing from the outrage of a famous Believer.

Although Merton may have characterized himself as the kind of believer not prone to reactionary bias when addressing the central question of God's existence, although he promises, in a headnote to "The Death of God and the End of History," that his discussion of the Death-of-God premise is reflective and not polemical, there is, even in the language of his summary descriptions, a touch of polemics which belies such evenhandedness. "What is meant by the current solemnization of the 'Death-of-God'?" Merton asks wryly. "It claims to be an act of fervent Christian iconoclasm which is vitally necessary both for Christianity and for the 'world' since without it (so the argument runs) Christianity cannot recover any relevance at all in the modern world and the world itself cannot discover its own implicit and unrecognized potentialities." Such a claim, he says, might as well be

> a declaration that the question of God's existence has now become irrelevant. An announcement of the 'good news': God as a problem no longer requires our attention.
>
> What is involved [in the Death-of-God movement] is a repudiation of *all* discussion of God, whether speculative or mystical: a repudiation of the very notion of God, even as "unknowable." Any claim whatever to know Him, or to know what one is talking about when discussing Him, is dismissed a priori as infected with mythology. [So] the language of theology and revelation has "died" on us, so the argument runs. The words have lost their meaning. Or the meaning they have kept is purely formal, ritual, incantory, magic. . . .
>
> The cornerstone of the whole . . . movement . . . is the formal belief that revelation itself is inconceivable. To say that God is dead is to say He is silent, that He cannot be conceived as speaking to man. . . . The whole concept of revelation has now become obsolete because modern man is simply incapable not only of grasping it but even of being interested in it at all (260).

Obviously unimpressed by some of the theological issues raised by the movement, Merton seemed more interested in the phenomenon of the movement itself as signaling a revolutionary new stage in the history of human consciousness, what he called "the expression of a 'happening' in the consciousness of man," "a psychological and epistemological assumption about human consciousness in the modern age." Beneath the popular rhetoric and the announced aims of the Death-of-God theologians to adapt theology to the collapse of Western Christendom and the advent of secular atheism, Merton sensed "the epiphany of a new state of consciousness, a new mode of being in the world, a new relationship to the secular world." With flashes of irony Merton caricatured that relationship as an Augustinianism in reverse, where the new Christian sings praises for secularity to the accompaniment of guitars while "the sin which is confessed is the sin not of infidelity but of belief."

Merton was not moved to such an unflattering and ironic treatment because he interpreted the Death-of-God theologians' central injunction as mere atheism or apostasy. "They are not 'atheists,'" he explained, "the old belligerent pseudo-scientific militant atheists." In fact, Merton grasped the real paradox of the God-is-dead Christian for whom God remains immanent, Merton writes, "empty and hidden in man and in the world," and "present more especially in those who deny him and repudiate him and refuse to recognize him." "The basic dogma," Merton then concludes, "of the God-is-dead theology is that any claim to an experience of the reality of God and his relevance for life on earth today is bound to be fraudulent or at least illusory." So the honest Christian has little choice except to confess to "having sinned against the world, of having insulted the adulthood of man by having believed in a transcendent God" (242).

Summarizing briefly, Merton featured the Death-of-God theology as radically *kenotic*: the God-is-dead Christian is emptied of the capacity to receive revelation, stripped of traditional metaphysical assumptions about Being or about God, and free of traditional formalistic rituals of worship and the trappings of dysfunctional, archaic symbolisms. He is emptied especially of God-talk. He is liberated in his modernness. And the test of the authenticity of that liberation, Merton writes, is whether the new Christian's "present subjective state of consciousness . . . corresponds to 'the world of our time' in its historical, technological, political actuality" (243).

Merton would have much to say about that issue of historical, technological, political realism. But first he made a point to affirm certain aspects of the Death-of-God theology before launching his critique. He noted, for example, that the claim made by certain radical Christian theologians that "God-is-dead" is, in itself, of indisputable cultural and religious importance. It has "special significance," he writes, as "a critique of traditional Christian ideas" and because it preaches "a radical 'Christian worldliness'" at a time when relations between the church and the modern world were undergoing revolutionary changes. The movement ought not to be dismissed out of hand, for it reflects, Merton felt, an appropriate exasperation with an abstract and formal religiosity which carries on about a God in heaven while showing too little concern for human persons on earth. Aside from simply appealing to his antinomian, iconoclastic temperament, Merton argued that the radical theologians should be listened to, especially because they had addressed "modern man's need for a religion he really feels to be authentic and not just a blend of pious imagination and submission to ethical and ritual prescriptions" (268).

Building from that foundation of affirmations, Merton then framed his critique. He was not convinced, first, that the "god" which Radical Theology had interred was ever alive in the first place. He in fact concurred with the central premise of the Death-of-God theologians if the god they had in mind—as he suspected—was "a God of hypotheses, a God of pious cliches, a God of formalistic ritual, a God invoked to make comfortable people more pleased with themselves." In addition, Merton detected a Madison Avenue mentality arising from the movement. Ever-critical of fashion and especially intolerant of the modern phenomenon of marketing ideas like soft drinks, Merton trained that critical disposition, in particular (though perhaps not altogether fairly), on John A. T. Robinson and his enormously popular book, *Honest to God*. Merton wondered whether *Honest to God* was little more than a sophisticated "manual of Christian salesmanship," an attempt to pitch a "reconditioned" Christianity—"worldly," "religionless," "free of myths" and basically "with it"—to a generation of disaffected believers who viewed Christianity as passé. Merton dressed down Robinson for trying to make Christianity palatable to the tastes of a new generation, and Merton dismissed *Honest to God* as merely a more refined and intellectually respectable version of the guitar-playing parish hootenanny.

In a similar vein, Merton could muster little tolerance for the fervent proselytizing he heard throughout the writings of the new radicals. Just as he had little sympathy for zealous Christians who aimed to share personal experiences of salvation with captive and undissenting converts, so too did Merton criticize the post-Christian "who is completely 'hip' to the modern world and will not listen for a moment to anyone who he suspects does not experience the modern world exactly as he does." Merton remained suspicious of some of the radicals' pretense to open dialogue, especially those who, he felt, "instinctively [regard] as suspect any tendency to question or criticize 'the world.' More precisely . . . any questioning of the pragmatic, technological, sociopolitical understanding of the world as autonomous and self-sufficient."

Of greater trouble to Merton was the "either/or" proposition he extrapolated from the logic of the radical theology, a proposition that led him to question whether the movement was really as modern as it was cracked up to be. As noted earlier, Merton viewed the new choice being offered modern Christians—to choose the world and reject God—as an Augustinianism turned inside out: thus, in Merton's mind, not a modern liberation from the old dialectics of the sacred and the secular as much as a retooling of the old hierarchies. "We can . . . easily understand," he writes, "a reaction against the stereotyped opposition by which traditional religion tended to set up God . . . over against . . . the secular, in a dualism that no longer seems valid or practical today. Unfortunately," he continues, "it seems that the God-is-dead Christian has simply perpetuated this same dualism by turning it inside out." He further questions whether "the dialectic [is] really valid, the tension really operative? Or is it simply, once again, a 'four legs good two legs bad' argument, as in Orwell's *Animal Farm* ?" (245–46). No doubt Merton's intolerance for such dialectical constraints issued from the fact that he himself had struggled for years with the existential consequences of such tensions. The personal difficulties and self-doubts, the crises of self-contradictions and ambivalences caused by his decision, decades earlier, to reject the world, left him naturally gun-shy of the "either/or" proposition, even when turned inside out.

The driving force behind Merton's critique hinged, above all, on his resolute rejection of an uncritical worship of the modern in its all-embracing modernness. Merton took careful aim at certain unnamed "secular city theorists in America," no doubt Harvey Cox and other intellectuals who had borrowed elements from the radical theology and fashioned what Merton considered a pop ideology of secularism. He wondered whether such theorists had merely reshuffled old formulas and replaced "metaphysics" and "revelation" with "history" and "politics"—whether they had negotiated a change of venue from

St. Augustine's City of God to a new earthly city where, Merton wise-cracked, Los Angeles becomes the New Jerusalem. That substitution, Merton feared, may only nourish a complacent praise of American affluence and further encourage a drift into "a quietism which simply celebrates and glorifies the muzak-supermarket complex." Some of Merton's toughest language surfaced as he pondered the ramifications of an unchecked and frenzied contemporariness and as he pictured the modern person submerged in the flux of changing fashion, uprooted into the "breathless dynamism of the ephemeral," and emboldened by "a quasi-Christian mystique of technological man as the summit of the evolutionary process." "The enthusiasm for the secular city," Merton warns, "coincides with a fervent praise of American affluence, which is in fact rooted in the enormous military-industrial complex." He further cautions: "though the God-is-dead movement repudiates transcendence, mysticism, inwardness, divine law and so forth, turning to immanence, outgoing love and creative innovation in interpersonal relationships, its substitution of 'history' and 'politics' for metaphysics and religion may run the risk of ending in conformism, acquiescence, and passive approval of the American managerial society, affluent economy, and war-making power politics" (247–48). Merton further questioned the efficacy of the historical/ political consciousness central to the New Theology's concept of modern ontology. He cites Camus and Hannah Arendt in an effort to show that the differences between historical fact and historical illusion, between political action and political manipulation, are by no means distinct or clear-cut.

> Today, with the enormous amplification of news and of opinion, we are suffering from more than acceptable distortions of perspective. Our supposed historical consciousness, over-informed and over-stimulated, is threatened with death by bloating, and we are overcome with a political elephantiasis which sometimes seems to make all actual forward motion useless if not impossible. But in addition to the sheer volume of information there is the even more portentous fact of falsification and misinformation by which those in power are often completely intent not only on misleading others but even on convincing themselves that their own lies are "historical truth" (250).

It followed, in Merton's reasoning, that the historical/political consciousness, allowed to evolve unchecked, will lead inevitably to "the death of history": a situation where, in the name of political realism, "we may altogether cease to know what is happening let alone understand it." He turned the axiom of the radical theologians against radical theology through recourse to a rugged Orwellian realism, claiming that just as God-is-dead so too history-is-dead, "for the idea of history . . . becomes fiction which keeps one from being aware of what is going on and from making decisions that are really capable of influencing man's destiny in a free and constructive manner." Merton saw no little naiveté as he looked beyond the bracing enthusiasms of the God-is-dead Christian. Blinded by a passion for the modern, intoxicated by "the constant unpredictable flux of existence," he must, Merton persistently warned, "be more aware of the deviousness of his own heart and of his own propensity to justify destructive tendencies with moral, religious, philosophical or even scientific rationalizations" (251–52). Merton could find, in a word, little value in trading a mystique of revelation for a mystique of secular liberation.

Although he ultimately rejected the most extreme claims of the new radicals, Merton's qualified reservations did not in the least derive from a sense of insult to his Christian beliefs and values, nor was his critique undertaken as an apologetic counterattack in defense of monasticism or, to be sure, Christian traditionalism. He turned against the New Theology because he viewed it as merely replacing old dysfunctional myths with a new secular mythology that did not promise, in his mind, human freedom and liberation from collective delusions. Unlike the countermodern polemics of Merton's earlier antisecular jeremiads, his critique of Secular Religion was not a sweeping renunciation of secularism per se; it did not issue from a conservative, reactionary Catholic sensibility lashing out at the New Theology as inherently malefic. Rather, Merton's position was that of a radical social critic defending the dignity and primacy of the human person against what he feared was a naive reconditioned Christianity that might, unknowingly, only worsen nihilism, conformism, and alienation in an age of mass cultures. In this sense, Merton's argument typified the social criticism of his later years: a criticism targeted on *dehumanization*, not apostasy; a criticism inspired by concern and compassion for the contemporary individual, not a criticism of bitterness and disdain for a post-Christian era that had strayed too far from a divine plan—a criticism, in short, of affirmation, not rejection. Above all, Merton may have detected in the New Theologians' all-embracing enthusiasm for the modern a violation of the balanced humanism he had struggled for years to attain: that amalgamation of traditional Christian compassion and a full, critical, responsible awareness of modern realities which he so admired in modern figures like Bonhoeffer and Camus. Merton articulated that sense of violation best by posing questions as he neared his final arguments in *Faith and Violence.*

Does the New Theology simply "liberate" the Christian from traditional Christianity in order to subject him to a ready-made political or a-political ideology of questionable worth? Or does it turn him loose in a world without values, to occupy himself with the infinite variety of possible metamorphoses in his own consciousness, his own awareness of himself in his self-creating milieu? Are we . . . drifting into a new world of total, predetermined necessity, a new "system" entirely closed to liberty and impervious to revolutionary change (except for its own immanent technical revolutionism, determined not by man's will but by technology's own capacity for self-perfection in its own realm, without consideration for man's real needs)? (252–53).

8

A Radical Humanist and the Radical Critique

Thomas Merton made two profoundly crucial decisions in his life. He announced the first decision with dramatic understatement in *The Seven Storey Mountain*. His casual remark to a friend—"You know, I think I ought to go and enter a monastery and become a priest"—set Merton's life on a course of two decades with an aim "to be lost to all created things, to die to them and to the knowledge of them." Twenty years later, almost to the day, Merton made another important decision that would alter the course of those previous years and send him in a new direction for the balance of his life. This time he announced the decision in a letter to a friend, a letter he selected to lead off his first collection of *Cold War Letters* which, in 1962, Merton began circulating in mimeograph to a formidable *samizdat* of friends, acquaintances and fellow travellers—a collection of letters showing Merton very much involved in "created things" and reaching out to refine his knowledge and understanding of them. "One thing that has kept me very busy in the last two weeks," Merton writes, "is the international crisis. It is not really my business to speak out about it, but since there is such a frightful apathy and passivity everywhere, with people simply unable to face the issue squarely, and with only a stray voice raised tentatively here and there, it has become an urgent obligation.

This has kept me occupied and will keep me even more occupied, because now I am perfectly convinced that there is one task for me that takes precedence over everything else: working with such means as I have at my disposal for the abolition of war" (*Ground*, 346–47). As if to underscore the urgency of his new obligations, Merton quickly follows, in "Cold War Letter #2," with a plea "to be in touch with anyone who is working for peace at this hour." And he continues to rattle off a string of superlatives to capture the totality of his new commitment. "I feel that the supreme obligation of every Christian, taking precedence over absolutely everything else, is to devote himself by the best means at his disposal to a struggle to preserve the human race from annihilation and to abolish war as the essential means to accomplish this end. Everything else must be seen in this perspective" (402).

Merton was well aware that his new undertaking would be fraught with personal difficulties and frustrations. Entering the public debate and even skirting the political arena may not have seemed appropriate or familiar terrain for a cloistered monk. He characterized his new task as that of a boxer who enters the ring blindfolded and with hands tied, and he had good reason to be wary of what lay ahead. As a writer he had already sparred with the Trappist censors over matters much more benign than the present international crisis. He stressed in the inaugural *Cold War Letters* that his new commitments certainly would not endear him to the censors who, he fully expected, would raise "all sorts of trivial objections . . . to everything that is not purely a matter of pious homilies for the sisters on how to arrange the veil during meditation." His hunch that "a lot of people are not going to like this and it may mean my head" was realized, in a manner of speaking, just two years later when Merton was no longer permitted to publish articles on war and peace. But he was willing and excited to press on despite such roadblocks. Inspired by a heightened sense of a personal mission to "speak as clearly, as forthrightly and as uncompromisingly as I can," he had never before been more convinced that it was "a question of conscience for me to enter . . . actively in the work that goes around this central problem of our time" (347).

The roots of that problem traced to the Cold War mentality that had governed relations between the superpowers for the previous fifteen years. And the international crisis that triggered Merton's decision to get actively involved in a campaign to abolish war was the Bay of Pigs debacle in Spring 1961. Merton's new commitments came at a time then when Cold War tensions threatened to reach a flash point, heightened by a new showdown between the superpowers in Berlin and the U2 incident in May 1960, in addition to an increasing crescendo of atmospheric nuclear testing and renewed anticommunist sentiment in America countered by more fist pounding in the Presidium—all of which would lead to the Cuban missile crisis the following year and the unthinkable consequences of nuclear brinkmanship. From Merton's vantage point, he couldn't help but picture, as he said in his first article on war and peace written shortly after the Cuba invasion, "the whole world . . . plunging headlong into frightful destruction, and doing so *with the purpose of avoiding war and preserving peace!* This is true war-madness, an illness of the mind and spirit that is spreading with a furious and subtle contagion all over the world."[1] Particularly alarming to Merton was the apparent acquiescence of the American public. Such apathy struck him as a mindless national numbing against a future perhaps just too frightful to even contemplate. But public resignation, Merton felt, could not mask the collective paranoia that surfaced in such ritual death dances as the fallout shelter frenzy during the early sixties. He continued in his inaugural statement, "The Root of War" with a subtle irony strained by revulsion: "On all sides we have people building bomb shelters where, in the case of a nuclear war, they will simply bake slowly instead of burning up quickly or being blown out of existence in a flash. And they are prepared to sit in these shelters with machine guns with which to prevent their neighbor from entering." Convinced that the bomb shelter mentality was a clear expression of the moral chaos and spiritual malaise which nourished the roots of war, Merton continued to write about the fallout shelter as a mass symbol of moral degradation and despair until his essay, "The Machine Gun in the Fallout Shelter," led to the writing ban in 1963. Setting the stage for a virtual tsunami of antiwar articles, books, and poems which would appear during the next seven years—either through normal channels of publication, or distributed in mimeograph through an international network of friends, or bootlegged pseudonymously into the pages of the *Catholic Worker* or the Fellowship of Reconciliation's pamphlet series—Merton asked in the autumn of 1961, then, "What are we to do?" What is the task of the Christian in such a time of crisis? He answered unequivocally.

That task is to work for the total abolition of war. *There can be no question that unless war is abolished the world will remain constantly in a state of madness and desperation in which, because of the immense destructive power of modern weapons, the danger of catastrophe will be imminent and probably at every moment everywhere.* Unless we set ourselves immediately to this task, both as individuals and in our political and religious groups, we tend by our passivity and fatalism to cooperate with the destructive forces that are leading inexorably to war. It is a problem of terrifying complexity and magnitude, for which the Church herself is not fully able to see clear and decisive solutions. Yet she must lead the way on the road towards non-violent settlement of difficulties and towards the gradual abolition of war as the way of settling international or civil disputes. Christians must become active in every possible way, mobilizing all their resources for the fight against war. First of all there is much to be studied, much to be learned. Peace is to be preached, nonviolence is to be explained as a practical method, and not left to be mocked as an outlet for crackpots who want to make a show of themselves. Prayers and sacrifice must be used as the most effective spiritual weapons in the war against war, and like all weapons they must be used with deliberate aim: not just with a vague aspiration for peace and security, but against violence and against war. This implies that we are also willing to sacrifice and restrain our own instinct for violence and aggressiveness in our relations with other people. We may never succeed in this campaign, but whether we succeed or not the duty is evident. It is the great Christian task of our time. Everything else is secondary, for the survival of the human race itself depends upon it. We must at least face this responsibility and do something about it. And the first job of all is to understand the psychological forces at work in ourselves and in society.[2]

— 2 —

Merton set himself to that initial task of understanding the psychological forces which animate human aggression even as he drafted his initial public statement on "The Root of War." That task came in the form of an aggressive "open" letter Merton wrote in early September 1961, addressed ostensibly to his friend Pablo Antonio Cuadra, a Nicaraguan poet and editor of *La Prensa* in Managua. Merton certainly had a wider audience in mind. By using an epistolary narrative, Merton hoped to capture an intimacy and immediacy which would enhance what has to be one of the decade's most virulent antiwar statements. At first, even Merton himself was shocked by the combative tone of the letter. Alarmed by the bitterness and anger that spilled over in the statement, Merton initially proposed that "A Letter to Pablo Antonio Cuadra Concerning Giants" be published, in Spanish translation, only in South America. If he was privately troubled by the letter's aggressiveness and revolutionary fervor, he nevertheless checked the temptation to restrict its circulation. Perhaps he felt that his new commitment to abolish war had to take precedence over matters of decorum, for not only was the letter published in South America, but it appeared, within a year, no less than five times in various American publications, including the widely circulated *Thomas Merton Reader* and *Emblems of a Season of Fury.* By December 1962, Merton seemed almost proud to remark, in a letter to a European correspondent, that his open letter had been widely read by an international audience of intellectuals and peace activists.

For our purposes, "A Letter to Pablo Antonio Cuadra Concerning Giants" is an ideal piece from which to launch an examination of Thomas Merton's mature humanism and its expression in the style of the radical critique. The letter is an exemplary model of the acerbic social criticism that grew out of Merton's radical humanism. And it also exemplifies a fusion of the religious, psychological, and aesthetic dimensions of that humanism which, taken together, form the inspirational bedrock for much of Merton's writing during the sixties. First, the letter shows that Merton's position on war—a position that would unify the entire range of his writings on social justice issues during the years ahead—grew out of a religious humanism centered on the power of redemptive love. Second, the letter is the earliest indication that Merton's understanding of the dynamics of contemporary mass culture was shaped by a social psychology of collective alienation which viewed the individual as estranged from authentic self-identity by the powerful manipulations of conglomerate ideologies. And third, the "style" of the letter—its pitch, tone, and strategy, its deadpan irony and mocking satire, its scrappy, street-fighting prose—reflects nascent elements of the "antiwriting" aesthetic that Merton would later refine through his postmodern innovations and experiments in poetry and prose.

Merton explained the theme of "A Letter to Pablo Antonio Cuadra Concerning Giants" to many correspondents in letters accompanying mimeograph copies. "It is an indignant letter," he wrote to Dona

Luisa Coomaraswamy, "which is long and irate (more than it should be) [and] about the merciless stupidity of the Great Powers and power politicians" (*Ground*, 132). He wrote to Erich Fromm and explained that the letter was prompted by the "serious and sickening" international situation. "There is no point in being bitter and disgusted," Merton admitted, "but I have written a rather angry tirade . . . to a friend of mine in Nicaragua . . . [and] am sending you a copy as I have done to other friends of mine whose intelligence I respect and who, I feel, may be in a position to sympathize. This at least gives me the chance to express myself, which I think is a human need at such a time, and a need which is not easily fulfilled in a society of open-mouthed and passive TV watchers" (315–16). And to Abdul Aziz: "The theme of this open 'letter' is the international situation and the deplorable attempts of the great powers to threaten one another and the world with nuclear weapons. There is no question that in these maneuverings of power we see a dire evil force at work, a force which is spiritual and more than human. It is my belief that all those in the world who have kept some vestige of sanity and spirituality should unite in firm resistance to the movements of power politicians and the monster nations, resist the whole movement of war and aggression, resist the diplomatic overtures of power and develop a strong and coherent 'third world' that can stand on its own feet and affirm the spiritual and human values which are cynically denied by the great powers" (50–51).

To emphasize the seriousness of the present international scene and to best characterize the suprahuman, demonic forces he saw at work in the global strategies of Cold War diplomacy, Merton chose to cast the United States and Russia in the Biblical images of Gog and Magog. Gog and Magog first appear in Ezekiel's Old Testament prophecies as monstrous foreign nations waging battle against each other, nations whose "ponderous brutality," Merton explains, "would exhaust itself on the mountains of Israel and provide a feast for the birds of the air." Gog and Magog return in *Revelations* once again as warring nations driven by Satanic powers and locked into a cataclysmic battle that ends with their mutual destruction when a fire comes down from heaven and consumes them. Such biblical allusions resonate with obvious connections to the actual historical situation. Gog (Russia), "a lover of power," and Magog (The United States), "absorbed in the cult of money," become locked into a titanic, self-consuming struggle which transcends human limits and control, as if genies had arisen out of "the storm of history"—"glorious characters," Merton writes, "revelling in paroxysms of collective power." Nuclear arsenals—echoing the prophecy of destruction by fire—become fitting, if not frightening, technological manifestations of the giants' unconscious phantasms. "The bright weapons that sing in the atmosphere, ready to pulverize the cities of the world, are the dreams of giants without a center." And given the strength of Merton's new determination to speak out about the international situation, it seems entirely fitting that he adopted the persona of the prophet Ezekiel in the Cuadra Letter. Just as God appointed Ezekiel "watchman" for the Israelites and charged him to stand guard over His people and warn them of approaching enemies, perhaps Merton felt similarly called to issue warnings in advance of the superpowers edging inexorably toward a catastrophic war. Although he claims to be no prophet and admits that the modern world must learn to get along without prophets, still the watchman persona was one of Merton's favorite self-images, while God's threat to hold Ezekiel accountable if he failed his duty captures something of the intense responsibilities Merton felt as he began a campaign as an antiwar spokesman.

By calling upon biblical allusions Merton did not intend a Bible-thumping lesson on the Apocalypse. But the images of Gog and Magog did enable him to capture the hugeness and suprahuman enormity of his subject, so much so that the effect of the entire letter is like that of a bad fever dream as the giants' delusions bloat up into frightening proportions. The grand scale also frees Merton to caricature the giants without losing some degree of realism in what might otherwise be an exercise in distorted political commentary. Most important, by shifting an actual political situation into a grand mythical dimension, Merton was able to explore the moral consequences of what happens when genuine human values—those of love, respect, mutual understanding, acceptance and fellowship, the kinds of human needs realized only in concrete relations between concrete individual persons—give way to the abstractions of collective power, those pragmatic and cynical doctrines of *Realpolitik*. What emerges, then, is a moral man/immoral society scenario where morality and ethics give way to the arrogance, "greed and cruelty," "moral dishonesty," "infidelity to truth," and "alienation, horror and insanity" of global giants drunk with power. Although Merton evinces great skepticism and frankly concedes that "Gog and Magog may wake up one morning to find that they have burned and blasted each other off the map during the night," the burden of pessimism eventually reaches a catharsis when Merton announces, with great conviction, a plea.

> I would say there is one lesson to be learned from the present situation, one of the greatest urgency: be unlike the giants, Gog and Magog. Mark what they do, and act differently. Mark their official pronouncements, their ideologies, and without any difficulty you will find them hollow. Mark their behavior: their bluster, their violence, their blandishments, their hypocrisy: by their fruits you shall know them. In all their boastfulness they have become the victims of their own terror, which is nothing but the emptiness of their own hearts. They claim to be humanists, they claim to know and love man. They have come to liberate man, they say. But they do not know what man is. They are themselves less human than their fathers were, less articulate, less sensitive, less profound, less capable of genuine concern. They are turning into giant insects. Their societies are becoming anthills, without purpose, without meaning, without spirit and joy (*CP*, 388–89).

Merton's strident condemnation of Gog and Magog's empty humanisms followed from what he saw as the obvious hypocrisy of two global superpowers who, with great official flourish, professed love and concern for humanity while openly hating each other. He discounted such official pronouncements of humanitarian concern as hollow abstractions born out of hatred and served up only to justify national self interest. He attacked the audacious hypocrisy of the giants who spoke of a "golden age of peace and love" while anxiously shooting "the rapids of a cold war waged with the chemically pure threat of nuclear war." "The love that is born out of hate," Merton argues, "will never be born." As he developed the operative logic of the Cuadra Letter, Merton scribed a bold line which the genuine humanist, he insisted, must never cross: "Ultimately there is no humanism without God." "Western civilization is now in full decline into barbarism (a barbarism that springs *from within itself*)," Merton writes, "because it has been guilty of a twofold disloyalty: to God and to Man. To a Christian who believes in the mystery of the Incarnation, and who by that belief means something more than a pious theory without real humanist implications, this is not two disloyalties but one. Since the Word was made Flesh, God is in Man. God is in all *men*. All men are to be seen and treated as Christ." This is a humanism rooted in the Christian doctrine of the Incarnation and realized only through the power of redemptive love. Any humanism which does not proceed from the fundamental "faith that God has become man and can be seen in man . . . [and] can speak in man and . . . can enlighten and inspire love in and through any man I meet"—including the enemy, the stranger, and the alien—is no humanism at all because "it refuses, *a priori*, to love." "It is dedicated not to concrete relations of man with man, but only to abstractions about politics, economics, psychology, and even, sometimes, religion" (375).

Merton targeted both the atheistic humanism of Gog and the unctuous Christianity of Magog as just such false humanisms which refuse to love. By surveying, for example, the Imperialist era in the history of western Christendom, Merton singled out the failure of missionaries and colonizers "to encounter the face of Christ already potentially present" in alien cultures as leading eventually to Magog's present day greed and cruelty and his "unmitigated arrogance toward the rest of the human race." A Christianity that refuses "to listen to the voice of Christ in the unfamiliar accents" of the foreigner and "in that part of humanity that is most remote from its own" becomes little more, Merton concludes, than a pseudo-Christianity of Magog. "Magog is himself without belief, cynically tolerant of the athletic yet sentimental Christ devised by some of his clients, because this Christ is profitable to Magog." And although Marx—to whom Merton refers as the Moses of Gog's atheistic humanism—was "a humanist, with a humanist's concerns," his revolutionary dogma that humanism had to be atheistic ultimately bankrupted, Merton felt, Marx's profound grasp of the meaning of human liberation. Like Magog, Marx "did not understand God any better than the self-complacent formalists whom he criticized. He thought, as they, that God was an idea, an abstract essence, forming part of an intellectual superstructure built to justify economic alienation" (390).

Merton's stinging critique of capitalist and communist ideologies which hypocritically professed genuine concern for human liberation and peace is reduced, then, to the rock-bottom premise that "ultimately there can be no humanism without God." Thus the Incarnation and its vision of the human person redeemed only through a redemptive I-Thou love serve as benchmarks from which Merton would begin to develop his radical religious humanism and base the logic of his social criticism. Throughout the Cuadra Letter he reaches, often overexcitedly, for various metaphors to illustrate the insidious destructiveness of any other humanism as, for example, "a humanism of termites, because without God man becomes an insect, a worm in the wood" (389).

By positing the premise that there can be no humanism without God and using it in a piece of vitriolic social criticism, it may seem as though Merton was harking back to a pious old line he had used in earlier antiworld jeremiads where he condemned the modern age as inherently wicked, evil, and godless. But Merton makes it clear in the opening paragraph of the Cuadra Letter that his reflections on the current scene are not "prophetic curses"—curses like those hurled by the vintage Merton who entered a monastery with his Bible dog-eared at the Apocalypse. Rather, "they are simply the thoughts of one civilized man to another, dictated by a spirit of sobriety and concern, and with no pretensions to exorcise anything" (312). In fact, Merton's criticisms of contemporary political affairs differ markedly from those of the young contemplative. They now issue from a deep sense of love for humanity and concern for the course of human events, so even the most bruising stretches of inflated prose do not read like misanthropic diatribes.

Besides, Merton's tough commentary on the Cold War mentality reflects a global and informed understanding of modern mass society, not the anxieties of a young man seeking to palliate the painful personal experiences of his own secular life. Specifically, the concepts of collective alienation and mass will-to-power surface as Merton explores the dynamic social forces animating the behavior of global giants. By cutting through the superficial bluster of Gog and Magog whose communiqués broadcast their proudly held differences, Merton sees more similarities than contrasts between the two giants. In spite of their mutual "thunderous denunciations" of the other side, in spite of their faces dead set against each other in the international ring of Cold War diplomacy, Gog and Magog, Merton argues, actually "resemble each other like a pair of twins." Each giant loves power. Each is possessed by an all-consuming xenophobia that leads to identical strategies aimed at liquidating the alien, the stranger, and the foreigner. And each twin is bent on reducing everyone—including his own followers as well as his enemy's citizens—to an undissenting and rigid conformity to his own outlook. Each twin demands, moreover, that his followers hold similar suspicions toward alien presences, so much so that citizens, through their passive submission to the delusions of collective paranoia, become estranged even from themselves. More frightful still, Merton suggests that the specters of Gog and Magog "are . . . the emanations of our own subliminal self!" They "have arisen out of our own hearts," "sprung unbidden out of the emptiness of technological man." Merton issues a sober warning to any reader moved by the hideous apparition of global twins inching toward mutual destruction. "We must be wary of ourselves," he cautions, "when the worst that is in man becomes objectified in society, approved, acclaimed and deified, when hatred becomes patriotism and murder a holy duty, when spying and delation are called love of truth and the stool pigeon is a public benefactor, when the gnawing and prurient resentments of frustrated bureaucrats become the conscience of the people and the gangster is enthroned in power, then we must fear the voice of our own hearts, even when it denounces them. For are we not all tainted with the same poison?" (373).

The theoretical framework of the Cuadra Letter is based, then, on two radical suppositions concerning the operations of modern mass culture, suppositions later bolstered by Merton's reading of Reza Arasteh, Erich Fromm, Camus, Marx, and especially the neo-Marxist philosopher Herbert Marcuse. First, the herding together of people into conglomerate supercultures expresses, on a collective scale, the unconscious fears and repressed instinct to violence harbored by individual men and women. If such is indeed the case, little wonder that citizens offer little dissent as their countries gird for war and "spend billions on weapons of destruction and space rockets when [they] cannot provide decent meals, shelter and clothing for two thirds of the human race." Second, by serving up collective fictions created by "giants without a center," mass societies effectively alienate individuals from authentic self-awareness. Unquestioning conformity to collective ideals—as manifested most obviously, for example, in the strident nationalisms of the United States and the Soviet Union—works to estrange individuals, Merton argues, from "a spiritual outlook which is not . . . pragmatic but hieratic, intuitive and affective rather than rationalistic and aggressive." While it may not have been Merton's aim to provide concrete advice on how to recover a human center and discover one's "true self," he does imply that we must first turn to ourselves and question whether the giants' behavior is an expression of our own aggressive proclivities. As if answering his own call made in the inaugural essay, "The Root of War"—the charge "to understand the psychological forces at work in ourselves and in society"—Merton proposes that purifying oneself of the poison of violence and aggressiveness may be the first step in challenging the giants and countering their plans for mutual suicide. "Out of [Gog and Magog's] negation and terror comes certitude and peace for anyone who can fight his way free of their confusion" (390).

In addition to a humanism founded on the Christian ideal of love coupled to a distinctly left-leaning cultural theory that stressed collective alienation, there are aesthetic elements in the Cuadra Letter that foreshadow the antipoetics seen throughout Merton's later poetry and experimental prose. By choosing an epistolary narrative which utilized biblical infrastructures, Merton was obviously experimenting with an unconventional context for contemporary political discourse. Adopting conventional modes of discourse, Merton believed, only serves to implicate the contemporary writer in the giants' crimes and perpetuates the impoverished sensibility of the mass-mind. There are moments in the Cuadra Letter, however, when Merton lapses into an altogether different aesthetic frame of reference, the antithesis of the divergent and non-traditional. Such instances illustrate what Merton would later refer to as a style characterized by a "deliberate ironic feedback of cliché" completely sanitized of editorial comment and stripped of moral imperatives. For example, Merton praises Gog and Magog's technological prowess in proposing development of the ultimate clean bomb without fallout as a "humanitarian kindness"— "a lovely, humane piece of surgery," "prompt, efficacious, [and] pure." By deliberately appropriating the insipid sensibility of the giants, Merton affects a subtle parody of stereotypes that results in brutal satire. These narrative elements reveal the two directions Merton's radical "antiwriting" aesthetic would follow during the next few years. While seemingly contradictory on the surface, each shares the deeper vision of the writer as a revolutionary engaged, as Camus would say, in dialectical combat with his or her culture: first, the later use—for example, in *Cables to the Ace*—of superabundant nonsense where an extreme departure from traditional grammars of human speech is intended as an epistemological riot against convention; and second, the parroting—as in "Chant to be used in Processions around a site with Furnaces"—of customary models of mass culture discourse, from journalese to deodorant ads, where vapidity and banality are mastered to the point of utterly abusing custom and convention.

In the Cuadra Letter Merton leans more heavily on the first of those narrative forms because he is too openly bitter and aggressive for the sort of calm reserve which subtle parody demands. As a writer, freshly charged with a sense of new obligations, he is giving himself the freedom "to let loose," as he later said to a writing class in Louisville, "what is hidden in our depths, to expand rather than condense prematurely. . . . [W]e need . . . to release the face that is sweating under the mask and let it sweat out in the open for a change, even though nobody gives it a prize for special beauty and significance."[3] The face that sweats openly in "A Letter to Pablo Antonio Cuadra Concerning Giants" is that of a radical humanist outraged by the dehumanizing strategies of global supertwins. Merton had much to question, however, when he shifted personae and viewed the umbrageous humanist from the vantage point of a contemplative whose spirit of humility, self-effacement, and surrender from the arena of secular affairs seemed antithetical to the aspirations of a writer lashing out at the arrogance of global superpowers. That showdown between the radical humanist, inspired by a call to mix it up in worldly affairs, and the contemplative monk, still scheming, we must remember, for greater solitude and isolation, suggests that Merton's decision of 1961 confronted him, once again, with a dynamic self-contradiction that had always nourished his creativity and, judging by the amount of writing yet to come, would continue to do so. In keeping with his custom, Merton analyzed that self-contradiction in a private journal where, shortly after drafting the Cuadra Letter, he asked himself, "How did it get to be so violent and unfair?" He answered,

The root is my own fear, my own desperate desire to survive even if only as a voice uttering an angry protest, while the waters of death close over the whole continent.

Why am I so willing to believe that the country will be destroyed? It is certainly possible, and in some sense it may even be likely. But this is a case where, in spite of evidence, one must continue to hope. One must not give in to defeatism and despair; just as one must hope for life in a mortal illness which has been declared incurable.

This is the point. This weakness and petulancy, rooted in egotism and which I have in common with other intellectuals in this country. Even after years in the monastery I have not toughened up and got the kind of fiber that is bred only by humility and self-forgetfulness. Or rather, though I had begun to get it, this writing job and my awareness of myself as a personage with definite opinions and with a voice, has kept me sensitive and afraid on a level which most monks long ago became indifferent. Yet also it is not good to be indifferent to the fate of the world on a simple level.

So I am concerned, humanly, politically, yet not wisely.[4]

By arguing for a God-centered humanism in the Cuadra Letter, Merton had in mind a dynamic, forward-looking, revisionist view of Christianity and its capacity to accommodate historical developments. In an era when religion itself had come under attack as an escape into mystification or a facile recourse to the past, Merton insisted that modern day Christians must not retreat to the humanism, say, of the Christian Renaissance for sufficient precedence that Christianity today can successfully adapt to revolutionary social changes never before played out on the stage of human history. He dismissed any reversion to a Christian humanism fixed in the halcyon centuries of Western Christendom as "historical apologetics," ambiguous and insincere. "To declare," he wrote in one of many essays on Christian humanism, "that Christian humanism is a living force in the world today simply because this world remains in cultural continuity with . . . the past would, in fact, be quite equivocal."[5]

Merton might not have gone to such lengths to distinguish a dynamic Christian humanism from a static conception of the efficacy of historical Christianity if he did not take so seriously the claims of certain modern day detractors like Marx, Camus, and Feuerback, which discounted conventional Christian hope as naive and leading ultimately to a tolerance of human suffering. Merton accepted those claims as credible. But he argued that such criticisms were leveled against an archaic conception of the Christian world view that he himself rejected, a conception impoverished by what he referred to as "facile historicism." The Christianity of the past, he admitted, had typically underestimated historical developments and resisted social change with suspicion, even hostility. Merton did not hesitate, then, to endorse the Marxist critique of such a monolithic Christianity as an acute and viable historic criticism, and he urged other present-day Christians to face it squarely too. If the Christian world view remains hemmed in by a static historicism, if Christian practice is confined to a fixation on the rewards of afterlife or the routine observance of formal worship rituals safely harbored outside the turbulent mainstream of history, then Marx was indeed right: Christianity dehumanizes, impoverishes, and alienates the individual into a fantasy life where he is incapable, as Marx argued, of a productive and creative life and prevented from taking charge of his own world and changing it. Recalling the Cuadra Letter, this is, in effect, the Christianity of Magog, formal, ritualistic, and complacent. It is a Christianity that willingly subordinates social witness and action in history and time to universal ideological conformism. It is a Christianity, Merton frankly conceded, incapable of any real human concern.

That critique of Magog's "pseudo-Christianity" became the departure point from which Merton subsequently urged contemporary Christians to reject a dysfunctional and antiquated Christian world view and move on to face, as he admonishes in his essay "Christian Humanism," "the much more disquieting task of inquiring under what conditions Christians can establish, by their outlook and their actions in the world today, the claim to be true participants in the building of a new humanism." Merton sought to articulate then a "new humanism" rooted in a more dynamic and resilient complex of traditional Christian principles, a humanism responsive to revolutionary social change and more relevant to urgent contemporary problems.

> There can be no mistake about it: at a time when progress and perhaps even the very survival of mankind depend on the solution of certain grave problems which are basically ethical as well as economic and political, Christianity can and must contribute something of its own unique and irreplaceable insights into the value of man, not only in his human nature, but in his inalienable dignity as a free person. *The course of these insights is, of course, redemptive love.*[6]

From the entire spectrum of traditional Christian teachings, Merton zeroed in on the principle of redemptive love as the linchpin of a dynamic new Christian humanism and as the basis for a practical course of Christian action in meeting such grave problems facing humankind today. He was well aware, however, that the notion of

Christian love had suffered considerable discredit through years of inordinate sentimentalization. And he knew too, more simply, that the very word "love," especially linked to Christian teaching, just did not resonate well in the modern ear. So Merton disclaimed from the outset what he called a "mere subjective disposition to love"—for example, "good works" through checkbook charity—as gestures which may only encourage Christians "to dispense . . . with more efficacious social action." He had in mind a more thoroughgoing, concrete, and practicable view of redemptive love for which he first sought theological justifications and rationale.

"Anyone," Merton writes, "who has read the Prophets and the New Testament with any attention recognizes that one of the most essential facts about Christianity is that, being a religion of love, it is also at the same time a religion of dynamic change." Since God's immanent love, Merton argued, entered into history through the Incarnation, Christian love expands along the same scale as human problems in history. Because of the Incarnation, the hieratic, unknowable love of God, he reasoned, becomes concretely "manifested and active, through man, in man's world." Merton offered a New Testament theology pitched in such a way as to sharply counter the Marxist critique of Christianity as alienating and antihumanistic, a theology which supported Merton's feeling that Marx and other secular humanists had underestimated the dynamism of Christian tradition by focusing solely on a decadent and static Christian world view. The teachings of the Apostles, Merton stresses, "were directed precisely against what we have come to know as religious alienation." The entire thrust of the New Testament, he further submits, is its constant emphasis on "the priority of human values over conventionally 'religious' ones." "All through the New Testament we find the explicit contrast between a mere interior religiosity, abstract, and intentional, or even purely a matter of fantasy, and that love which, in uniting man to his brother of flesh and blood, thereby also unites him to the truth in God." Such an emphasis on Christian love as essentially experiential—a love, Merton contends, "manifested in actual love, not only in pious ideas and practices"—reveals "the heart of true Christian humanism . . . as a principle of divine life and love in man." As a corollary to the theology of redemptive love, Merton called upon the Christian mandate of *forgiveness* to shore up further his contention that Christian humanism was a humanism capable of transformation and dynamic change. "Above all," he writes, "we must understand the crucial importance of forgiveness as the heart of Christian humanism. Christianity is not merely a religious system which attempts to explain evil; it is a life of dynamic love which forgives evil and, by forgiving, enables love to transform evil into good. *The dynamic of Christian love is a dynamic of forgiveness"* (*L&L*, 145).

Merton mustered four theological justifications, then, in a effort to fashion a dynamic Christian humanism which could, and could alone he felt, yield insight into the profusion of problems unique to the modern scene. These are, summarized briefly, the concept of redemptive love and its empowering doctrine of the Incarnation; a New Testament theology stressing the primacy of the human person over the claims of legalistic religion; and the mandate of forgiveness fundamental to Christian ethical standards. We should note that these same canonical emphases were being simultaneously rejuvenated by a ferment of broader church reforms following Vatican II. At a time when Merton himself was struggling to rediscover a "new humanism" responsive to the realities of a post-Christian era, the church was similarly engaged in its own efforts to accommodate Catholicism to what it too recognized as "a new age of human history." Merton wrote several commentaries on the Council's *Constitution on the Church in the Modern World*. He pressed the Council's initiatives into the service of his own call for a more dynamic Christian world view and for a more thoroughgoing Christian involvement in the political, cultural, economic, and technological life of an increasingly complicated, interdependent global community.[7] By stressing, in particular, the essential altruistic character of Christian practice, the Council furthered Merton's own appeal for a "redemptive humanism" realized only through social action. "We are witnesses," the Council states, "of the birth of a new humanism, one in which man is defined first of all by his responsibility to his brothers and to history." "Nothing must [then] obscure the obligation of the Christian *to work with all men* in the building of a more human world" (Quoted in *L&L*, 139).

While Merton cited theological justifications to support a more socially responsible Christianity, he was clearly more concerned, as was the Council, with existential and pragmatic ramifications of the "new humanism." He proposed a litmus test for the redemptive love which undergirds that humanism as, simply, whether an individual attains a real union of love with other persons "through a realistic collaboration in the work of daily living in the world of hard facts in which man must work in order to eat." Redemptive love is not realized, he insisted, through such effete abstractions as, for example, "the speculations of pseudomysticism." Christian love manifests itself rather in the midst of common, even banal everyday realities. This pragmatic and utilitarian humanism is not, then, a strictly contemplative operation. It is not a Christianity of stoic quiescence. It does not "teach man to attain an inner ideal of divine tranquility . . . by abstracting himself from material things." It carried Merton well beyond the parameters of the monastic agenda. His proposal for a new humanism, that is to say, stressed salvation *of* the world over salvation *from* the world. A humanism that "unites man to man [in] authentic love" bears further witness, then, to Merton's evolution of self-images: from the ascetic and his claims on interiority to the pragmatic humanist whose spiritual progress was measured, not by degrees of self-transcendence, but through the quality of his interpersonal relationships and whether they advanced, as a practical matter, "the unity," Merton says, "of the human family."

— 4 —

While by no means prosaic, Merton's proposal for a new humanism based on a fine tuning of traditional Christian sources may not seem all that revolutionary. Its radical character resulted from Merton linking his religious humanism to social criticism. Merton could not divorce his evolving humanist commitments from an accompanying attitude increasingly critical of mass culture. His humanist inclinations deepened and clarified at a time when he furthered his understanding of the psychosocial forces at work in modern society. As he became more convinced of the dehumanizing effects of mass social organizations, he must have sensed a threat to the efficacy of his religious humanism, so naturally the pace of his social criticism quickened.

Merton's interest in the psychodynamics of mass culture traces back at least to 1954 when he first chanced upon the work of Erich Fromm. A profitable reading of Fromm's *Psychoanalysis and Religion* lead Merton to question the suspicion he had previously harbored toward modern psychology. After following up with *Man for Himself* and *Escape from Freedom*, he wrote Fromm and told him that his books had indeed inspired a reevaluation of "my originally premature judgment of psychoanalysis." "I notice a profound agreement," Merton went on to say, between Fromm's humanistic psychology and Christianity, itself "fundamentally humanistic" (*Ground*, 309).

Thus began a long and collaborative friendship in which the impress of Fromm's ideas became evident in the truculent social criticism Merton wrote during the decade following their initial exchange of letters. Much evidence points to Fromm's theory of social pathology, in particular, as a strong catalyst for Merton's later views. Judging from his reading journals and his letters to Fromm, *Escape from Freedom* and *The Sane Society* were most instrumental in shaping Merton's outlook on mass culture and its potential, as Merton said to Fromm, to debase "man's fundamental dignity as the image of God" (*Ground*, 309).

Of most interest to Merton was Fromm's proposal for a "pathology of normalcy." Based on anthropological speculation, sociological analysis, and clinical psychiatric evidence, Fromm postulated an inverse relationship between evolving social and institutional refinements and the general standard of mental hygiene among individuals. Economic, technological, and scientific innovations which contribute ostensibly to a higher standard of living, Fromm discovered, were accompanied by increased incidence of neuroses and other more serious psychiatric disorders—both self-destructive acts, like suicide and alcoholism, and behaviors of gross social maladjustment such as homicide. He speculated, then, that advanced industrial societies—whether totalitarian regimes (*Escape from Freedom*) or capitalistic societies (*The Sane Society*)—alienate individuals from the deepest and most profound of human needs. Modern social agglomerations, in short, *dehumanize*. Speaking as a psychotherapist, Fromm observed that individuals express their humanness through love and relatedness to other persons, through the exercise of imagination, creativity, reason, and ethical responsibility. As a social analyst, however, Fromm discovered that the prevailing authoritarianism, collective narcissism, and conformism characteristic of modern mass societies counter, frustrate and oppose the expression of such fundamental human needs. Runaway conformism, for example, seriously hinders, he argued, an individual's capacity to define himself authentically and spontaneously both in relation and contradistinction to his world.

We may detect a parallel here to Merton, for he later developed a similar dichotomous relationship between the individual and the social order in his writings on Christian humanism. In "Christian Humanism," for example, Merton argued that the redemptive love of the Christian humanist degenerates, in a culture of narcissism, to the regressive, infantile, and undeveloped love of alienated man. Fromm's contention that "much of modern society and its attitudes can be summed up as highly organized narcissism" easily carries over into Merton's claim in "Christian Humanism," that "narcissism is hostile to the true development of man's capacity to love," thus alienating him, as Fromm suspected, from the most basic of human needs.

There are several other avenues of influence from which we can trace Merton's social critique back to Fromm's social pathology. Merton's "Devout Meditation in Memory of Adolf Eichmann," for example, owes much to Fromm's view of the social order as sick and maladjusted. Astonished by a psychiatrist's report pronouncing Eichmann perfectly sane, Merton probes a scenario where definitional standards of sanity are turned inside out. "We equate sanity," Merton writes, "with a sense of justice [and] humanness." Given clinical evidence of Eichmann's "sanity," however, "it begins to dawn on us that it is precisely the sane ones who are the most dangerous."[8] In other words, to be perfectly well adjusted to a sick society is not to be "sane." This is exactly the position Fromm takes in *The Sane Society*. Whereas most therapies treated neurosis as an expression of an individual's maladjustment to social norms, Fromm turns that around and defines neurosis as an individual's successful adaptation to a neurotic society. For Merton, the case of Eichmann became a perfect expression, then, of Fromm's "pathology of normalcy." Here was a mass murderer, Merton reflected, by all clinical standards apparently "sane"—a consummate bureaucrat who had a good appetite, slept well, and who was kind to his pets. As Merton said in a letter to Fromm while reading *The Sane Society,* "I certainly agree with you that we ought to scrap the notion that mental health is merely a matter of adjustment to the existing society—to be adjusted to a society that is insane is not to be healthy" (*Ground*, 313).

There is an even more striking resemblance between Fromm's concluding remarks in *The Sane Society* and Merton's Cuadra Letter, his inaugural foray into radical social criticism. Such parallels suggest that Merton surveyed the Cold War political landscape in much the same terms as Fromm. In his psychological analysis of mass culture, Fromm attributes the growing disenfranchisement of the individual partly to the United States and the Soviet Union's mounting ideological retrenchment—the "two great social collosi," Fromm writes, who, "being afraid of each other, seek security in ever-increasing military rearmament."[9] Both countries—like Merton's colossal supertwins— "claim that their system promises final salvation for man, guarantees the paradise of the future. Both claim," Fromm continues, "that the opponent represents the exact opposite to himself, and that his system must be eradicated . . . if mankind is to be saved." Both countries profess radically conflicting, but nonetheless noble ideals. Turning to an examination of the similarities between the two superpowers, however, Fromm exposes the utter bankruptcy of such ideals—the same maneuver Merton would later use to condemn Gog and Magog's hypocritical, abstract professions of humanitarian concern. Fromm argues that each society aims only to insure its system's smooth functioning efficiency. The result is a subordination of individual needs to the successful operation and survival of the social system: the exploitation and alienation of the population, in other words, whether through psychological conditioning and manipulation, mass suggestion, monetary rewards or gross terror. Such a complex of alienating social forces contributes much to the anatomy of Merton's own hard-edged portrait of the global superpowers in which he shifts Fromm's political and economic analysis into an eschatological framework and arrives at the same conclusion: the "automatization" and "ever-increasing insanity," as Fromm feared, of collective life.

One would think that such a gloomy reading of modern affairs might have brought both Merton and Fromm to the verge of despair. But their rigorous humanist dissent spoke, too, of their mutual hope. The fact that their social critiques were tempered by a thoroughgoing humanism prevented Fromm and Merton from giving in to utter pessimism. "You and I certainly agree in being dissenters first of all," Merton wrote Fromm, "and in having much the same kind of dissent: in favor of basically human values" (*Ground*, 321). Their dialogue eventually turned, then—especially after Merton's pivotal decision of 1961—to a sustained discussion about appropriate remedies for the estrangement, insecurity, anxiety, and ennui which, both agreed, seriously imperiled the quality of modern life.

If both men basically agreed on a diagnosis of modernity's ills, strong differences surfaced in their prescriptions for a cure. Owing to his Marxist leanings, Fromm preferred to treat alienation from the structural perspective of political economy, whereas Merton naturally turned his inquiry into alienation through the prism of "the Christian concept of man." Healing the divisions between basic human needs and modern social structures became, for Fromm, a question of political and economic reform; for Merton, it was a matter of spiritual and moral renewal. Like Camus, Fromm discounted Christian proposals for human progress. Since "theistic concepts," he believed, "are bound to disappear in the future development of humanity," he proposed instead a social agenda that he called "Humanist Communitarian Socialism." Merton must have detected what he later criticized as a static Christianity at work in Fromm's agnostic doubts. Nonetheless, any fundamental disagreement between Fromm's socialism and Merton's theism did not flare into open contention between them. A deeper bond informed their dialogue. Their humanist dissent "in favor of basically human values" helped sustain a solidarity in spite of what Merton once confessed were "grave doctrinal differences."

In his letters to Fromm, Merton speculated informally on the Christian response to self-estrangement. He articulated a more rigorous formal position in a 1963 essay entitled "Note on the Psychological Causes of War by Erich Fromm," a response to Fromm's monograph "War Within Man: A Psychological Inquiry into the Roots of Destructiveness" in which Fromm formulates the concept of "the death wish" as an ultimate expression of modern man's self-estrangement. In his reply Merton accepts Fromm's psychological analysis, but he felt that the question of alienation needed further exploration beyond what he considered the limits of sociology and depth psychology. Merton could then use Fromm's psychological insights as a springboard to explore the religious dimensions of alienation, "a more fruitful avenue, at least for one in my field" (*F&V*, 112).

As he turned to pursue that avenue, Merton first defined alienation through recourse to a religious language that would complement Fromm's psychological terminology. Alienation, Merton argues, cuts off the modern person from entering "the spiritual and metaphysical substratum of . . . being." In defining alienation in terms of a religious ontology, Merton carefully constructs a dichotomy between "the empirical ego" and "the spiritual self," a dichotomy upon which his later social criticism firmly rests. As such, we may reasonably conclude that the groundwork of Merton's own radical humanist critique was laid through what he himself acknowledged as his "stimulating dialogue" with Erich Fromm. "When our empirical ego is taken," Merton writes, "as the true 'person,' the true 'self,' as the being who is the genuine subject of life, freedom, joy and fulfillment, or indeed of religious salvation, then we arrive at the most tragic frustrations and errors, because this implies a radical alienation of our true being. . . . There is no real love of life unless it is oriented to the discovery of one's true, spiritual self, beyond and above the level of mere empirical individuality, with its superficial enjoyments and fears" (113). Obviously, then, the problem of alienation was, for Merton, essentially a problem of *spiritual* alienation in which the individual perceives identity from the stunted perspective of a "transient, exterior self" and becomes estranged from what all higher religions, Merton reminds Fromm's readers, have recognized as the "ground" of being or the "base" of the soul.

Merton was not at all sanguine about the potential of popular religion to heal such divisions and reconnect the modern individual to that higher metaphysical ground of being. In fact he criticized contemporary religious trends, as he would the Death-of-God theologians, for having "betrayed man's inner spirit and turn[ing] him over, like Sampson, with his hair cut off and his eyes dug out, to turn the mill of a self-frustrating and self-destroying culture" (116).

Quick to dismiss the "organizational jollity [and] moral legalism" of popular religious trends, Merton nevertheless saw great potential in traditional religious wisdoms as he turned to the question of how to mend divisions in the modern psyche. He urged that more attention should be paid to traditional contemplative wisdoms which, he argued, "help man transcend his empirical self and find his 'true self' in an emptiness that is completely 'awake' because completely free of useless reflection"—in particular, such disciplines as prescribed by monastic practice. If the central aim in his exchange with Fromm was to cure modern alienation by transcending, as Fromm urged, the debilitating concept of the human person as an organic machine going about its biological business, then Merton offered a discipline of contemplative wisdom as "the highest . . . expression . . . of man's extraordinary capacities" (114). Simply put, Merton identified in Christian monasticism—especially in its procedures of training for self-unification—insights which both complemented and extended Fromm's social and psychological analysis of modern alienation. He discovered, moreover, potential therapeutic resources in contemplative practice appropriate to reclaiming the "vital spiritual energy" necessary, Merton believed, for personal integration *and* creative action in the world.

Most significantly, much of Merton's writing on solitude would bear an entirely new stamp after his dialogue with Fromm. Prior to that dialogue, Merton had pitched contemplation strictly as a discipline of self-transcendence. We may recall, in particular, Merton's earlier treatment of "infused contemplation"—the highest degree of contemplative practice to which the monk aspired—as a negating of the self and a severing of its ties to the quotidian world. Now, however, he reformulated that view into a perspective much more attuned to the psychological problem of alienation in modern life. Contemplation-as-asceticism, that is to say, gave way to a new emphasis on contemplation-as-rehabilitation. Merton evolved, then, from a sapiential, apophatic theory of contemplation—in which the self is lost in darkness as the soul plunges into the abyss of God's unknowability—to a cataphatic, therapeutic, more practicable view of solitude where the "authentic self" breaks through a surface of false social selves and is affirmed in the light of its true being.

Merton's encounter with Fromm's analysis of alienation further illustrates the broader revisionist pattern we have seen elsewhere in the evolution of Merton's mature humanism. Just as his study of Bonhoeffer and Camus led Merton to redefine a more socially responsible Christianity and arrive at a renovated literary identity as *artist engagé*, so too did Fromm's social critique force Merton to reconstitute traditional Catholic monasticism in such a way as to complement his newly refurbished Christian humanism. Like his "new humanism," Merton's curative solitude is much more amenable to the ordinary lives of ordinary people; it is not an ascetic regimen reserved for the monastic elite. In order to recover personal authenticity in modern mass society, Merton offered nothing less than a practical program of renewal through moratoriums of solitude. Simply break away, if only momentarily, he seemed to be admonishing, from the superficial charms and seductions of collective existence in order to regain "a sense of personal integrity, a sense of one's own reality and of one's ability to give himself to society."[10] In a later essay entitled "Creative

Silence," Merton writes, "we have to come to terms [with our inner selves] in silence [where] we recognize the need to be at home with ourselves in order that we may go out and meet others, not just with a mask of affability, but with real commitment and authentic love" (*L&L*, 41). It is doubtful that Merton would have arrived at this existential and humanist perspective on contemplative practice without, I am suggesting, his stimulating dialogue with Erich Fromm. At the very least, Merton's reformulation of the monastic agenda marks a change of course in his own journey. He abandoned a desert of selfless asceticism and entered a new "desert of loneliness," as he says in *Raids on the Unspeakable*, where one finds "the gifts of peace and understanding not simply in personal illumination and liberation, but by commitment and empathy, for the contemplative must assume the universal anguish and the inescapable condition of mortal man. The solitary, far from enclosing himself in himself, becomes every man. He dwells in the solitude, the poverty, the indigence of every man" (*Raids*, 18).

— 5 —

Thomas Merton's new humanism and his claims for the therapeutic potential of solitude shared two things in common. Each were responses to alienation as the distinguishing feature of life in advanced technological civilization. And each was forged from the crucible of critical social theories which sought, through rigorous dissent, to revitalize that civilization with humanist reforms.

Nowhere are those common elements more pronounced than in Merton's late poetry, especially *Cables to the Ace*, his radical experiment with the language of alienation and its implications for a new poetry—an antipoetry—of pure signs. Beginning with "Original Child Bomb" in 1962 and culminating in 1968 with the "Liturgies of Misunderstanding" which comprise *Cables*, much of Merton's new poetry entirely abrogates conventional symbolism in favor of *indicative signs*. The distinguishing hallmarks, especially of *Cables to the Ace*, include Merton's wholesale renunciation of conventional syntax, patterns of rational cognition, and inherited standards of poetic truth— which help account for the opacity and, at times, the utter abstruseness of his later poetry and its startling departure from his previous work. Merton's antipoetics suggests generally, then, that he believed a poetry stripped of symbolic language and moral imperative was a poetry essentially of unmeaning. Merton's new humanism, as we have seen, was the response of a committed humanist outraged by mass culture's potential to dehumanize. Similarly, his new poetry was the reaction of a poet angered by what Merton once described as "the spasmodic upheaval of language" reflected in mass culture modes of discourse.

This issue of Merton's antipoetics has been widely discussed in recent Merton scholarship,[11] and it is difficult to pin down a convincing consensus among literary critics, some of whom have gone to extraordinary lengths to unslip the Gordian knot of *Cables to the Ace*.[12] It may well be, in the final analysis, that Merton's purpose in *Cables* was only to frustrate critical good sense and create a postmodern paean to unmeaning whose sole aim was to dislocate decoding efforts. *Cables* might only be a repository of jokes, in fact, where Merton pokes fun at literary scholars who seem bent, as he once said of Joyce studies, on pursuing "an academic treasure hunt which [Joyce] took far less seriously than they." In any event, in the following discussion of Merton's late poetics we will try to avoid springing the playful traps strewn especially throughout *Cables*, choosing instead a safer, less problematic course: namely, that Merton's denatured antipoetics was his way of entering, as a poet, into the consciousness of alienated man and mimicking his style of speech—his way, he himself remarked, of declaring war on dehumanizing modes of contemporary discourse which exacerbate human alienation. Like Merton's radical humanism, his new poetry is, above all, a poetry of dissent.

One thing is certain: any discussion of Merton's antipoems cannot be separated from his continuing interest in critical social theories. Among important direct influences and models—such poets as Merton's friends Robert Lax and the Chilean antipoet Nicanor Parra[13]— Merton also needed a firm theoretical and philosophical basis for his experiments with a new poetry. He found that substratum in the writings of Herbert Marcuse whose model of a one-dimensional society easily merged into a partnership with the other dissident social theorists and culture critics who had previously shaped Merton's radical humanism.

Like Fromm's pathology of normalcy, Marcuse's critical social theory—set forth in *One-Dimensional Man*—uncovered serious deficiencies in modern industrial society which had led to an advanced state of human alienation. Marcuse argued that contemporary society was so dominated by technological processes such as production, distribution, and consumption that it had succumbed, in effect, to a technological totalitarianism. A society under the domination of its technology not only determines the occupations, skills, and attitudes of workers necessary to sustain its technological apparatus, but it must also control and define those workers' needs and aspirations. Technological totalitarianism—defined by Marcuse as "a non-terroristic economic-technical coordination which operates through the manipulation of needs by vested interests"[14]—effectively obliterates any distinctions between private and public life and individual and societal needs, thus creating a "one-dimensional society" comprised of one-dimensional persons. When economic and technological contingencies prevail, such things as individuality, dissent, and nonconformity lose their critical function—indeed, Marcuse claimed, they become socially useless.

With its emphasis on repression and subjugation of individual needs, Marcuse's theory carries profoundly antihumanistic consequences. He insisted that the prevailing societal forces of process, technique, and operation subvert the economic, political, and intellectual freedom of individuals. Individual needs, he stressed, collapse under the tyranny of vested collective interests "which perpetuate toil, aggressiveness, misery, and injustice." "The more rational, productive, technical, and total the repressive administration of society becomes," Marcuse concludes, "the more unimaginable the means and ways by which the administered individuals might break their servitude and seize their own liberation."[15]

Of particular interest to Marcuse, and more germane to his influence over Merton's new poetics, was the way in which one-dimensional behavior and thought are expressed in modern modes of communication.[16] Discourse in a one-dimensional society, Marcuse considered, must reflect the same repressive characteristics as the economic and political forces which manipulate individual needs in order to sustain the collective technological agenda. One-dimensional man's language, Marcuse claimed, testifies then to those societal forces responsible for his repression. Thus, language in a one-dimensional society has yielded to a progressive "functionalization" which repels nonconformist and idiosyncratic elements from the patterns and movement of speech. One-dimensional language is dominated by "operationalism"; it is the language of "technological reasoning" which rigorously promotes positive thinking and action, a language "that orders and organizes, that induces people to do, to buy, and to accept." Moreover, Marcuse argued, this functional language stifles "transcendent, critical notions"; it disables such rhetorical elements as "symbols of reflection, abstraction, development, contradiction." Above all, by devaluating transcendence, dissension, contradiction, and critical reflection, functional discourse *"militates against a development of meaning,"* Marcuse writes, because "it does not search for but establishes and imposes truth and falsehood."

Marcuse analyzed examples of one-dimensional discourse in such areas as contemporary patterns of syntax and usage, historical writing, political language, and advertising copy. He summarizes: "Abridgment of the concept in fixed images; arrested development in self-validating, hypnotic formulas; immunity against contradiction; identification of the thing (and of the person) with its function—these tendencies reveal the one-dimensional mind in the language that it speaks."[17] And he concludes: "In and for the society, this organization of functional discourse is of vital importance; it serves as a vehicle of coordination and subordination. The unified, functional language is an irreconcilably anti-critical and anti-dialectical language. In it, operational and behavioral rationality absorbs the transcendent, negative, oppositional elements of Reason."[18]

Ample evidence—stated explicitly or otherwise implied—suggests that Merton interpreted Marcuse's functional discourse as the language of alienated man. In *Zen and the Birds of Appetite,* for example, Merton announces his complete agreement with Marcuse's critique of one-dimensional thinking and discourse "in which," Merton writes, "the very rationality and exactitude of technological society and its various justifications, add up to one more total mystification" (*ZB,* 139–40). A close reading of Merton's essay "Symbolism: Communication or Communion?"—a commentary on the fate of symbolism in technological society—reveals most clearly the full extent of Marcuse's influence. Although Merton doesn't cite *One-Dimensional Man* directly, the essay resonates with Marcuse's ideas. I would argue, then, that Merton used Marcuse's insights into the functionalization of modern language as a springboard to discuss its spiritual ramifications, just as Merton had done with Fromm's psychological analysis of alienation in *The Sane Society.* If, as Marcuse claimed, modern language has succumbed to sheer operationalism, Merton argued, by extension, that the functionalization of discourse had been accompanied by a gradual *dysfunctionalization* of symbolic language. And it followed, for Merton, that this erosion of the symbol's efficacy and the accompanying deterioration in the modern person's capacity to respond to symbolic language are "alarming symptoms of spiritual decay."

In "Symbolism: Communication or Communion?", Merton attributes the degradation of symbolic language in scientific and technological society to "an incapacity to distinguish between the *symbol* and the *indicative sign.*" The sign's preeminent function, Merton explains, is to communicate practical and factual information. The symbol, in contrast, has no utilitarian value whatsoever; it does not convey information or *explain.* Given then the overwhelming premium set on function, operation, and process in modern mass culture, as Marcuse had argued, the nonutilitarian symbol is inevitably routed from the language of mass-man.

Although the symbol is useless as a means of communication, Merton emphasizes its higher purpose, "the purpose of going beyond practicality and purpose, beyond cause and effect" (*L&L,* 67). He stresses the transcendent function of symbolism, its role as a vehicle of union and synthesis, and its power to awaken "spiritual resonances" and evoke a deeper awareness "of the inner meaning of life and of reality itself." Symbols mobilize and animate vital resources of creativity and spirituality. Merton draws on the power of symbolic language itself in an effort to approximate the function and purpose of symbolism:

> A true symbol takes us to the center of [a] circle, not to another point on the circumference. A true symbol points to the very heart of being, not to an incident in the flow of becoming. The symbol awakens awareness, or restores it. Therefore, it aims not at communication but at communion. Communion is the awareness of participation in an ontological or religious reality: in the mystery of being, of human love, of redemptive mystery, of contemplative truth.
>
> The purpose of the symbol, if it can be said to have a "purpose," is not to increase the quantity of our knowledge and information but to deepen and enrich the *quality* of life itself by bringing man into communion with the mysterious sources of vitality and meaning, of creativity, love, and

truth, to which he cannot have direct access by means of science and technique (68).

The vital role of the symbol [then] is precisely this: to express and encourage man's acceptance of his own center, his own ontological roots in a mystery of being that transcends his individual ego (65).

As Merton positions his discussion of symbolism's transcendent function into the context of modern technological civilization—a context clearly identifiable as Marcuse's one-dimensional society—Merton's commentary pivots sharply into critique and lament. One-dimensional society, after all, obliterates the distinction between public and private existence; therefore, it bars contact with those ontological roots of which symbols aim to evoke awareness. Modes of modern communication, which Marcuse showed to be dominated by utilitarian processes, effectively disable the higher purpose of symbolism to transcend, as Merton argued, practicality and cause and effect. The operational and functional rationality of modern discourse—a central premise in Marcuse's critique—absorbs and denies transcendent vocabularies. In one-dimensional society, the symbol as a vehicle of communion, in short, surrenders to a discourse of signs with its sole purpose of identifying facts and conveying information.

Merton also acknowledges, at least implicitly, Marcuse's claims for the totalitarian character of functional language, a language that, as Marcuse says, serves only to induce people into consumption habits. Elsewhere—for example in Merton's "War and the Crisis of Language," a much sharper protest against denatured contemporary prose than his jeremiad on the degradation of symbolism—Merton cites many examples in modern usage which illustrate the breakdown of communication into deception. By analyzing advertising copy, political jargon, and even religious language, Merton parallels Marcuse's argument that such discourse modalities reveal a language of "power," "self-enclosed finality," and "totalist dictatorship" in action. This is a language of final utterance and hypnotic formulation, a language, Merton writes, where "the insatiable appetite for the tautological, the definitive, the *final*" (*NVA,* 238) defies contradiction and dissent and, as Marcuse stressed, militates against the development of meaning, what Merton prefers to call "the contamination of reason . . . by inherent ambiguity." Merton culls specific examples from military terminology—such as "kill ratio," "pacification," "free zone," "liberation"—which reflect precisely those operational characteristics that Marcuse claimed preclude the genuine development of meaning. Such terms are, first and foremost, rooted in cliché. They exemplify what Marcuse described as the abridgment of concepts in fixed images: that is, they oversimplify and economize to the point of either obscuring or trivializing the concepts which underpin them. This is a terminology, as Merton would say, that contaminates reason through purposeful ambiguity. Specifically, Merton explains, a "free zone" is an area where anything that moves can be assumed to be the enemy and shot. He cites the case of an army major who explained the shelling of a South Vietnamese village as "liberation"; "It became necessary," the major reports, "to destroy the town in order to save it." More recent examples would include the CIA's training manual for anti-Sandinista rebels in Nicaragua which urges "the selective use of violence" against government officials (assassination) and proposes the "elimination" of a popular Contra supporter in order to create a "martyr" for the cause (disloyalty and murder).

This is, by and large, a discourse of gross deception, evasion, euphemism. It is a businesslike and antiseptic terminology in which clinical certainty successfully masks sinister connotations. Such terms seem immune to contradiction in their masterful and unsentimental justifications of the otherwise ugly business of war. Although the above examples are drawn from military jargon, their distinguishing features, as Marcuse and Merton show, extend to all manner of linguistic forms in one-dimensional society. What unifies the discourse in such a society is the will to power which dictates ethically neutral speech patterns. As Merton explains, the logic of power speaks the language of power, "a language that is all the more pervasive because it is proud of being ethically illiterate and because it accepts, as realistic, the basic irrationality of its own tactics." It is, above all, a language inherently dehumanizing and contemptuous of fundamental human values and needs—a discourse, Merton writes, "of double-talk, tautology, ambiguous cliché, self-righteous and doctrinaire pomposity, and pseudoscientific jargon that mask a total callousness and moral insensitivity, indeed a basic contempt for man" (NVA, 246).

Returning to Merton's discussion of the degradation of symbolism, the dynamics of his argument reduce to a basic conflict between Marcuse's totalitarian functional discourse and Merton's own interpretation of the purpose of symbolism, between a language which indoctrinates truth and falsehood and a language which promotes the search for truth. Drawing on a line from *Cables to the Ace*, Merton maintains that nothing less is at stake than the survival of symbolic language in "a culture of bare-faced literal commands." Sounding a note of serious alarm, Merton questions that survival as long as the modern person, he suggests, remains "cut off from any reality except that of his own processes . . . and that of the extraordinary new world of his machines." "When man is reduced to his empirical self and confined within its limits, he is, so to speak, excluded from himself, cut off from his own roots, condemned to . . . a wilderness of externals . . . [where] there can be no living symbols" (*L&L*, 65).

Not willing to conclude his reflections on the dysfunctionalization of symbolic language on such a pessimistic note, Merton calls on artists and poets—"the ones most aware of the disastrous situation [and] for that very reason the closest to despair"—to restore vitality to the already corrupt and degenerate state of symbolism and check the process which continues to devalue symbolic language in technological society. He calls for a renewal of wisdom that, like his new humanism, "must be more than a return to the past, however glorious. We need a wisdom appropriate to our own predicament," a wisdom that recognizes and cooperates with the "spiritual and creative vitality" of symbolism and refuses, above all, any complicity with the logic and language of power. "One thing is certain," he notes finally; "if the contemplative . . . and the poet . . . forsake [that] wisdom and join in the triumphant, empty-headed crowing of advertising men and engineers of opinion, then there is nothing left in store for us but total madness" (79).

That last comment is somewhat perplexing, considering especially *Cables to the Ace,* in which Merton, contrary to his own advice for fellow poets, eschews symbolic language. By extrapolating modes of mass culture discourse into a new poetry devoid of symbolism, the practicing poet of *Cables* sounds as if he is compromising the essayist of "Symbolism: Communication or Communion?" At least it may appear as though Merton fails to heed his own counsel because *Cables*, while by no means an exercise in "total madness," is nonetheless an antipoetry that shuns the vitality and wisdom of traditional symbolism; it is a poetry that prefers instead to join in what Merton elsewhere condemns as empty-headed crowing along the road to lunacy. Any hints of conflict, however, between Merton's advice to other poets and his own practice of antipoetry should not be construed as such clear evidence of cross-purposes or contradictions. After all, by mimicking the discourse of admen and engineers of opinion in *Cables* Merton is, in effect, condemning that discourse. Besides, Merton's approach to the fundamental issue of language, and especially the fate and the practice of poetry in contemporary society, is complicated by a familiar separation of perspectives, by two distinct personae with separate obligations.

As a priest, for example, Merton viewed the degradation of symbolism in technological society as evidence of spiritual decay. This is the voice, then, that issues apocalyptic warning signals in "Symbolism: Communication or Communion?" This is the persona that, in "Answers on Art and Freedom," calls on contemporary poets to liberate themselves from society's "coercive or seductive pressures" and assesses the poet's responsibility as "a moral obligation to maintain his own freedom and his own truth" (*Raids*, 170–71). It is as a priest that Merton addresses a gathering of Latin American poets whom he urges, in "Message to Poets," "to remain united against . . . falsehoods, against all power that poisons man, and subjects him to the mystifications of bureaucracy , commerce and the police state." Modern poets must seek their salvation, he further intones, by renouncing "tutelage to established political systems or cultural structures" and their "impurity of language and spirit" (155–59). As a spiritual counsellor, Merton defines the poet in such homilies as these as a prophet who restores a spiritual vision to reality and the future.

But as a practicing poet, Merton seemed more interested in parody than prophecy. As a poet himself, Merton viewed the degradation of symbolism in technological society as opening up new possibilities for an innovative poetics: a radically experimental, postmodern antipoetry notable for its lack of moral fervor or prophetic inspiration, a poetry that does not resist "the mystifications of bureaucracy, commerce and the police state" but rather submits to such mystifications. Both the poet and the priest recognized, as Merton—echoing Marcuse—says in *Zen and the Birds of Appetite*, that "Western culture . . . [had] reached the climax of entire totalitarian rationality of organization and of complete absurdity and self-contradiction" (*ZB*, 140). The priest resisted that recognition because it raised the specter of a modern ethos alien to his spiritual traditions. But the poet, especially of *Cables to the Ace*, accepted it and sought an aesthetic appropriate to what Marcuse had shown to be a one-dimensional society distin-guished by one-dimensional thought and behavior. If, when speaking as a priest, Merton urged other poets to liberate themselves from that ethos, as a poet he entered it and began experimenting with a poetry, as he notes in a review of Roland Barthe's *Writing Degree Zero*, "which reminds the reader not to get lost . . . in false complicities with the message or the emotion, not to get swept away by illusions of inner meaning, a slice of life, a cosmic celebration, or an eschatological vi-sion" (*LE*, 142). This is a poetry—an *antipoetry*—that does just the opposite of what traditional poetry, empowered by symbolism, should do. Antipoetry does not bring the reader "into communion with . . . mysterious sources of vitality and meaning, of creativity, love, and truth." Merton defines the purpose of antipoetry and the role of the antipoet most succinctly in an entry in *The Asian Journal:* "The anti-poet 'suggests' a tertiary meaning which is *not* 'creative' and 'original' but a deliberate ironic feedback of cliché, a further referential meaning, alluding, by its tone, banality, etc., to a *customary and abused context*, that of an impoverished and routine sensibility, and of the 'mass-mind,' the stereotyped creation of quantitative response by 'mass-culture'" (*AJ*, 286). The antipoet abandons traditional poetic discourse because "he can no longer trust the honesty of his custom-ary dialogue with the rest of society." He must surrender "all charis-matic exaltation, all aspiration to power, all *numen*, all that would seem to give him some ascendency over the reader" (*LE*, 145). Even as early as *Conjectures of a Guilty Bystander* Merton had already begun to suspect that in a culture dominated by double-talk and propaganda there is not much left for the poet to do except mimic the speech of propagandists. (*CGB*, 241ff.).

In a manner of speaking, then, the antipoet declares himself poet laureate of Marcuse's one-dimensional society. "Marcuse," Merton ac-knowledges in *The Asian Journal*, "has shown how mass culture tends to be anticulture—to stifle creative work by the sheer volume of what is 'produced,' or reproduced. In which case, poetry . . . must start with an awareness of this contradiction and *use* it—as anti-poetry—which freely draws on the material of superabundant nonsense at its disposal . . . and feed [it] back . . . into the mass consumption of pseudo-culture" (*AJ*, 118).

So the following discussion of entries selected from *Cables to the Ace* (*CP*, 395–454) builds on the fundamental proposition that Merton's radical antipoetics incorporates many elements of Marcuse's "functional discourse" in one-dimensional society. As indicated earlier, however, any effort to give a comprehensive and unified reading of *Cables* is bound to be frustrated by its apparently purposeful uncenteredness in which disparate elements tumble together in disarray. While melancholic (as in Cable 12, for example), it is at times utterly comedic, as when a midget suddenly pops out in Cable 27 and cries, "Hats off! Hats off to the human condition!" In a prologue which is bullying to the point of insult, Merton sets the stage for an aggressiveness that also surfaces in many Cables, the same sort of aggression that heated Merton's Cuadra Letter and prompted him to confess, once he cooled down, to a certain petulance rooted in egotism. Some Cables are grossly, though playfully nonsensical, while in others the babble gives way to pensive utterance (Cables 37 and 38). One may wonder too why Merton saw fit to include some of the love poems he wrote for the nurse in Louisville: for example Cable 78, "Harmonies of Excess," where a serene lyricism seems so discordant and compromised as it jostles against the opposite moods of its neighboring entries. All of this makes for a disorienting reading experience, a disruptive, automatic, random conjoining of oddball elements—"mosaics," Merton called them, or "Familiar Liturgies of Misunderstanding"—where poetry and antipoetry, verse and prose blocks fire, so to speak, in cylinders oddly out of time. Nonetheless, we can at least identify a major leitmotif that trails through *Cables to the Ace:* it can be read profitably as a sustained Marcusian meditation on the dysfunctionalization of symbolic language in technological society—an antipoetry *qua* social criticism.

In Cables 1 and 2, for example, Merton immediately pits the quantitative function of signs against the qualitative values of the symbol and judges the outcome. "Cables"—as in *telegraphic* cables—are themselves signs because their purpose is to convey information, to communicate not commune. In Cables 1 and 2, then, messages skip across the page like electric pulses—short syntactical bursts—"played and sung" as if Merton scored them for a discordant technocratic symphony.

1

Edifying cables can be made musical if played and sung by full-armed societies doomed to an electric war. A heavy imperturbable beat. No indication where to stop. No messages to decode. Cables are never causes. Noises are never values. With the unending vroom vroom vroom of the guitars we will all learn a new kind of obstinacy, together with massive lessons of irony and refusal. We assist once again at the marriage of heaven and hell.

2

A seer interprets the ministry of the stars, the broken gear of a bird. He tests the quality of stone lights, ashen fruits of a fire's forgotten service. He registers their clarity with each new lurch into suspicion. He does not regret for he does not know. He plots the nativity of the pole star, but it neither sets nor rises. Snow melts on the surface of the young brown river, and there are two lids: the petals of sleep. The sayings of the saints are put away in air-conditioned archives.

"Cables are never causes. Noises are never values." The higher critical functions of causation and value judgment are drowned out here by the hypnotic "heavy imperturbable beat" of Cable (sign) language and absorbed into the omnipresent white noise of vrooming guitars, captured elsewhere, in Cable 77, in a better image as "the copyrighted tornado / Of sheer sound." The seer in Cable 2 speaks a different language. He interprets and tests and registers clarity. His knowledge derives from intuition. His plotting of the origin of a star does not follow the precise mathematical procedures of astronomy. He exercises higher order cognitive and intellectual faculties, in other words, which Marcuse claims are essentially those of the nonconformist. But the fate of Merton's nonconformist poet-seer in a world where there are "no messages to decode" is hinted at by the nature of the objects that the seer trains his intuitive powers upon. Those objects are metallic and strangely funereal: "the broken gear of a bird," "stone lights" and "ashen fruits," objects which might clutter a sterile, even irradiated landscape. The potential symbolic value of a bird or of lights and fruits is negated anyway by the adjectives which modify them. The seer's ultimate fate is indeed sealed when Merton negotiates a final nonsequitur leap: "The sayings of the saints are put away in air-conditioned archives."

Merton arrives at a similar judgment in Cable 5 where the form of commentary first changes from prose blocks to verse.

Gem notes
Of the examiner
Or terminal declarations:

> The Directors
> Have engineered a surprise
> You will not easily discover:

The speech—the "notes"—of the examiner in these lines is that language of self-enclosed finality, or "terminal declaration," which Marcuse identifies as the chief characteristic of totalitarian discourse. It is the speech of directors and dictators and those "engineers of opinion" whom Merton had previously ostracized in his essay on the degradation of symbolism. Their surprise is not only hard to discover but, once discovered, it quickly slips away.

> Come shyly to the main question
> There is dishonor in these wires
> You will first hesitate then repeat
> Then sing louder
> To the drivers
> Of ironic mechanisms
> As they map your political void

Functional discourse dehumanizes; there is dishonor in the language of cables and electric wires. But even if the "you" addressed in the stanza hesitates through faint recognition, he still seems doomed to a hypnotic speech of drives and mechanisms. Cut off from participation in a deeper ontological reality, he enters a landscape of his own emptiness where the directors happily survey his "political void." And among the "many original / Side effects" of residence in that wasteland of mechanisms, that ethos of operationalism, is that "Each nominal conceit / Will be shot down by an electric eye" and "Events are finally obscure forever." Symbol and metaphor, along with critical self-reflection and indeed the very evidence of history itself—those things that Marcuse identifies, in short, as "transcendent functions"—are stifled and incapacitated until

> You wake and wonder
> Whose case history you composed
> As your confessions are filed
> In the dialect
> Of bureaux and electrons.

Merton had previously defined symbolic language as awakening awareness or restoring it; he characterized the symbol as a vehicle of self-discovery. But here functional and operational speech prevail—

"the dialect," that is to say, "Of bureaux and electrons"—so the case history of self-awareness, arrived at through self-reflection and confession, becomes little more than fodder for the filing cabinet, like those sayings of saints shelved away in hermetic archives. Little wonder that Merton immediately follows in Cable 6 with Caliban's curse: "The red plague rid you / For learning me your language!"

Throughout these early entries Merton establishes clear links between his own Cables and those various features that Marcuse identifies as preeminent hallmarks of functional discourse in advanced technological society. In the Cables which follow Merton continues to expand those linkages by further developing the controlling image of electricity, an especially ironic choice in light of Merton's own death by accidental electrocution. Electricity is exquisitely organized power transmitted through networks of highly organized circuits, cables, conduits. It is a perfect image for the coordination of functional energy, and Merton uses it to portray a social environment, as Marcuse might say, entirely dominated by its technological apparatus, a social order wired-in to process and technique. Merton charts patterns of electrical flow from the specific to the global—from "academies of electric renown" to "the electric village" and "the electric world" and finally to an "electric universe." Ultimately the "electric cosmos" itself comes to resemble a macrocosmic circuit board where everything— commerce, industry, agriculture, politics, education, metaphysics, religion as well as all modes of human discourse—flows through "imitable wires," "everlasting carbon vines," and "electric walks." Time itself marches in the electronic parade, for even "the next ice-age [is programmed] from end to end."

Technological totalitarianism—the politics of Merton's electric village—must insulate itself, as Marcuse further reasoned, against any nonconformist or idiosyncratic elements which might challenge the organization and control of vested collective interests. It stands to reason that errant pulses or surges are to Merton's electric ethos what dissent, nonconformity, and individuality are to Marcuse's one-dimensional society. Following the metaphor, an electric cosmos must be glitch-proof and protected against anything that threatens to blow a fuse or trip a circuit.

In a further allusion to the operational and behavioral rationality that Marcuse claimed necessarily governed one-dimensional thought and behavior, Merton devotes Cable 19 to a vignette depicting a man wired to a rat's brain in a behavioral scientist's laboratory. It is a morbid presentation of human behavior shaped and controlled by the mechanisms of pleasure and punishment. "Split second doses of motivation / Keep you in stitches," Merton writes, and human ecstasies are triggered by rats pushing "pleasure buttons"—a wretched nightmare that effectively underscores Marcuse's contention that "the more total the repressive administration of society becomes, the more unimaginable the means and ways by which the administered individuals might break their servitude and seize their own liberation." Portraits of such "administered individuals" abound throughout *Cables*. Merton uses the behavioral scenario, for example, in Cable 52 where strictly controlled and ordered human behavior is likened to the robotic activity of an ant, obediently carrying out "his appointed task" and mindlessly following "his appointed round / In the technical circuit." Or consider the businessman in Cable 50 whose entire being is shaped by the pleasures of "Crackling new money." He worships "truth-telling twenties / And fifties that understand," and he offers a prayer to "the cunning dollar": "Make me numb / And advertise / My buzzing feedbacking / Business-making mind." His consciousness and conscience and spirit owe allegiance to a cult of commerce that provides for all his values, aspirations, and needs. "The dollar . . . tells me no lie /. . . [It] knows and loves me / And is my intimate all-looking doctor." Like this disciple of commerce, all of Merton's portraits of administered, alienated individuals reflect operational minds in action: minds that define objectives—pleasure, wealth— and identify means—conformity, commerce—while betraying an astonishing ineptness in such things as ethical calculation, moral reasoning, and critical self-reflection.

Rats, ants, robotic businessmen . . . these, as Merton would no doubt prefer to say, are antiportraits of human beings reduced to ciphers by the cult of order and organization. These are persons dehumanized, alienated, stripped of their individuality, just like the woman in Cable 43 who is transformed into an empty caricature of the Ideal Woman by the adman—the shaman of one-dimensional society—who sells her a new face. Here again the operational mind springs into action: a mind that defines an objective (beauty) and identifies a means (cosmetics) without the slightest pause for or interest in any authentic self-awareness. Here is a ritual seduction, an esoteric initiation into the cult of eternal youth, a baptism in cosmetics full of magic and mysterious charms. "Let us cool your bitter sweet charm," chants the adman, "with incense and verse." He conjures a "rich pigment," "a new glaze of ours

> . . . to melt away
> Stubborn little worries known as lines
> To restore with magic lanolin our flawless picture of YOU
> Yes you, our own pity-making sweet charade of oils

This is only one entry among many others in *Cables* where Merton parodies the popular genre of Madison Avenue. Like Marcuse, Merton was fascinated by the language of advertisement, especially its incantory and charismatic power, as Marcuse said, to induce people to do, to buy, to accept. While working on *Cables* Merton received regular consignments of ad copy which he requested from friends. "I would much appreciate good, gaudy, noisy *ad* material," he mentioned to W. H. Ferry, noting "how conscious [I am] of the wacky material there is to exploit in ads." (Apparently Merton had his limits. After receiving a bundle of such ads, he quickly returned notice: "enough! . . . Am still retching. Weak stomach, getting old. . . . Old gut won't take it. This will be quite enough to produce the long poetic retch I was planning.")[19] As he said in "War and the Crisis of Language," it is "the vocation of the poet—or the antipoet—*not* to be deaf to [advertisements] but to apply his ear to their corrupt charms." Among such consignments of ad material, and perhaps as a prototype for the cosmetics ad that he parodies in Cable 43, Merton cites in that essay the example of an Arpège hair spray advertisement culled from *The New Yorker:* "A delicate-as-air-spray / Your hair takes on a shimmer and sheen that's wonderfully young. / You seem to spray new life and bounce right into it," etc. He celebrates this hair spray verse as a "masterpiece" of antipoetry that stands "inviolate in its own victorious rejection of meaning." Like the lanolin magic of Cable 43, Arpège "is endowed with a finality so inviolable that it is beyond debate and beyond reason . . . at once totally trivial and totally definitive." That "it has nothing to do with anything real" seems of such little consequence or concern. And like the "flawless picture of YOU" captured in Merton's own ad parody, Arpège "is so magic that it not only makes you smell good, it 'coifs' you with a new and unassailable identity." By applying his ear to the charm of ad copy in *Cables*, Merton not only parodies its linguistic features but he enters into the mentality of salesmanship and what he firmly believed to be its morally illiterate consciousness. That, as Merton said, is the antipoet's duty: to "feed back" for mass culture consumption a language that testifies to the impoverished and dehumanized sensibility of the mass mind.

That sensibility, moreover, is so vulnerable to the persuasive and hypnotic power of manipulation, as Marcuse argues, that its higher order intellectual skills are crippled. Such cognitive functions as abstraction, conceptualization, synthesis, demonstration, and critique atrophy when operational logic (designation, identification, assertion, imitation, etc.) dominates consciousness and modes of thought. If modes of discourse reflect modes of thought, it follows that language itself becomes what Marcuse calls a "closed language" that "does not demonstrate and explain—it communicates decision, dictum, command."[20]

Much of the abstruseness and the frankly annoying nonsense of *Cables*, then, might well be the result of Merton implementing a Marcuse-like "closed language" and capitalizing especially on the disruption of meaning inevitable in a language closed to higher order cognitive functions. The antipoet not only "feeds back" an impoverished sensibility, he taps the rich resources of "superabundant nonsense" at his disposal, as Merton notes in *The Asian Journal* with direct reference to Marcuse, and returns it to mass culture circulation. Throughout *Cables* Merton often taps into that reservoir; he borrows popular discourse modalities and parodies their formal structures while simultaneously disrupting and disjointing patterns of meaning.

For example, after culling jargon common to manufacturing and industry, Merton assembles such terminology into a syntactical cackle in Cable 25: "Elastic programs to draft nonspecialist energy and rotate funds to speedup intake of output." In addition to ad copy, similarly farcical constructions are used to parody business memoranda (Cable 26), academic discourse (Cable 33), gossip columns (Cable 41), even cut lines for newspaper photographs (Cable 70): "Clean-cut pirate meets and befriends priceless stolen owl." The ultimate dismembering of semantics occurs in Cable 48, a ludicrous burlesque of a newscast. It is sufficient to quote only the first stanza.

> Children of large nervous furs
> Will grow more pale this morning
> In king populations

> Where today drug leaders
> Will promote an ever increasing traffic
> Of irritant colors
> Signs of this evident group
> Are said to be almost local

Here are typical references to time and place: this morning, today, local. And Merton selects stock verbs common to any news broadcast: promote, are said to be. But the factual certainty one expects from a newscast is derailed by the passive voice. Besides, time, place, and action are mediated by nonsensical constructions. Absurd adverb and adjective clauses, random modifiers, and nonsequitur transitions sabotage logical semantic relationships until meaning is so disrupted that the broadcast collapses into an inane babble, into "a copyrighted tornado / Of sheer sound."

Let's consider finally Cable 30 where these previously discussed elements of antipoetry fuse together into a distinctly Orwellian meditation on the utter banality of an utterly ordinary day: the day, we might say, of a typical one-dimensional citizen in a typical one-dimensional society. During this day, events are strung together by a chain reaction of signals, and people go about their activities as if switched on and off by terminals in a grid. The functional discourse of signs and its potential to dehumanize; the controlling image of electricity; totalitarianism, operationalism, automatization; the parody of ad copy; and the broken syntax of nonsense—all of these are indiscriminately conjoined to depict the narcosis of human routine in an environment cluttered with signs. Morning begins with the ubiquitous sounds of sizzling bacon and perking coffee ("the chatter of meats" and the "Nine o'clock boil"), which in turn trigger an exodus of crowds and traffic into high-rise buildings topped with flashing neon signs—"An electric goat's head / Turns and smiles / Turns and smiles"—which in turn switch on a counter-exodus back through "Names Omens Tunnels" to "Night sanctuaries / Imaginary refuge / Full of flowers" and "The solemn twittering of news," until the entire day disappears into a vortex of ultimate unmeaning as

> The iron voice in the next apartment
> Cries NOW
> And you flush the toilet.

Cable 30 is probably the purest example of antipoetry in *Cables to the Ace*. It is composed entirely of signs, like the literal blinking tautology of that absurd flashing neon goat's head. The crowds that shuffle along "in cotton mist / And chloroform" are composed of entirely alienated individuals bereft of ontological roots, so the poem itself is bereft of symbolic language. Cable 30, that is to say, refuses any participation in an ontological or religious reality which, as Merton claimed, symbols evoke awareness of. There is no "mystery of being, of human love, of redemptive mystery, of contemplative truth" in Cable 30's "energy of motors." Even the pitiful clergyman in the anti-poem joins the mindless semiotic march as he "goes by / With a placard / 'You can still win.'" Christian confidence in salvation—The Good News—is just another message, another billboard ad in this ethos of signals and signs.

Young Man Merton:
A Speculative Epilogue

> Greatness . . . harbors massive conflict.
>
> —*Erik Erikson on Martin Luther*

The cleric swept up in Cable 30's stuporous cavalcade of mass men bluntly illustrates that religious were not exempt from Merton's critique as he surveyed a contemporary social landscape of dehumanization and alienation. That stark image of the cleric as adman for Christian hope also reveals the extent to which Merton's associations with the clerical identity had changed during a long struggle with his own self-image as monk. In his religious verse two decades earlier, Merton's rigorous affiliation with Christian mystics' and martyrs' heroic otherworldliness circumscribed his unassailable fidelity to the religious vocation. With awe and trembling, Merton described his first encounter with a Catholic priest as he sketched, in *The Seven Storey Mountain*, a portrait of an enigmatic Jesuit walking the streets of Montaubaun. During his first retreat at Gethsemani, the monks impressed Merton as superhuman dynamos innervating the entire universe and single-handedly preventing America's spiritual doom and material destruction. Yet twenty six years later, Merton could openly question his solidarity to the monastic identity. In an antipoem that bore not the slightest resemblance to his pious psalmody of the forties, Merton could cast a cleric as a player in a tragic burlesque. An ideal role model, once above reproach and completely immune to the vicissitudes of worldly life, could later give way to an unflattering caricature of a religious seduced into the humdrum march of one-dimensional men. While Merton continued to profess an unconditional affection for his fellow monks, he could, on occasion, betray uneasiness about living among "lotus eaters" and, in a rare moment of uncharacteristic callousness and insensitivity, seem even to imply that "they are for the most part idiots."[1] During the period of his early monastic formation, Merton invariably insisted that his role as monk could only be fulfilled through a selfless detachment found in infused contemplation. Two decades later his "opinion [that] a monk did not become a monk until he had gone through Luther's experience and knew that the monastic life was futile"[2] was forged as much by Merton's renovated identity as a humanist/dissident as it was by his empathy for the experience of monastic crisis. This profound revolution in identity—from an institutional role model to an independent, fully autonomous self-image—was captured poignantly by an old friend of Merton's who observed that he had literally traded uniforms over the years and switched "from cowl to blue jeans."[3]

Throughout this study of Thomas Merton, I have avoided, for the most part, using any theory of human development to explain the shifts in self-image described above—or indeed to justify the particular stresses apparent in my reading of Merton's life history. I have chosen instead to focus on Merton's own narrative as he himself constructed it through an extraordinary and painstaking record of self-reflections. I have tried to let Merton speak for himself. I have followed him through a prodigious canon of autobiographical writing which at times may seem to verge on self-obsession, but which always reflects integrity and tenacity as Merton reports on the private conflicts and public crises gradually shaping the evolution of his identity and marking the stages toward an eventual breakthrough to his "quiet but articulate place" in modern letters. Perhaps I may be permitted, then, to reconstruct in these closing comments a broader overview of an otherwise exceptionally complicated personal history. If only to stimulate further study and continued fascination with the Merton biography, a synthesis is in order. In seeking a critical framework appropriate to that task of consolidation, I have found no paradigm more suitable to the general configurations of Merton's life history than the psychoanalyst Erik Erikson's pioneering work on human development and identity formation. In what follows, I offer an Eriksonian mapping of Merton's evolving identity, hoping that what may be lost in nuance and detail can be more than compensated by a thought-provoking analysis worth serious consideration and perhaps further investigation.

— 1 —

A survey of Erik Erikson's major writing quickly reveals just how applicable his psychoanalytic investigations are to the evolution of Thomas Merton's radical humanism. *Identity: Youth and Crisis* stands as Erikson's major theoretical and clinical statement. He is best known, however, for his ground-breaking contributions to psychobiography, a field of social science which aims to apply psychoanalytic practice and clinical evidence to the lives of creative individuals. In his clinical studies, Erikson frequently turns to such figures as George Bernard Shaw, William James, and Freud as case illustrations of his developmental theories, but it is in his full-scale studies of major religious personalities that Erikson offers most convincing evidence for the central premise of his developmental theory: namely, the early adulthood identity crisis traces back to unresolved conflicts encountered during previous stages of an individual's psychological development. In his books on Gandhi and Luther, for example, Erikson focuses particular attention on their early adulthood; he discovers in each man that an acute early mid-life identity crisis constituted a moratorium during which old childhood identity conflicts were revived and "re-resolved." This period of isolation, withdrawal, and critical inner searching, Erikson argues, is essential to understanding the dynamic process of confused and conflicted young men becoming great ones.

While a bit premature, a scenario derived from Erikson's *Young Man Luther* nonetheless reveals a psychobiographical pattern by no means unlike the general outline of Thomas Merton's life history. A somber and harsh childhood, Erikson maintains, laid the psychological groundwork for a severe identity crisis Luther suffered in his early twenties. Acute identity confusion drove Luther to the silence of a monastery; he entered into a prolonged identity moratorium during which regressive conflicts continued to plague him. Running their course toward eventual resolution, such identity conflicts gradually led to a creative identity breakthrough: a catharsis, Erikson concludes, that simultaneously healed the emotional wounds of Luther's childhood and liberated him to "formulate for himself and for all mankind," Erikson writes, "a new kind of ethical and psychological awareness."[4]

Generally speaking, Erikson treats the major developmental crisis of early adulthood as, in effect, an identity conflict. Negative identity fragments remaining from previous developmental stages collide with positive identity elements that the young adult discovers in new idealized role identifications. This is best illustrated by two mutually exclusive existential assertions: "I am what I will myself to be" versus "I am what my past has shaped me to become." Erikson argues that such fundamental identity conflicts seek resolution during the identity moratorium of early adulthood so that one can negotiate the remaining developmental stages unified and reconciled, prepared to accept oneself and to embrace with less resignation and ambivalence one's place in society. The identity crisis shapes and tempers a sense of adult duty. Once resolved, an individual is ready to engage the balance of the life course with ideological commitment, caring, trust, a capacity for intimacy and sharing, and, above all, a sense of obligation to future generations.

Most important, the process of identity formation, according to Erikson, does not take place in a vacuum outside of history. His psychobiographies of Gandhi and Luther are psychohistorical investigations as well. Erikson's greatest contribution to our understanding of the human life cycle lies in his yoking of the individual life course to its social, cultural, and historical contexts. For Erikson, identity is, in short, a psychosocial phenomenon. In *Life History and the Historical Moment,* for example, Erikson develops a dynamic matrix of biographical and historical interactions as they apply more theoretically to his psychobiographical study of Gandhi.[5] A given episode in Gandhi's autobiography—an account, say, of his father's death—must not only be situated, Erikson argues, in relation to the autobiographer's previous developmental stages, but also be keyed into the state of Gandhi's community at the moment his father died and the continuity of that moment in the community's cultural history. An autobiographical record is shaped by a complementarity of related conditions: autonomous experience and its relation to an individual's earlier unresolved identity conflicts played out at a given historical moment and its relation to undercurrents of historical change. In *Young Man Luther*, Erikson states the matter more simply in terms of what the psychosocial components of identity mean for the psychobiographer. "We cannot even begin to encompass a human being," he writes, "without indicating for each of the stages of his life cycle the framework of social influences and of traditional institutions which determine his perspectives on his more infantile past and on his more adult future" (*Luther*, 20).

In applying that framework to Merton, we can identify two principal social influences in his identity formation: the anticulture of modernism (from Merton's youth through roughly the mid-fifties), and the counterculture humanist revolt of the 1960s which, as we have seen, coincided with Merton's profound retooling of self-image as a humanist social critic. Looking at the former, we cannot separate the moment Merton entered the monastery from a historical moment when the anticulture of modernism was in its ascendency. Just as Merton's conversion of manners in 1941 cannot be isolated from the unresolved conflicts of his "lost childhood," neither can the modernist ethos be divorced from collective moral and ideological trends in post-Enlightenment history which challenged the Christian vision of human progress governed by divine law. The modernist sensibility may be viewed, then, as an ideological by-product of the post-Enlightenment tension between human purpose defined through faith (religion), on the one hand, and through a conquest of objective truth (science), on the other. If Merton's embrace of the monastic persona tentatively resolved a personal crisis of identity, Erikson's psychosocial theory encourages us to view that resolution as a simultaneous enactment of Christian culture itself reacting against the modernist vision of human society abandoned by God. From Erikson's contextual perspective, *The Seven Storey Mountain*, then, is properly both autobiography and cultural history. That perspective may help explain, in part, the book's extraordinary popularity as well. Merton's triumph over unresolved conflicts in his personal past extends to the wider society's triumph over residual conflicts rooted in its collective history. As I have argued all along, Merton's recourse to a monastic self-image, however, failed to resolve his crisis of identity. It follows that his reactionary assault in *Mountain* on secularism and material determinism was ultimately insufficient to resolve the cultural identity crisis of post-Christian society. We have only to recall Aelred Graham's criticism of Merton as a propagandist of mysticism for the masses and Graham's fear, in particular, that Merton's retreat into a premodern ideology of world renunciation might exonerate his readers from moral and ethical responsibility at a moment in history that called for Christian action.

Given the interdependence of identity formation and the historical process, the early adulthood identity moratorium is, for Erikson, a "psychosocial moratorium"—a period, that is to say, when an individual must reconcile the often conflicting tasks of settling on an authentic self-image and finding a niche in society. Erikson considers the psychosocial moratorium an interregnum of often-exaggerated role experimentation. It is an interval for resynthesizing residual childhood identity conflicts in accordance with role models sanctioned by the society at large. "A moratorium," Erikson writes, "is a period of delay granted to somebody who is not ready to meet an obligation. . . . By psychosocial moratorium, then, we mean a delay of adult commitments [which] also often leads to deep, if often transitory, commitment."[6] Such exaggerated moratoria may be especially acute among very gifted people whose enthusiastic embrace of an identity niche frequently accompanies an excited, reactionary, even militant rejection of contrary role identifications. Individuals so deeply committed, Erikson says, "may learn only much later that what [they] took so seriously was only a period of transition." They may come to feel estranged from a self-image which once seemed so firmly and uniquely suited to them. During this pivotal stage of identity formation, "any experimentation with identity images means also to play with the inner fire of emotions and drives and to risk the outer damage of ending up in a social 'pocket' from which there is no return" (*ID*, 158).

Erikson further argues that residual identity crises unresolved from earlier stages of identity development influence the degree of commitment to experimental identity images during the psychosocial moratorium. He refers to especially exaggerated identity convictions as "radical psychological realignments" which serve to compensate an impoverished sense of wholeness as one arrives at the threshold of adult life. Erikson is especially concerned with analyzing ideologies and ideational systems ("Gestalts") and their role as agents for the collective restitution of personal wholeness. Organized religion is preeminent among these cultural gestalts. (Others include educational institutions, fraternal organizations, military training, secret societies, and gangs.) As such, Erikson treats religion as a cultural agent which helps shepherd the identity crisis of young adulthood—a revival of old childhood conflicts—into a fully integrated psychosocial identity. Institutional religion "offers to man by way of rituals a periodic collective restitution of trust which in mature adults ripens to a combination of faith and realism. . . . Religion restores, at regular intervals and through rituals significantly connected with the important crises of the life cycle . . . , a new sense of wholeness, of things rebound" (*ID*, 83).

The dynamic interplay of cultural constructs (ideologies, in general, and specifically institutional religion) and components of identity formation (the psychosocial moratorium and radical psychological realignments) may seem less abstruse when applied to actual case histories, such as Erikson's penetrating and insightful study of Luther. As a biographer, Erikson methodically screens fragmentary evidence from Luther's childhood and reconstructs a family milieu dominated by the presence of a punitive father. The father's prohibitory harshness, expressed through an "extreme degree of moralistic paternalism," was undercut, Erikson finds, by Hans Luder's cruel alcoholic and sexual self-indulgence. As a psychoanalyst, Erikson interprets that family milieu as a breeding ground which denied young Luther the freedom and autonomy necessary to develop an integrated self-image through the stages of his early identity formation. The result was that Luther arrived at the crucial juncture of young adulthood in a condition of acute identity confusion which could be reconciled only through recourse to a radical psychological realignment. Erikson describes Luther's mood before entering the monastery at Erfurt as one of extreme sadness and emotional debilitation. His sense of self was fractured to a degree that Luther could "see only one way out: the abandonment of all of his previous life and earthly future it implied for the sake of a total dedication to a new life" (*Luther*, 39–40). Both forward-looking and retrospective, Luther's radical psycho-ideological transformation was tantamount to a totalist rejection of his past— particularly his father's dogmatic foisting upon Luther an identity expectation of a first generation ex-peasant who demanded that his son gain a foothold in a newly emerging managerial class.

Erikson considers the period of Luther's early monastic formation, then, as his psychosocial moratorium. Because Luther plunged himself into monastic life with the intensity of a radical psychological realignment, his new monastic identity was not, however, as viable a commitment as might have been implied by the monastic vow, but rather, according to Erikson, a dilemma of overcommitment for the young Luther. Luther's monastic moratorium became a period of postponement, of marking time toward a later crossroad of adult commitment where Luther arrived in his late thirties—after an interim of self-doubt, depression, persistent melancholy (what Erikson refers to as an admixture of "mental disease and religious creativity")—as the leader of a rebellion called the Reformation. Examining the monastic experience from the twin perspectives of ideological commitment and psychosocial development, Erikson writes: "The monastery offers methods of making a meditative descent into the inner shafts of mental existence, from which the aspirant emerges with the gold of faith or with gems of wisdom. These shafts, however, are psychological as well as meditative: they lead not only into the depths of adult inner experience, but also downward into our most primitive layers, and backward into our infantile beginnings" (109).

We can derive a general conclusion from Erikson's analysis of a young man overcommitted to monastic silence, meditation, and compulsive self-inspection who later became a voice heard around the world: to wit, when a young man negotiates the psychosocial moratorium of early adulthood driven by a radical psychological realignment, that moratorium may not liberate a fully integrated identity, but it may deepen instead the crisis of identity. "The crisis in such a young man's life," Erikson writes, "may be reached when he half-realizes that he is fatally overcommitted to what he is not" (*Luther*, 43).

If we soften the stresses slightly, Erikson's insights into Luther's identity crisis may not seem all that incompatible with my reading of Thomas Merton's conflicts over identity. In fact, Luther and Merton's life histories reflect developmental scenarios remarkably similar, at least in their general contours. Viewed from an Eriksonian angle, those developmental scenarios appear charted on roughly parallel courses. Both biographies are narratives of personal histories interacting with historical moments in such a way as to produce voices that shape history. Each man experienced childhood milieus which groomed them, so to speak, for radical psychological realignments in their twenties; their gestalts of identity restructuring were expressed as monastic separations. Both men subsequently entered a psychosocial moratorium of identity confusion—periods of self-denial and self-doubt during which regressive identity conflicts resurfaced. Nearly a decade passed until Luther and Merton emerged from their moratoria and achieved an integration of adult identity. In both cases, a resolution of the identity crisis was accompanied by a new ideological commitment: for Luther, a Protestantism that vigorously sought to redress the excesses of papal authoritarianism; and for Merton, as we have seen, a post-Christian humanism aimed at healing the alienation and dehumanization that he had come to associate with the dominant culture of modernism. It is most important to note that Luther and Merton's revisionist ideologies were rooted in residual conflicts with their fathers. Luther's Protestantism, that is to say, echoes a certain residual dissent against a harsh, authoritative, punitive father and a triumph over his dogmatic, tyrannical expectations for his son. Merton's radical humanism resonates, as well, with a triumph over sources of alienation and dehumanization buried in his lost childhood. He managed to settle a score with a well-meaning, even benevolent father who was nonetheless seduced, in his son's eyes, into a bohemian cult of art where moral responsibility in interpersonal affairs—especially, as we have seen, paternal obligation—was sacrificed to the tenuous rewards of artistic self-expression.

— 2 —

Armed with rudimentary definitions and a conceptual understanding of the developmental processes underpinning Erikson's insights into identity formation, we can sketch a preliminary Eriksonian mapping of Merton's identity formation by following its course through key introspective texts. Spanning three decades, Merton's canon of self-reflections amounts to nothing less, in fact, than a dynamic record of what Erikson calls "the ontogenic unfolding of the main components of psychosocial vitality." That record can be indexed briefly as follows: *My Argument with the Gestapo*, an autobiographical novel of identity diffusion; *The Seven Storey Mountain,* an autobiography of radical psychological realignment; *The Sign of Jonas,* a diary of psychosocial moratorium; and *Conjectures of a Guilty Bystander,* a journal of final identity integration.

Before pressing much further, we need to review the procedural methodology of psychobiography as practiced by Erikson. Briefly, Erikson maintains that primary identity estrangements left over from early stages of psychosocial development (and, as such, largely unconscious) resurface as *subsymptoms* of identity confusion during a pivotal identity crisis in young adulthood, the fifth stage, according to Erikson, of identity formation. The young adult, as it were, reencounters episodic crises keyed into previous stages of ego synthesis in the form of such subsymptoms. For example, Erikson tracks the subsymptom of "time confusion" back to a basic sense of mistrust experienced during early infancy, the first stage of identity formation. Among "regressed young people," Erikson writes, a mistrust of time manifests itself as a feeling that "every delay appears to be a deceit, every wait an experience of impotence, every hope a danger, every plan a catastrophe, every possible provider a potential traitor" (*ID,* 181). And clinical evidence led Erikson to connect this diffusion of temporal perspective and expectancy to an "absence or impairment . . . that arises out of the encounter of maternal person and small infant, an encounter which [should be] one of mutual trustworthiness and mutual recognition" (105). Another example is Erikson's subsymptom of "self-consciousness": "a painful self-consciousness," he defines, "which dwells on discrepancies between one's self-esteem, the aggrandized self-image as an autonomous person, and one's appearance in the eyes of others" (183). Self-consciousness carried to such a morbidly calculating degree expresses "shame and doubt," a primary identity estrangement common to Erikson's second stage of psychosocial development. Similarly, "role fixation" is a subsymptom of residual "guilt" during the third stage, "work paralysis" a subsymptom of Stage Four "inferiority," and so on.

Erikson's model of interconnections between these subsymptoms and their residual identity estrangements means, above all else, that the early adulthood identity crisis aims to reconstitute the adult identity through a reenactment and "re-resolution" of latent identity conflicts. By restoring "temporal perspective," for example, out of "time confusion," one simultaneously recovers a basic sense of trust from the mistrust of a deprived infancy. By reestablishing self-certainty from the wounds of a painful self-consciousness, the young adult resolves the second stage identity crisis and recovers personal autonomy and independence from the remnants of lingering self-doubt. Thus, the developmental crisis of early adulthood is, in effect, the major crossroad in identity formation; its outcome determines the direction of one's future life course. And, once again, Erikson relies on a vocabulary of moral antinomies to describe the avenues which may follow, as he says, "beyond identity": whether one travels the remaining life course with a capacity for intimacy in interpersonal relationships or impoverished by persistent self-isolation, with generativity or stagnation, with integrity or despair.

In short, then, the psychobiographer's task is, first, to isolate subsymptoms of identity confusion during his or her subject's fifth-stage identity crisis and extrapolate them back to primary identity estrangements folded into earlier layers of the life cycle. Second, the psychobiographer interprets the balance of a life history from the perspective of successful, partial, or failed efforts at resolving the major identity crisis of young adulthood.

It would take a separate full-scale study to flesh out a detailed psychobiographical portrait of Merton—something well beyond the scope of a speculative epilogue. However, we can briefly investigate selected features of *My Argument with the Gestapo* from an Eriksonian angle, evaluate it generally as a novel of identity confusion, and analyze specifically one subsymptom—time confusion—as a principal motif.

Merton wrote *Gestapo* while teaching at St. Bonaventure University. This was a brief but pivotal period in Merton's life history: a restive and searching interregnum between his graduate studies at Columbia and his successful petition to enter the monastery. The novel is situated, then, in Erikson's fifth-stage identity crisis. Such crises, Erikson notes, may be especially pronounced for creative individuals who are inclined to "resolve [the identity crisis] for themselves . . . by offering to their contemporaries a new model of resolution such as that expressed in works of art . . . , and who furthermore are eager to tell us all about it in diaries, letters, and self-representations" (*ID*, 134). *Gestapo* is such a model. Merton's principal aim, however, is not to resolve his identity crisis, but rather to articulate, as it seems to me, the extent of identity confusion that eventually—within a matter of weeks, in fact—brought him to the threshold of monastic life. *Gestapo* records, in journal format, the misadventures of a young poet—clearly an autobiographical protagonist—who sets out for England and France at the height of World War II. Not only does the sensitive and perplexed young poet try to come to terms with the social and political realities of a London raked by buzz bombs and a France cowed by Nazi occupation (something that has led many critics into misreading *Gestapo* as an intentional antiwar novel), but, more importantly, he struggles as well to rediscover his own past in some meaningful continuity with his present circumstances. Merton says in a preface written twenty-seven years later that the novel concerns "the crisis of civilization in general" and "an attempt to define its predicament [in light of] my own place in it." "Dreamed in 1941," the novel, Merton concedes, is a work of personal mythmaking. Viewed as such, Erikson's framework of psycho-moral polarities provides a stimulating critical vantage point from which we can decode the Joyce-like narrative fracturing—"the fantasy . . . tone of divertissement," Merton later demurred—that stamps *Gestapo* with the somewhat artificial, self-conscious impress of an experimental modernist aesthetic.

Identity confusion is apparent even in *Gestapo's* narrative technique. A bifurcation of Merton's personality quickly reveals a familiar conflict between a modernist aesthetic, on the one hand, and a moral imagination counter to the modernist sensibility, on the other. This sets up a narrative tension between the author of the novel and T. J. Merton, the novel's central character: a tension between a novelist who writes in an innovative, flauntingly unconventional style reminiscent of James Joyce and a poet/protagonist whose traditionalist Judeo-Christian sensibilities leave him ill at ease with the audacious desperation that is the *sine qua non* of modernism's ethical consciousness. Throughout the novel, the protagonist is trying to escape from the very conditions imposed upon him by his creator. Originally titled *Journal of My Escape from the Nazis*, the novel, in a word, is a journal of Merton's attempted liberation from identity confusion.

In one representative episode, for example, two officers, suspicious of the authenticity of T. J. Merton's passport, harass him on a London street corner. The interrogation scene—one of many scattered throughout the novel—comes to resemble a vaudevillian dialogue between two officious arbiters of the status quo—Caesar's henchmen—

and a self-described "Citizen of Casa" whose anarchic flippance fuels the officers' indignation. The officers insist on the viability of a passport; to them it is a document of pragmatic utility that underwrites identity. A passport, they insist, endorses its bearer as "a social animal, a creature of ethics," a citizen of Caesar's sworn "to sacrifice yourself for the good of the state." T. J. Merton rejoins:

> "I gave you my social animal's passport. I will wear any label you hitch onto my collar, in the world's wide prison. But though you give me a license that says I am a social animal, I continue to know I am a child of God, and while you talk about your abstract ethics, which is a science, I will pray to learn, on another level that overcomes and includes all other levels, a concrete love which is not an abstract science but a way of life, and only exists in actions. I will buy all the passports required of me by Caesar's petty clerks, but my passports do not tell anything like my real identity, nor do they have anything much to do with what I live for." (*AG*, 157)

This exchange illustrates the fundamental identity dichotomy that Merton wrestled with throughout his pre-Gethsemani days (and well into, as I have argued, his monastic moratorium). A "sacred self," so to speak, struggles to define itself in contradistinction to a secular identity. A "child of God" affirms himself by renouncing his identity as a "social animal." The officers—agents of an ethic "of total allegiance to human systems"—interrogate their suspect—an agent of a morality of selfless "concrete love"—and such an exchange between mutually exclusive ontological visions inevitably collapses into "a set of equivocal jokes." Simply put, the polarities of religion and worldliness, the sacred and the secular, cannot be bridged. The same tyranny of oppositions immediately carries over into the opening chapter of *The Seven Storey Mountain* where, as we have seen, Merton describes his parents as "captives . . . [in a] world that was the picture of Hell," "knowing they did not belong with it or in it, and yet"—like the angry and chagrined protagonist in *Gestapo*—"unable to get away from it" (*SSM*, 3).

I would suggest, then, that *My Argument with the Gestapo* is driven by the same identity confusion that formed the basis of my thesis in chapter four. Merton renders into fiction a tension between his calling as artist/writer and his deep-seated fear that the artist/writer is inextricably bound, as he says in *Gestapo*, in a "negative allegiance" to a corrupt society, to "abstract ethics," to the science of "Caesar's petty clerks." It is particularly fascinating to note that Merton fashioned the same provisional resolution in *Gestapo* that he had in his masters thesis on William Blake and his revisionist portrait of Owen Merton as painter/saint in *The Seven Storey Mountain:* namely, the persona of the sacred artist. Having finished his autobiographical novel of identity confusion, Merton closes *Gestapo* inspired by a new authorial self-image as pure and innocent as the "new paper, white, untouched" that he cranks lovingly into his typewriter. "I think suddenly of Blake," Merton writes, "filling paper with words, so that the words flew about the room for the angels to read. . . . That is the only reason for wanting to write, Blake's reason" (*AG*, 259).

Against a general backdrop of creative identity diffusion, Merton blocks in a peculiar time-consciousness in *Gestapo* that has striking parallels to Erikson's subsymptom of time confusion that I mentioned earlier. Symptomatic of the fifth-stage identity crisis, Erikson characterizes the mistrust of time as a "mistrustful difficulty with mere living in time." Time-consciousness is fractured. Linear associations to time come unglued. Fluid temporal connections between activity and rest, work and recreation, interactions with other people and periods of isolation are broken. Even "the usual alternation of day and night," Erikson finds, may be ignored. Time is experienced as a malaise of apprehensions in which one may feel to be waiting, as we say, for the other shoe to drop. It is as if one "were waiting," Erikson concludes, "for some event, or some person, to sweep him out of this state by promising him, instead of the reassuring routine and practice of most men's time, a vast utopian view that would make the very disposition of time worthwhile" (*Luther*, 101).

This may help explain why Merton treats time with such suspicion, indignation, and tragic indifference in *Gestapo*. In one especially revealing entry, Merton lampoons a civic ceremony in which a time capsule—crammed with the trivial cultural detritus of 1941—is officially dedicated to the year 6939. He writes about the time capsule in a letter to himself after several failed efforts to draft letters to relatives, friends, and past acquaintances—"people," Merton comes to realize in a moment of paralyzing self-isolation, "who have become strangers to me." The time capsule is filled with the "signs and tokens" of a civilization on the verge of destruction, poised "perhaps the minute before the invading army of barbarians appears." It contains thousands of photographs which meld, in Merton's mind, into a single snapshot of the secular Everyman: the "unassuming, unimaginative, pathetic, miserly, envious little hypochondriac that you are, . . . the unembellished snapshot of your completely unimportant self" (127)! As a symbol of profane time, Merton gazes upon the capsule with loathing and fear. His description of the dedication ceremony, laden with invective, is at the same time the confession of a young man "terrified by the nightmare in my mind of [the] . . . future." The entry is nothing short of a meditation on hopelessness. "I am," Merton admits, "afraid of the Time Capsule: and of the things that are neatly compressed into it like vitamins into some kind of a pill. All the things the Time Capsule contains will only carry on, for thousands of years, the dreadful, futile, and trivial worries of the dead" (126).

Like all subsymptoms of identity confusion, time mistrust, Erikson argues, signals a regressive trend in the identity crisis. Merton's loathing and dread in the face of future time can be seen, then, as a new edition of an original doubt and fear which, according to Erikson, concerns the trustworthiness of one's parents. As I argued in chapter three, Merton's "lost childhood" harbored deep psychological wounds not unlike the primary identity estrangements Erikson describes as mistrust, fear, and a persistent, overbearing sense of rejection. From Erikson's perspective, we can evaluate the time capsule entry in *Gestapo* as a retrogression to a preadolescent doubt that Merton later transferred to a larger social universe where he found himself—a young adult in the clutches of an identity crisis—regressing to a painful, semiconscious state of incomplete self-certainty. The narrative technique Merton uses throughout *Gestapo*, in fact, relies heavily on these dynamic regressions. Present fears frequently fuse into past fears. Dilemmas of uncertainty, rejection, shame, and self-doubt immediately trigger onrushes of past experiences as prototypes of present dangers. When T. J. Merton is grilled by a Gestapo agent, for example, the interrogation scene quickly transfers to memory flashes of the Lycée Censeur at Montauban who had punished Merton, fourteen years earlier, for reading pulp novels and smoking cigarettes. The interrogation room itself evokes past fears of the dark, cold classrooms at the Lycée Ingres where Merton had been shipped after a secure but brief vacation with his father at St. Antonin. The German soldiers goosestepping through the corridors become the cruel boys with fox faces who pulled Merton's ears during recess on the Lycée playground.

"[W]hat are the various avenues," Erikson asks, "which cultures offer to . . . youths so that they may overcome the forces that pull them back into [such] infantile regressions and find ways of mobilizing their inner strength for future-oriented pursuits?" (*ID*, 180). Keeping with the motif of time confusion, Erikson explains that ideologies and ideational systems provide temporal perspectives that counteract time confusion. Fidelity to a new ideology brings a compelling change in the entire quality of temporal experience. According to Erikson, "there is an indispensable temporal aspect to all ideology [that yields] a sensually convincing *time perspective* compatible with a coherent world image" (*ID*, 182). I have suggested that Cistercian monasticism filled an identity breach for the young Merton and supplied him with a new ideological orientation that he adopted with the impelling commitment of a radical psychosocial realignment. And with that ideological reorientation, as Erikson predicts, came a profound change in the quality of temporal experience for Merton. For evidence, we need only turn to Merton's *Secular Journal* where he records his initial impressions of Gethsemani. Most striking in Merton's account of his first monastic retreat—an account written just a few weeks after he completed the draft of *Gestapo*—is the powerful sense of "centering" captured in the passage. Merton finds himself suddenly *centered* in both space and time. "This [monastery] is the center of America," he writes. He had finally found a place that quietly stood in such stark contrast to the geopsychological fracturing and uprootedness associated with his youth. Gethsemani becomes a *locus* of unifying forces, the eye of a geocultural hurricane. The monastery "hold[s] the country together." It "keep[s] the universe from cracking in pieces and falling apart" (*SecJ*, 183). And Gethsemani also provides a unifying *focus* for the movement of time. Merton contrasts the chaos and pointlessness of secular time—profane time, that is to say, the time that governs work routines, railway schedules, "money-making"—with the symmetry, order, balance, and coherence of monastic time. The day coheres around a highly organized, predictable, and ritualized cycle of Canonical Hours in which High Mass forms "the center and foundation and meaning of the day here. It *is* the day." "The Mass is the real center, and life is ordered as it should be" (194–95). Time confusion gives way to time perspective through a therapeutic transformation that reverses itself the moment Merton finishes his retreat and departs. "Leaving Gethsemani was sad," he writes. "I left early Monday morning, got to Louisville at 8. This would have been the middle of the day, at the Abbey—not its beginning. It was confusing. What a difference between the monastery and the outside world!" (204).

As Merton's novel of identity confusion amply demonstrates, he was ready in 1941 for a new time perspective that would help marshal forces to heal a young man in "terror and confusion," "without harmony, in a state full of contradictions" (*AG*, 110). In a parting episode, we can leave Merton at a point of departure from his secular life as his protagonist stands on a Paris street corner, slouching dejectedly with his hands stuffed into empty pockets. He suddenly notices that all the public clocks in the city are dead; they have stopped. "The calendars . . . are unchanged." "I would scarcely know how to locate myself in time at all if it were not for my missal," he admits, "which I follow from day to day, and for the bells of a convent locked away among the houses somewhere behind my hotel" (231). The bells lure his imagination to the "serious, undramatic" life inside the walls of the convent where "all nonsense is locked out." The bells bring a peaceful interlude that mutes for a moment the sounds of "the world outside . . . filled . . . with the unmistakable accents of serious, suffering stupidity" (233).

The protagonist of *My Argument with the Gestapo*, adrift in a world without moral bearings, searches desperately and fruitlessly for his place in that world and for continuities between his past and present so that his future may come to mean something to him. Caught in an identity crisis, the novel places Merton at that crucial juncture of young adulthood where the uncertainties of self-image are perhaps best described by Arthur Miller in *Death of a Salesman* when Biff confesses to his mother, "I just can't take hold, Mom, I can't take hold of some kind of life."

It is in *The Seven Storey Mountain* where Merton manages a provisional breakthrough into a "kind of life" he could take hold of. An autobiography of radical psychological realignment, *Mountain* offers, in many respects, a solution to the dilemmas of identity diffusion suffered by the conflicted young poet in Merton's first and only surviving novel. *Mountain* is an autobiography of dynamic self-restructuring, of abrupt and dramatic separations, of reified and exaggerated likes, predilections, and convictions. In both an ideological and a temporal sense, Merton's story of conversion "evokes a Gestalt," as Erikson says, "in which an absolute boundary is emphasized: given a certain arbitrary delineation, nothing that belongs inside must be left outside, nothing that must be outside can be tolerated inside" (*ID*, 81). Such clarities of arbitrary delineation empower *The Seven Storey Mountain*. Gethsemani's gatehouse is a symbolic curtain, a ritual threshold which, once crossed, opens a passage into a whole new world of separations and changes. In the monastic tradition, such transformations are embodied in the monastic vows, especially the *conversatio morum* (conversion of manners) which, as Merton once said, aims to "deliver [a monk] from the uncertainties and cares and illusions that beset the man of the world" (*SJ*, 9). In terms of the dynamics of developmental processes, Erikson reminds us too that these transformations are self-restructurings, especially pronounced in individuals who have lost a feeling of essential wholeness. As such, a radical ideological transformation can also be said to deliver a conflicted young man from the sources of his conflicts.

When the Abbey gate locked behind him, Merton experienced an oceanic liberation from the "terror and confusion" which had buffeted the protagonist of *Gestapo* and left him "without harmony, in a state full of contradictions." "I was enclosed in the four walls of my new freedom" (*SSM*, 372). The monastery comes to represent, then, not only a spatial delineation between the City of God and the Secular City, but an ideological separation as well between the evils of secular modernism, associated with the painful discontinuities of Merton's personal past, and the purity of contemplative faith promised by the monastic regimen's new order and continuity. Most important, the monastery stands as a crossroad in Merton's life: a turning away from past divisions into a diametrically opposed new investiture of identity. "I was out of my secular clothing," Merton announces with great relief, "and glad to get rid of it forever." *The Seven Storey Mountain* bristles, in short, with the sort of recourse to totalism that seems fitting to Erikson's definition of a "totality . . . as absolutely inclusive as it is utterly exclusive" (*ID*, 81).

I have argued, however, that Merton's rapt plunge into the new uniformity of monastic life may only have masked deeper uncertainties as he sought, through recourse to a group identity, to rewrite his personal history and liberate himself from the clutches of modernist culture that had gripped, indeed paralyzed, the young poet in *Gestapo*. Erikson's comment that "an incomplete self-certainty, for a time, can hide in a group certainty" may indeed apply to Merton's conversion narrative. I would argue, then, that Merton's resolution of his identity crisis was not simply a matter of discarding his secular clothing or attempting an exorcism of his shadow image as writer in the epilogue to *The Seven Storey Mountain*. The transience of his monastic persona may account for Merton's persistent efforts after 1958 to dissociate himself from his much-acclaimed autobiography. Besides, a conflict between self-images was by no means stilled by 1948, as Merton himself admits in the closing pages of *Mountain* when he says that problems over his "true identity" continue to haunt him. Such problems quickly resurface in *The Sign of Jonas*, the journal of Merton's missing years. *Jonas* may be viewed, then, as the diary of Merton's psychosocial moratorium: a synthesis or redramatization of his identity crisis played out as a conflict between the highly polarized self-images of contemplative and writer/poet.

Erikson's treatment of positive identity elements and negative identity fragments during psychosocial moratoria seems especially germane to the literary strategy of *Jonas*. Through his monk persona, Merton projects certain positive role identifications that Erikson describes as trust, autonomy, initiative, and industry. Merton's writer persona, on the other hand, carries the signature of negative identity fragments or identity estrangements revived from childhood conflicts, such as guilt, mistrust, doubt, and inferiority. The negative identity, Erikson explains, is "based on all those identifications and roles which, at crucial stages of development, had been presented . . . as most undesirable or dangerous and yet also as most real" (*ID*, 174). In Merton's case, his negative identity as writer traces to the dominant image of his father as artist that continued, well into Merton's young adulthood, to stir painful, semiconscious recollections of loss, mistrust, fear, and loneliness—an identity, in other words, that experience had warned him not to become. His provisional identity as monk simultaneously provided Merton with a highly idealistic self-image "diametrically opposed," in Erikson's words, "to the dominant values of an individual's upbringing," and such compensatory values as stability, security, authority. In a manner of speaking, then, *The*

Sign of Jonas is inspired by Merton's need to discover and define for himself an ideal identity niche entirely of his own making against the excessive ideals demanded of him by an ambitious but failed artist/father, the sort of "unexpressed wishes," Erikson warns, which are "recognized by [a] child with catastrophic clarity" (*ID*, 175).

The negative identity, according to Erikson, is always treated with scorn and hostility. It looms as an intolerable shadow cast by identity estrangements unresolved from previous stages of psychosocial development. This seems to be the case with Merton. Throughout his monastic moratorium he persisted in heaping contempt on his self-image as writer. He sustained a pattern of denials despite relentless vague dissembling and, at times, outright contradiction. Erikson reminds us, however, that a radical psychological realignment to an idealized role identification may never be sufficient to resolve the deeper conflicts harbored by the negative identity. This seems, too, to be the case with Merton. His renunciations of the writer/poet persona only aggravated, as we saw in part I, his identity ambivalences.

And, as we saw in part II, a crisis of self-doubt eventually lead Merton to a new identity synthesis. In *Conjectures of a Guilty Bystander*, Merton announces that creative breakthrough into a new psychosocial persona: a simultaneous integration of his self-identity and Merton's reintegration into society and history. Facing the discontinuities of his past life and unsuccessfully (though courageously) reconciling the identity polarities of monk and writer in *Jonas*, Merton emerges in *Conjectures* with an entirely new identity configuration as a radical Christian humanist. That configuration combines ideological resolve and a commitment to meaningful work in the form of a dissident writer/social critic compelled to uphold Christian moral and ethical standards against the increasingly amoral and unethical proclivities of contemporary techno-culture. In the social and ethical undercurrents of *Conjectures*, Merton at last discovered, in short, a "quiet but articulate place," a final integration, as Erikson titled one of his books, of life history and the historical moment. Merton's eventual identity breakthrough as a post-Christian humanist freed him, as Erikson says of Martin Luther, "to formulate for himself and for all mankind a new kind of ethical and psychological awareness"—a formulation that inspired *Conjectures of a Guilty Bystander* and shaped the literary agenda for Merton's remaining years.

— 4 —

In his journal of final identity integration, Merton's reflections on "the psychology of crisis and change" bear marked similarities to Erikson's view that adult identity derives from a restructuring of the self that incorporates, as Merton says, "irreconcilable opposites in oneself." Merton acknowledges too that identity conflicts cannot be resolved by building a unity on the most desirable persona polarity and projecting the other upon the world and other people. This seems to be precisely what Merton had persisted in doing throughout his own psychosocial identity moratorium: namely, projecting his negative identity as writer/poet onto a profane and hostile secular world and taking shelter in a positive role identification as hermit/mystic/saint. But Merton came to realize, he writes in *Conjectures,* that "a personal crisis is creative and salutary if one can accept the conflict and restore unity on a higher level, incorporating the opposed elements in a higher unity. One thus becomes a more complete, a more developed person, capable of wider understanding, empathy, and love for others" (*CGB,* 189). Erik Erikson considers that process of self-acceptance as the endgame, so to speak, of identity formation—a psychological stillpoint of self-awareness from which an individual can travel the future life course, Erikson concludes, emboldened by personal integrity, a renewed capacity for intimacy with others, and, above all, a heightened obligation to lead and guide subsequent generations, a quality Erikson refers to as "generativity." I have argued throughout this study that Merton's crisis of identity confusion gradually nourished his wisdom to care in entirely new ways for persons and institutions, his extraordinary capacity for ultimate concerns, and his devotion to the moral and ethical maintenance of the human condition in his time. There may be no better way to estimate Merton's legacy than what is implied in Erikson's capstone virtue of generativity. Erikson illustrates that virtue as an existential assertion: "I am what survives of me." That declaration, I believe, is the common inspirational thread that united Merton's prodigious outpouring of letters, poems, essays, and books after *Conjectures of a Guilty Bystander,* a body of humanist discourse in which Merton could be as gentle in expressions of love for his brothers and sisters as he could be acerbic in condemning their collective acts of human hatred. The degree of Merton's generative commitment was nowhere stated with greater clarity and simplicity than in his comment to a teenaged correspondent (his source for the latest rock-and-roll releases). He declared that they must work together to make the world a better place, to leave it in better shape than they had found it. On the occasion of his correspondent's graduation from high school, and just six months before his own untimely death, one generation addressed the next. Merton's advice: "Go forth into the world and help it, if possible, make some kind of sense. Or anyway less nonsense."[7]

Against that standard, Thomas Merton measured up.

NOTES

Unless otherwise indicated, the letters and manuscripts cited below are in the Thomas Merton Studies Center [TMSC], Bellarmine College, Louisville, Kentucky.

Prologue

1. *See* John F. Teahan's excellent overview in "A Dark and Empty Way: Thomas Merton and the Apophatic Tradition," *Journal of Religion* 58, no. 3 (1978): 263–87.

Chapter One: The Letter Killeth

1. George Woodcock, *Thomas Merton/Monk and Poet: A Critical Study* (New York: Farrar, Straus & Giroux, 1978), 62.

2. Thomas Merton, "Poetry and the Contemplative Life," *Commonweal* 46 (4 July 1947): 285.

3. TM to MVD, 30 March 1948. Used with permission of the Merton Legacy Trust.

4. Thomas Merton, "Todo y Nada," *Renascence* 2 (Spring, 1950), 90.

5. MVD to TM, 14 March 1948. Used with permission of Dorothy Van Doren.

6. TM to MVD, 30 March 1948.

7. CD to TM, 14 October 1941; 25 October 1941.

8. "Todo y Nada," 101.

Chapter Two: The Art of Denial, I

1. NBS to TM, 15 July 1952. Used with permission of Naomi Burton Stone.

2. NBS to TM, 31 March 1950. Used with permission of Naomi Burton Stone.

3. RG to TM, 20 April 1950. Used with permission of Robert Giroux.

4. Censors' Reports: TMSC. Used with permission of the Merton Legacy Trust.

5. TM to JLq, 9 October 1950. Used with permission of the Merton Legacy Trust.

6. TM to JLq, 18 May 1953. Used with permission of the Merton Legacy Trust.

7. TM to BA, December 1952. Used with permission of the Merton Legacy Trust.

8. BA to TM, 29 January 1953.

9. Quoted in Monica Furlong, *Merton: A Biography* (San Francisco: Harper & Row, 1980), 212.

10. TM to JLq, 3 June 1955. Used with permission of the Merton Legacy Trust.

11. Dom James Fox to Dom Jean LeClerq, quoted in Furlong, 212.

12. TM to JLq, 11 August 1955. Used with permission of the Merton Legacy Trust.

13. Ibid.

14. Ibid.

15. Dom James Fox, "The Spiritual Son," in Brother Patrick Hart (ed.), *Thomas Merton/Monk: A Monastic Tribute* (Kalamazoo: Cistercian Publications 1983), 150–51.

16. TM to NBS, 4 August 1955. Used with permission of the Merton Legacy Trust.

17. NBS to TM, 15 April 1955. Used with permission of Naomi Burton Stone.

18. Fox, "Spiritual Son," 151.

19. Furlong, 212.

20. TM to JLq, 3 December 1955. Used with permission of the Merton Legacy Trust.

21. TM to MVD, 30 December 1955. Columbia University. Used with permission of the Merton Legacy Trust.

22. TM to BA, January 1953. Used with permission of the Merton Legacy Trust.

Chapter Three: The Art of Denial, II

1. Louis Lekai, *The Cistercians: Ideals and Reality* (Kent, Ohio: Kent University Press, 1977), 263.

2. Otto von Simsom, *The Gothic Cathedral: Origins of Gothic Architecture and the Medieval Concept of Order* (New York: Pantheon Books, 1956), 47–48 and 56–58.

3. Thomas Merton, "Art and Morality," *New Catholic Encyclopedia*, (New York: McGraw-Hill, 1967), 1:866.

4. TM to NBS, 27 January 1951. Used with permission of the Merton Legacy Trust.

5. Ibid.

6. Mott, 17.

7. Furlong, 8.

8. TM to Rosemary Ruether, 24 March 1967.

9. Owen Merton to Esmond Atkinson, 16 January 1916, TMSC. Used with permission of the Merton Legacy Trust.

10. Robert E. Daggy, "Birthday Theology: A Reflection on Thomas Merton and the Bermuda Menage," *The Kentucky Review*, 7, no. 2 (Summer 1987), 62–89.

11. Unidentified, n.d. [1925], TMSC.

12. *The Observer*, 31 May 1925, n.p., TMSC.

13. "A Little-Known Painter," *The New Zealand Herald*, 23 August 1930, n.p., TMSC.

14. *The Referee*, 31 May 1925.

15. *The Morning Post*, 25 May 1925.

16. David D. Cooper, ed., "Thomas Merton and Henry Miller: An Exchange of Letters," *Helix* 19/20 (1984), 23.

17. Quoted in Daggy, 73.

18. *See* Arthur Callard, "Father of the Man: An Investigation into the Roots of Thomas Merton," *The Merton Seasonal of Bellarmine College* Spring/Summer (1986): 5–8; Daggy, "Birthday Theology"; Mott, 23–26.

19. Quoted in Mott, 25.

20. Anthony Padovano, *The Human Journey: Thomas Merton—Symbol of a Century* (New York: Doubleday, 1982), 81, 88.

21. Unless otherwise indicated, all quotations in this section are from Daggy, "Birthday Theology."

22. Quoted in Arthur Callard, "Pretty Good for a Woman: A Quest for Evelyn Scott," *London Magazine*, Oct. 1981, 57.

23. Evelyn Scott to Lola Ridge, October 1924. From material supplied to the author by Arthur Callard.

24. Callard material.

25. Quoted in Daggy, 70.

26. Mott, 21–22.

27. Daggy, 85.

28. ES to LR, 17 July 1925. Callard material.

29. Quoted in Callard, "Father of the Man," 7.

30. TM to Robert Lawrence Williams, 16 July 1968, *Ground*, 605.

31. Quoted in Daggy, 71.

32. Ibid.

33. Callard, "Father of the Man," 8.

Chapter Four: The Art of the Sacred

1. T. S. Eliot, "The Waste Land," in *The Waste Land and Other Poems* (New York: Harcourt, Brace & World, 1930), 33.

2. Owen Merton to Esmond Atkinson, 16 January 1916.

3. TM to Ad Reinhardt, 1962.

4. *See* William H. Shannon, *Thomas Merton's Dark Path* (New York: Farrar, Straus & Giroux, 1981), 34–50; Donald Grayston, "The Making of a Spiritual Classic: Thomas Merton's *Seeds of Contemplation* and *New Seeds of Contemplation*," *Studies in Religion* 3 (1974): 339–56.

5. RG to TM, 26 November 1958. Used with permission of Robert Giroux.

6. RG to TM, 18 November 1958. Used with permission of Robert Giroux.

7. RG to TM, 25 November 1959. Used with permission of Robert Giroux.

8. TM to RG, 28 November 1959. Used with permission of Merton Legacy Trust.

9. RG to TM, 19 December 1958. Used with permission of Robert Giroux.

10. NBS to TM, 2 November 1959. Used with permission of Naomi Burton Stone.

11. Eloise Spaeth to RG, July 1960.

12. RG to TM, 13 July 1960. Used with permission of Robert Giroux.

13. TM to ES, 18 July 1960. Used with permission of the Merton Legacy Trust.

14. Anon. to ES, n.d. [mid-1964].

15. TM to NBS, 10 May 1963. Used with permission of the Merton Legacy Trust.

16. Ad Reinhardt, "Art-as-Art," *Monks Pond* 1 (Spring, 1968), 2.

17. Quoted in "Five Unpublished Letters from Ad Reinhardt to Thomas Merton and Two in Return," *ArtForum*, December 1978, 24.

18. Ibid.

19. *In My Disc of Gold: Itinerary to Christ of William Congdon* (New York: Reynal & Co., n.d.), n.p.

20. "Five Unpublished Letters," 25.

21. Reinhardt, "Art-as-Art," 2.

22. TM to AR, July, 1960, Cold War Letters #45.

23. *Victor Hammer: A Retrospective Exhibition* (Raleigh: North Carolina Museum of Art, 1965), 4.

24. Ibid, 75.

25. Victor Hammer to TM, 2 May 1959. Used with permission of Carolyn Hammer.

26. TM to VH, 9 November 1963. Used with permission of the Merton Legacy Trust.

27. "Conference Notes," TMSC. *See* Thomas Merton, "Notes on Sacred and Profane Art," *Jubilee,* November 1956, 26. Used with permission of the Merton Legacy Trust.

28. "New Notes on Art," Novitiate Conference, Summer 1964, Ms. TMSC. Emphasis mine. Used with permission of the Merton Legacy Trust.

Chapter Five: A Modern Man in Reverse Looking Forward

1. TM to Rosemary Ruether, 19 March 1967.

2. TM to Cecilia Corsanego, 31 January 1964.

3. Aelred Graham, "Thomas Merton: A Modern Man in Reverse," *Atlantic* 191 (January 1953): 71.

4. *Vow of Conversation* [Ms.: TMSC]: 10 March 1964.

5. TM to DD, 10 November 1941, *Ground,* 7.

6. Thomas Merton, "A Life Free from Care," *Cistercian Studies* 5 (1970), 226.

7. TM to RR, 21 June 1965.

8. TM to RR, 9 March 1967.

9. TM to Erich Fromm, 13 October 1966.

10. TM to RR, 19 March 1967.

11. TM to DB, 4 August 1964.

12. TM to Etta Gullick, 1 August 1966, *Ground,* 376.

13. TM to EC, 25 February 1963. Used with permission of the Merton Legacy Trust.

14. TM to DD, 23 August 1961, *Ground,* 140.

15. Censors' Reports, TMSC.

16. TM to DB, 25 June 1963.

17. TM to Lord Northbourne, 30 August 1966.

18. Quoted in Patrick F. O'Connell, "Sunken Islands: Two and One-Fifth Unpublished Merton Poems," *The Merton Seasonal,* 12, no. 2 (Spring, 1987): 6–7.

19. TM to EC, 24 November 1959. Used with permission of the Merton Legacy Trust.

20. TM to EC, 17 August 1959. Used with permission of the Merton Legacy Trust.

21. TM to EC, 24 December 1961. Used with permission of the Merton Legacy Trust.

22. TM to EC, 11 March 1967. Used with permission of the Merton Legacy Trust.

23. TM to EC, 24 December 1961.

24. For more on this much-discussed incident, see Mott, 290–99, and Padovano, 35–36.

Chapter Six: Failed Mysticism—The Crisis of a "Finally Integrated Man"

1. Robert E. Daggy (ed.), *Thomas Merton: Introductions East and West* (Greensboro: Unicorn Press, 1981), 43.

2. TM to EC, 17 August 1959.

3. TM to Czeslaw Milosz, 6 May 1960. Used with permission of the Merton Legacy Trust.

4. Thomas Merton and Robert Lax, *A Catch of Anti-Letters* (Kansas City: Sheed, Andrews and McMeel, 1978), 11.

5. Thomas Merton, *Vow of Conversation* [Ms.]: 20 January 1964.

6. Ibid., 25 January 1964.

7. Ibid., 2 June 1964.

8. TM to DB, 4 August 1964.

9. Thomas Merton, Private Notes, Volume 3, 1965. Quoted in John Howard Griffin, *Follow the Ecstasy: Thomas Merton, The Hermitage Years, 1965–1968* (Fort Worth: JHG Editions/Latitudes Press, 1983), 56.

10. From "Cancer Blues" in *Eighteen Poems* (New York: New Directions, 1985) n.p.

11. From "Six Night Letters" in *Eighteen Poems*.

12. TM to RR, 14 February 1967.

13. TM to RR, 25 March 1967.

14. Restricted Journal: 5 July 1968. Quoted in Mott, 527.

15. Furlong, xiv, xx.

16. Quoted in Griffin, 39.

17. Erik H. Erikson, *Identity: Youth and Crisis* (New York: W. W. Norton, 1968), 91–92.

18. Quoted in Griffin, 112.

19. TM to Reza Arasteh, 22 March 1968.

20. Furlong, 234.

21. TM to Cardinal Jean Danielou, 21 April 1960.

22. Quoted in Griffin, 89.

23. Ibid., p. 80.

24. Quoted in Griffin, 44–45, 79.

25. Ibid., 108, 89.

26. Ibid., 99, 112, 100.

27. Ibid., 108.

28. Quoted in Griffin, 108.

29. Ibid., 111, 130.

30. *Eighteen Poems*, n.p.

Chapter Seven: The Secularization of Thomas Merton— Modernity Reconciled

1. Dietrich Bonhoeffer, *Prisoner for God* (New York: Macmillan, 1954), 122.

2. John A. T. Robinson, *Honest to God* (Philadelphia: The Westminster Press, 1963), 17.

3. Dietrich Bonhoeffer, *Letters and Papers from Prison* (New York: Macmillan, 1972), 360.

4. TM to E. I. Watkin, 11 January 1966.

5. TM to Bruno Schlesinger, 16 January 1966.

6. Karl Barth, *Dogmatics in Outline* (New York: Harper and Row, 1959), 20–21. Quoted in *CGB*, 303.

7. Dietrich Bonhoeffer, *Ethics* (New York: Macmillan, 1963), 61, 101.

8. Ibid., 101.

9. Quoted in Mott, 451.

10. Thomas Merton, "Three Saviors in Camus: Lucidity and the Absurd," *LE*, 291.

11. Thomas Merton, "The Plague of Albert Camus: A Commentary and Introduction," *LE*, 192.

12. Thomas Merton, "Terror and the Absurd: Violence and Nonviolence in Albert Camus," *LE*, 238.

13. Albert Camus, "The Unbeliever and Christians," *Resistance, Rebellion, and Death* (New York: The Modern Library, 1963), 52–53.

14. Albert Camus, "Create Dangerously." Ibid., 202.

15. Albert Camus, "The Wager of Our Generation." Ibid., 184.

16. Ibid., 182.

17. TM to Marco Pallis, 17 June 1965, *Ground*, 471.

Chapter Eight: A Radical Humanist and the Radical Critique

1. "The Root of War," *Catholic Worker* 28 (October 1961). Reprinted in *The Merton Seasonal*, 10, no. 3 (Summer, 1985), 5.

2. Ibid.

3. "Why Alienation Is for Everybody," *LE*, 382.

4. Quoted in Mott, 365.

5. *L&L*, 137. Merton's major essays on Christian humanism can be found in Part III of *L&L*. Unless otherwise noted, the following discussion is based on the lead essay, "Christian Humanism," 135–50.

6. Ibid., 138. The emphasis is mine.

7. See esp. "Christian Humanism in the Nuclear Era." *L&L*, 151–70.

8. *Raids*, 46. *See also CGB*, 261–63.

9. Erich Fromm, *The Sane Society* (New York: Rinehart, 1955), 357–58.

10. Thomas Merton, *Thoughts in Solitude*, 13.

11. *See* Ross Labrie, *The Art of Thomas Merton* (Fort Worth: Texas Christian University Press, 1979), 135–47; Sister Therese Lentfoehr, *Words and Silence: On the Poetry of Thomas Merton* (New York: New Directions, 1979), 97–114; and Woodcock, *Thomas Merton: Monk and Poet*, 173ff.

12. *See*, e.g., Luke Flaherty, "Thomas Merton's Cables to the Ace: A Critical Study," *Renascence*, 24, no. 1 (Autumn 1971), 2–32.

13. On Lax, *see* Merton and Lax, *A Catch of Anti-Letters*. On Parra, *see* Merton's translations in *Poems and Antipoems*, Miller Williams, ed. (New York: New Directions, 1966).

14. Herbert Marcuse, *One-Dimensional Man* (Boston: Beacon Press, 1964), 3.

15. Ibid., 6–7.

16. *See* Marcuse, Chapter 4, "The Closing of the Universe of Discourse," 84–120.

17. Marcuse, 96–97.

18. Ibid., 103.

19. TM to W. H. Ferry, 17 September 1966, 4 October 1966.

20. Marcuse, 101.

Young Man Merton: A Speculative Epilogue

1. TM to RR, 25 March 1967.

2. TM to RR, 4 August 1967.

3. Carolyn Hammer to the author, 22 September 1986.

4. Erik Erikson, *Young Man Luther* (New York: W. W. Norton, 1962), 47. Further references appear parenthetically in the text.

5. *See* Erik Erikson, *Life History and the Historical Moment* (New York: W. W. Norton, 1975), 136ff.

6. Erik Erikson, *Identity: Youth and Crisis* (New York: W. W. Norton, 1968), 157. Further references appear parenthetically in the text.

7. TM to Susan Butorovich, 4 June 1968.

INDEX

DATE DUE			

R0122164642 humca   810
                         .9
                        M55C

Houston Public Library
Humanities

4/10